UGANDA SINCE INDEPENDENCE

Phares Mukasa Mutibwa was born in July 1936 in Bulemezi county, now part of Luwero district in the former kingdom of Buganda, and educated at Ndejje Secondary School, King's College Budo and Makerere University. He served as a diplomat in Uganda's Foreign Service for two years, before joining Makerere University as a lecturer in history. After obtaining his Ph.D. at the University of Sussex, England, he was promoted to a senior lectureship at Makerere, and was Professor and Head of the History Department there in 1976-7 and 1979-83. He has served as professor at the Universities of Nairobi and Swaziland. He was Director of Research and Political Affairs in the National Resistance Movement (the ruling party in Uganda, since 1986) and is currently a member of the Uganda Constitutional Commission.

Besides articles in learned journals, Professor Mutibwa is the author of *The Malagasy and the Europeans* (Longman, 1974) and *African Heritage and the New Africa* (East African Literature Bureau, 1977), and co-author of *A Century of Christianity in Uganda, 1877-1977* (Uzima Press, 1978). Since 1975 he has been a member of UNESCO's International Scientific Committee for its *General History of Africa*, contributing a chapter on Madagascar to volume VI.

PHARES MUTIBWA

Uganda since Independence

A Story of Unfulfilled Hopes

Africa World Press, Inc.

P.O. Box 1892
Trenton, New Jersey 08607

Africa World Press, Inc.
P.O. Box 1892
Trenton, N.J. 08607

© Phares Mutibwa, 1992

First American edition 1992
Originated by C. Hurst & Co. (Publishers) Ltd.,
London, England

Printed in Hong Kong

Library of Congress Catalog Card No. 92-53941

ISBN: 0-86543-356-9 *HB*
       0-86543-357-7 *PB*

CONTENTS

Contents   vii

PHOTOGRAPHS

MAPS

PREFACE AND ACKNOWLEDGEMENTS

If the attention of the world today is focused on Africa, it is not because of the vast natural resources of the continent. It is rather because of the scale of violence that has been unleashed upon it, to which no end seems to be in sight. Although we cannot deny the existence of this violence, it is too often seen in a false perspective. Commentators, especially in the Western press, tend to give the impression that never before in history, and in no other continent since the dark ages, has such violence been seen. Yet glaring violations of human rights and acts of savagery have been, and are still being committed, by regimes of both left and right in Europe, Asia and Latin America.

But two wrongs do not make a right. We Africans should not take comfort because these acts are also committed by others. We have every reason to be concerned about the violence that has scarred our continent – in Angola, the Central African Republic, Chad, Equatorial Guinea, Ethiopia, Liberia and Somalia to name only some instances. The continent that has produced Amin, Bokassa, Samuel Doe, Mengistu, the Nguemas and Tombalbaye cannot be called a safe place to live in.

It is common for our leaders and those who support them and their policies, or lack of them, to brand the evils of feudalism, colonialism, imperialism and neo-colonialism as responsible for all Africa's miseries and agonies. The rise of such butchers as Macias Nguema, Amin and Bokassa was, so the argument goes, the work of foreigners and outsiders, and cannot be laid at the door of the citizens of the countries from which they emerged, and whom they subsequently tried to annihilate.

Such views may contain some truth, but they do not tell the whole story. The real danger facing black Africa today lies less in foreign interference than in the growing conflicts within the continent itself. What the African masses have to protect themselves against are not so much foreign forces as their own leaders. The irony of our recent history is that the agonies to which people have been subjected often did not start with the *arrival* of the European colonisers but with their *departure* in the 1960s. It is hard for us African nationalists to say this, and it is not to underestimate the evils of colonialism. But the truth is that among ordinary people in many parts of Africa the colonialists have never been so popular. The people have gained little from the efforts they made to help the nationalists capture power from the white exploiters of our continent. Ordinary Africans, the governed, are perplexed and angry when, having helped to achieve independence, they see around them oppression, coercion and mass-murder. As Hilary Ng'weno, editor of the Nairobi-based *Weekly Review*, noted,

Before independence, the cry of the African nationalists was for freedom. The assumption was that the nationalist leaders were talking about freedom for their people – all of their people. There may have been a time when African leaders fighting colonialism actually believed in individual liberties. But in retrospect, it now appears as if the freedom they fought for was freedom for them to rule the people.

The people watch a deteriorating situation in which the gap between the rulers in their mansions and the masses in their slums and huts is widening.

This brings me to Uganda, my motherland, which has suffered more than its fair share of Africa's violence and tribulation since it became politically independent in the 1960s. The appalling events which have taken place in this once prosperous country, once named 'the Pearl of Africa' by Winston Churchill, cannot be denied and need explanation. On this explanation hangs the success or failure of our efforts to reverse the course of its turbulent history, especially now that the country has been rescued from the clutches of its murderous former leaders and their henchmen. For without a coherent as well as a sympathetic understanding of the roots of those ills that have plagued Uganda since independence, no true reconciliation and reconstruction can be achieved.

As with the rest of Africa, Uganda's problems have been looked at from two different perspectives. According to the first, Uganda is the victim of an international neo-colonialist and imperialist conspiracy. A package of anti-colonialist jargon attempts to explain the miseries and grotesque savagery which Ugandans experienced in the 1970s and 1980s. This view asserts that most of the tragic events now experienced by Third World countries are consequences of an international economic order of which the Western world is the chief beneficiary.

The second explanation for the tragedy of Uganda is one which can be termed a 'personality cult'. According to this view, a former leader is responsible for all the country's troubles, present as well as past. To the enemies of Idi Amin – and they are many – he and his henchmen alone were responsible for the collapse of Uganda's economy and even for its failure to revive after his overthrow. The state of lawlessness and unrest which continued for so long after his removal were, and still are, attributed to the ousted ruler. To the enemies of Milton Obote – and they too are many – he was solely responsible for these evils, including the constitutional crisis of 1966, back to which all the subsequent problems and horrors are traced. As for the sufferings of Ugandans under Idi Amin, was it not Obote who raised Amin to be head of the Ugandan army? When, during his second presidency, Obote proceeded to exterminate a great part of Uganda's population, all the blame was placed on him personally. The explanations which have so far been offered are simplistic and therefore inadequate.

The best example of a fusion of these two approaches is by Dan Nabudere, the author of a document entitled 'Historical Development of Classes in Uganda'. In his judgement responsibility for Uganda's agonies and problems lies both with imperialism and with Uganda's elected or self-imposed leaders:

> We submit that the real enemy of the people of Uganda is imperialism and the imperialist bourgeoisie. . . . This same class continued to make . . . trouble through their chosen man, Dr Obote, who denied Ugandans their basic rights of independence, freedom and democracy; and in the name of Idi Amin who took away *the little rights we enjoyed even under colonialism* [emphasis added].

My contention, however, is somewhat different. I do not deny that foreign influences have had much to do with the agony of Uganda since independence, nor do I deny the individual responsibility of Amin and Obote. We cannot deny the influence of international organisations which control our economies and thus continue to exert a tight grip over Third World countries. We readily agree that Uganda suffers from underdevelopment, the cause of which is its structural involvement with the developed economies of the West on an unequal basis. Such a situation would disrupt the stability of any country and be likely to result in the emergence of bad political leadership. But we reject the view that blames the rise of Amin and Obote and the inhumanity of their regimes exclusively on outside forces.

We need to recognise that the fascism of Amin and Obote was a bad animal; and to dissect its every nerve and muscle so as to identify the conditions that made it possible. But we are unhappy about the frequent over-emphasis on external factors in explaining our situation in Uganda. It implies that Africans are such good folk that left to themselves they would never harm one another. To ignore or underrate the internal factors is not only a distortion of our history; it can also proceed from a deliberate attempt to ignore reality in favour of a preconceived ideological position. This could be a dangerous hindrance to our efforts to fight those forces and conditions *within our country* which might allow new Amins or Obotes to emerge.

This brings us to our second point which, for lack of a better term, we refer to as the 'personality cult', one of the conditions *within*

Uganda that was a product of and embedded in our society. I believe in the importance of individual personalities in history, but there are greater forces at play than them. Notwithstanding the importance of Obote and Amin, the roots of Uganda's tragedy are more deeply embedded in the country's history. Uganda's tragedy cannot be explained simply in terms of those two men. It is the backwardness of the country which allows such people to climb to positions of leadership. And while backwardness may be partly the result of foreign forces, they alone cannot explain the disasters that have befallen countries such as Uganda.

Let me explain how I came to this realisation. In 1981 I was commissioned by the London publisher, Christopher Hurst, to write a book on the effect of Idi Amin and his regime on the social and state structures in Uganda. I welcomed the venture, for I had not only been a victim of Amin and been forced to flee the country into exile, but had participated in his overthrow and was anxious both to expose his crimes and to warn my 'fellow-liberators' what we should avoid if we were to establish a humane regime in our country. However, after completing a few chapters, I no longer had the heart to continue, not because I ceased to hate Idi Amin and the savagery he unleashed on Uganda, but rather because, as the months grew into years, lawlessness increased and fresh tragedies were unfolding. Amin's rule alone was not the whole story. One now had also to explain the continued suffering of Uganda after the return to civilian rule under Obote in December 1980. The issues therefore had to be more basic than we previously thought.

In saying this I do not absolve Amin and Obote from blame for the agonies of our country, but I hope to show that the colonial history of Uganda did much to shape the events that the personalities of Obote and Amin manipulated. However, what concerns me most is to look at Uganda since 1962 – and not merely in terms of personalities. The same historical factors which shaped Uganda's destiny up to the time of independence continued to shape it afterwards, and it is those which we must examine first if we are to understand what happened and build a better future for our country.

The second point we wish to stress is that men such as Amin and Obote were *produced by our own society*. They alone could not have caused such agony had they not been supported by key figures in the country who benefited from the chaos they created. Take the case of Amin: those who condemn him most are the very ones who not only supported him when he was most vulnerable, but ate from his hands when the loot was still big and flowing freely. They abandoned Amin either when things were getting too hot for them or when they had satisfied their appetite and collected enough booty to last them a lifetime either in exile or at home. Some of them even had the gall to write sensationally about Amin's atrocities – atrocities which had earned *them* thousands of pounds. Perhaps this is one of the most important lessons we can learn from our study: that dictators thrive on those they maim and kill, and that they are products of the societies from which they spring and in which they live. We have to examine the depth of popular support for Amin and Obote. Some Ugandans fall into the same trap as Germans who treat Hitler's Nazism as something alien to German society. The truth is that Uganda's two fascistic and barbaric rulers and their henchmen did not belong to a different species from the ordinary folk of Uganda. People confuse the system with those who become its instruments, and this is why they emphasise removing the leaders when they should be reforming the underlying system. When Amin and Obote were dominant, 'they as individuals', as one commentator (Yoweri Museveni) has remarked, 'were inaccurately seen as the sum total of Uganda's problems. They were therefore blindly equated with a system, that is, with the state.' The same commentator remarks: 'This logically meant that with their removal from power all would be fine.' But this was not and could not be so, because the system remained.

We should also remember that the system is not created by the leaders alone. It is created over a long period, and is the product of the history, traditions and character of the people. We are all jointly responsible for what our country has gone through since 1962: By the same token we are also responsible for its future.

The early part of this book is about Uganda before independence. Our purpose is to show how the historical developments of the colonial period are among the main sources of the agonies that have afflicted our country since. Uganda is poor and much stems from this fact. But it is wrong to say that we are poor because of colonialism, although that may be part of the explanation. Colonialism, harsh as it may have been, produced certain benefits, some of which weathered the ravages of the post-independence era. We shall examine colonialism, not *per se* but only in so far as it tended to emphasise the differences and rivalries between one region and another. The diversity of peoples was used by the colonising power to divide and rule. This policy created societies which saw themselves as states within the state and others which were relegated to second-rate positions. The political, educational, economic and social policies that were pursued not only sharpened existing differences, but also introduced new class formations, stratifications and cleavages. Such a situation, persisting as it did for sixty years, did not favour the achievement of national unity.

The second part of the book discusses Uganda since 1962 – the period when, instead of enjoying the fruits of independence, Ugandans have reaped a terrible harvest brought about by their failure to deal with the problems of decolonisation. It is the heart of the book, but in all of it I have had my fellow-Ugandans particularly in mind. It is they who have experienced the agonies it relates. At the same time, I do not forget our friends outside, who have been with us in spirit, and some in person, during our sufferings.

If it seems to some of my friends that it would have been better to leave certain parts of the book unwritten, so be it; I cannot agree with them. The holocaust in our country has left a stain on our moral standing in the world community, and it is best not to mini- mise that fact. At the same time, I feel only confidence in the poten- tial of our country and its people. I repeat that it is first and foremost for them that the book has been written.

I owe the reader a brief word about my personal background. I am a Muganda from a humble family, which rose through hard work to a position of prominence in the *ssaza* (county) of Bulemezi in the kingdom of Buganda. I was brought up in the traditions of Buganda culture, and offered the best education available to a Muganda in colonial Uganda. I went to King's College, Budo, and Makerere University and from there to France and the United Kingdom to pursue post-graduate studies. This kind of background and upbringing is supposed to be responsible for making some Baganda seem proud and arrogant. I disclaim that description for myself!

There is, of course, a problem involved in writing contemporary history when one's own country is involved and even more when, as in my case, one's family has suffered directly – and terribly – at the hands of agents of the regime in power. I must, there- fore, mention for the record something of what has befallen my family. My elder brother, Ephraim Nsubuga, was murdered by Nubian soldiers of Amin's regime at the time of the first liberation in April 1979. My second elder brother, Zeviriyo Luganda, and his two daughters were killed by Acholi soldiers of Milton Obote's regime in March 1983. My father's entire home and my own home in Kyamutakasa, near Nakaseke in the Luwero District, were ran- sacked and completely destroyed by Obote's soldiers in 1983. My father, Musa Mukasa, was subsequently gunned down in cold blood by Obote's soldiers and buried in a mat because the Acholi soldiers who murdered him took everything that was on him, leaving him absolutely naked. My stepmother, Norah, died when fleeing from the UNLA in Bulemezi to Lukoola in Ssingo. My elder sister, Loyi, died a few months after the NRM/NRA entered Kampala in 1986, after having lived in the bush with the NRA liberators for over two years. Lastly my mother, Omumbejja Zulia Nakayenga, was forced to live like a wild animal in the forests of the Luwero Triangle for three months before she found shelter and was finally rescued by officials of the Red Cross.

Thousands of families in Uganda have suffered in much the same way during the various turbulent periods since independence. In the case of my family, it was after the overthrow of Amin and during the second civilian administration of Milton Obote; for many others it began even before Amin seized power in 1971. I regard Uganda's tragedy as a collective one, for although many feel that the Langis and Acholis suffered worst during Amin's rule and the Baganda during Obote's two rounds of leadership (the West Nilers shared Obote's wrath in his second presidency), it is clear that not one ethnic group, nationality or region was spared. Every part of Uganda has suffered.

Acknowledgements

This whole typescript was read and commented on by my friend and colleague Samwiri Lwanga-Lunyiigo of Makerere University. The Hon. Jotham Tumwesigye read and commented on Chapter 10 (on the UNLF administration); and Mr Justin Okot did likewise with Chapters 11 (on Obote's second regime) and 12 (on the short-lived regime of the Okellos). I am very grateful to these three scholars and colleagues. I am particularly indebted to Thomas B. Byatike, for a long time a close friend and critic of mine, for his advice and guidance in many of my writings. My thanks go to them all. However, I must make it clear that I alone am responsible for any short-comings in the book.

I wish to express my profound gratitude to Christine and John Ssebaana-Kizito who provided me with much needed accommodation at their beautiful home in Kansanga when I had just returned to Uganda early in 1986; some of these chapters were written there. I am also grateful to my daughter, Jacqueline Mutibwa, for her moral support while I was preparing the book.

As a member of the National Resistance Movement, which I now serve, I have to state that the views expressed in this book are mine alone and in no way reflect the views and policies of the National Resistance Movement.

Finally, my thanks go to Anne Lutta and Mrs Teopista Mayanja who typed the final version of the manuscript.

Kampala
January 1992   PHARES MUKASA MUTIBWA

MAPS

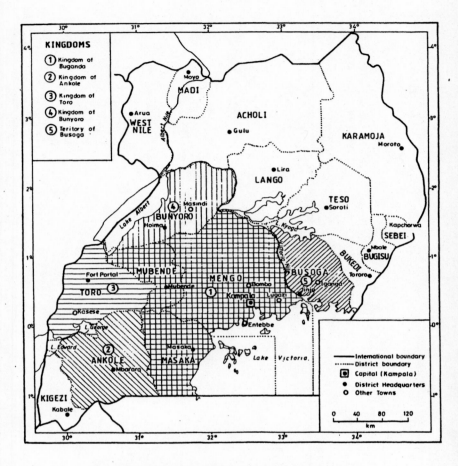

KINGDOMS

1. Kingdom of Buganda
2. Kingdom of Ankole
3. Kingdom of Toro
4. Kingdom of Bunyoro
5. Teritory of Busoga

International boundary
District boundary
Capital (Kampala)
District Headquarters
Other Towns

0   40   80   120
km

Uganda at Independence, 1962: the kingdoms

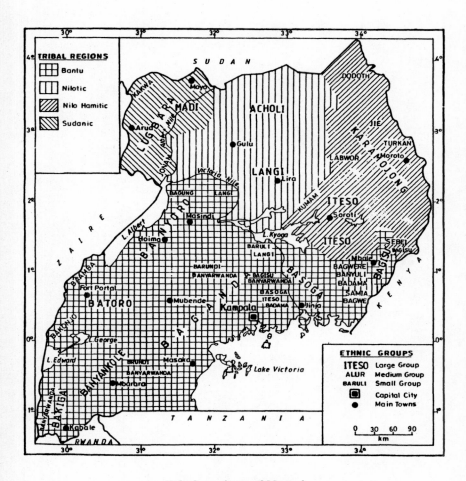

Ethnic regions of Uganda

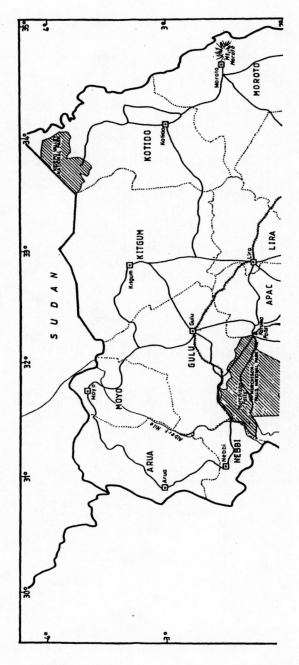

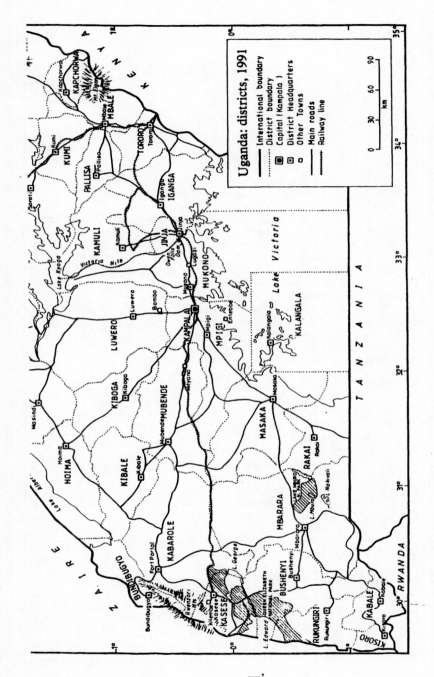

Uganda: districts, 1991

International boundary
District boundary
Capital (Kampala)
District Headquarters
Other Towns
Main roads
Railway line

0   30   60   90
km

xxi

ABBREVIATIONS

COG	Commonwealth Observer Group
CP	Conservative Party
DP	Democratic Party
FEDEMU	Federal Democratic Movement
Fronasa	Front of National Salvation
FUNA	Former Uganda National Army
FUTU	Federation of Ugandan Trade Unions
GSU	General Service Unit
IBRD	International Bank of Reconstruction and Development
IMF	International Monetary Fund
KAR	King's African Rifles
KY	*Kabaka Yekka* ('The King Alone')
NAAM	National Association for the Advancement of Muslims
NASA	National Security Agency
NCC	National Consultative Council
NEC	National Executive Council
NRA	National Resistance Army
NRM	National Resistance Movement
NTC	National Trading Corporation
NUSU	National Union of Ugandan Students
OAU	Organisation of African Unity
PMB	Produce Marketing Board
PP	Progressive Party
RC	Resistance Council
TPDF	Tanzania People's Defence Forces
UFM	Uganda Freedom Movement
ULC	Uganda Labour Congress
UMC	Uganda Muslim Community
UNC	Uganda National Congress
UNLA	Uganda National Liberation Army
UNLF	Uganda National Liberation Front
UNRF	Uganda National Rescue Front
UPC	Uganda People's Congress
UPDM	Uganda People's Democratic Movement
UPM	Uganda Patriotic Movement
UPU	Uganda People's Union
UTUC	Uganda Trade Union Congress

1

COLONIALISM ESTABLISHED: SOWING THE SEEDS OF DISUNITY

Precolonial Uganda; establishment of the Protectorate

Uganda, like many other countries in Africa, is an amalgam of different nationalities and religions. It also includes two major linguistic groups, Nilotic in the north and Bantu in the south. In the southern part of present-day Uganda lived peoples who for centuries had been welded into centralised states with highly sophisticated political systems. These states not only had kings but also *nkiikos* (parliaments), a hierarchy of chiefs, and laws that governed the relationship between the rulers and the ruled. These orderly and settled communities had extensive contacts with the outside world. A different situation existed in the north and east of Uganda. There most of the peoples had not yet developed centralised states or settled modes of life. Theirs were what are generally referred to as segmentary societies. Such contacts as they had with the outside world were with slave-traders from Khartoum who had devastated the area, particularly Acholi. The British Protectorate therefore consisted of many distinct regions, inhabited by people who were not only ethnically different but who were also at different stages of development. The people in the south were able to steal a march upon their counterparts in the north.

The British did not invade Uganda in the classic sense of the term. The first Britons, Speke and Grant, to visit Uganda in 1862 were looking for the source of the Nile and their visit had therefore more a geographic than a political significance. The next European to visit the court of the Kabaka (king) of Buganda, Henry Morton Stanley, became a celebrity with his dashing and adventurous journeys in Africa. It was he who, after speaking to the Kabaka about Christianity, became the bearer of the Kabaka's famous letter which appeared in London's *Daily Telegraph* asking Queen Victoria to send missionaries to Buganda to teach his people the Christian religion and 'Western knowledge'. At the time the letter was sent, Buganda was faced with the possibility of military incursions from Egypt and by a threat from Kabarega, king of Bunyoro, immediately to the north. Mutesa's overture to the British should be seen against this background.

The British missionaries who arrived in 1877 were followed two years later by French Catholics. The court of Mutesa I became a battlefield for the two missions, the Church Missionary Society and the White Fathers. The initial grounds for disagreement were religious, but the disagreements did not remain purely religious. When the proselytes took sides in support of their masters, political divisions in Buganda society became accentuated, and in 1892 degenerated into civil war. The issue at stake was which group would triumph over the other, and thus control political sovereignty in Buganda. Thus religion had already divided the country, and it was this civil war which prompted the initial declaration of a British protectorate in 1894. The crucial battle of Mengo in 1892 was a triumph for the Protestant faction and this determined the nature of the establishment in Uganda for the next seventy years. It meant the rise to power of a minority wing of the Baganda ruling élite, and power and influence were disposed and enjoyed according to religious affiliation. This pattern was reproduced throughout the protectorate of Uganda. Catholics, who were in the majority numerically, were relegated to second place, and Muslims, who had been a considerable power in the 1880s, fared even worse. Muslim education emphasised study of the *Qur'an* rather than secular education, with the result that very few Muslim children received a modern education, but became the milk-carriers and butchers of the protectorate. Thus religion became a divisive rather than a unifying force right from the very beginnings of colonialism in Uganda.

Extension of British rule to areas outside Buganda

An important aspect of the establishment of British rule in Buganda was the extension of that rule to the territories surrounding Buganda. Equally important was the manner in which it was done, because in that process seeds of discord were sown that were detrimental to the establishment of peaceful and harmonious relationships between the different peoples of Uganda.

Bunyoro and Buganda had been arch-enemies throughout the nineteenth century, and in the latter half of that century Buganda had encouraged and assisted Toro and Nkore (Ankole) to ward off the pretensions of Bunyoro to their territories. The British now sided with Buganda and came to accept that Bunyoro was hostile to 'civilisation' and European contact. They used the Baganda to fight and conquer Bunyoro, and the Baganda were rewarded with territory torn away from Bunyoro, which became known as the Lost Counties and was a source of discord and hatred between Bunyoro and Buganda, in particular because it contained the burial-places of the kings of Bunyoro. The extension of British rule to Toro and Ankole was more peaceful.

In the extension of colonial rule to Kigezi and to most of the north and east, the British employed the Baganda as agents of their imperialism, a policy often referred to as 'Buganda sub-imperialism'. The Baganda were used as agents at a time when the British lacked the financial resources and manpower to do the job themselves, and the Baganda embraced the opportunities offered to them and used them to their own advantage, exercising their own version of leadership and rule over non-Baganda, gaining in wealth and personal aggrandisement. Men who had been mere chiefs became lords overnight, and there were military glories to be won. Memories of the misrule and atrocities of the Baganda agents are still vivid, particularly in Mbale and the surrounding areas, where the system of using Baganda agents was most fiercely resisted. It is little wonder that the modern Democratic Party, which has always been led by a Muganda, has little support in this region today.

Administrative and military policies

Thus one of the major features of British rule was the creation of Buganda into a state within the state. The manner in which missionaries were seen to have been invited and the enthusiasm with which the Baganda embraced Christianity clearly appealed to the sentiments of Victorian England. Secondly, the support which the Baganda oligarchy gave to the British administration inclined the British towards Buganda. Thirdly, the manner in which the Baganda were used as agents to extend British rule outside Buganda made them into a privileged group. Fourthly, we should not forget that Buganda was the most powerful kingdom in the interlacustrine area and was well-armed. It was imperative to persuade the Baganda to surrender their guns, but this could only be done by appeasing the Buganda oligarchy, making Buganda into a mini-state within the protectorate. The consequence of this policy was to increase division and disunity in Uganda as a whole.

Another major problem of post-colonial Uganda, as of other African countries, was the way in which its boundaries were drawn. When the imperial powers met in Berlin in 1884-5 to divide up Africa among themselves, they looked not at peoples but at mountains, rivers and other physical features of our continent, which in fact united people rather than dividing them. By the end of the exercise people who belonged to the same ethnic group or even clan found themselves in separate colonies, soon to be further separated by the introduction of new foreign languages and cultures. The end-result of the partition, as Mahmood Mamdani puts it, 'brought within the fold of one country peoples at different levels of social development and without close historical contacts, while splitting nationalities and tribes into, or among, several countries.' When British colonial policy went on to emphasise differences in order to implement their policy of divide and rule, it is not surprising that the peoples of Uganda remained · foreign to each other. This never erupted into physical conflict while the *pax britannica* remained, but as soon as the protecting powers departed, these different groups started jumping at each other's throats.

At the time when the boundaries of Uganda were being negotiated, a colonial administrator seriously suggested that in view of the glaring disparities between the peoples north of Lake Kioga and those south of it, the Nile should be the national boundary, and the territory north of it should be joined to Sudan. The history of Uganda would certainly have been different if this suggestion had been adopted.

Yoweri Museveni rightly says that we should reject as backward, tribalistic and nonsensical the view that it is the northern people of Uganda who have been the cause of all the country's woes. But today people are pointing out that Amin, Obote and Okello-Lutwa all came from across the Karuma bridge. Has it nothing to do, they ask, with what people these days call 'the northern factor' in our politics? Museveni also makes the point that the peasants of these regions have suffered as much as anybody from 'the backward and disastrous policies of these evil men'. It is further argued by some that Amin, Obote and Okello-Lutwa are the products of their societies, a point we have also made about dictators in general. Are southerners to blame for expressing the opinion that there has always existed more backwardness and perhaps a more disorganised and evil society in the regions north of the Karuma bridge? They are speaking out of their frustration and their bitter experience over several decades of suffering, an experience which would have been different, they believe, had the boundaries of Uganda been drawn differently. This is a historical problem, one of those negative legacies bequeathed to us by colonial masters who created the present-day Uganda.

Now to look at the agreement made with Buganda in 1900, which was of considerable importance, not only to the parties that concluded it, but also – perhaps more important – to the non-contractual parties that were to be affected by it. There are two main reasons for this. The first is the significance which the Baganda attached to it and the manner in which it defined their relationship with the other peoples of the protectorate. The second is the significance which the British themselves, both in Entebbe and in White-hall, attached to the Agreement. Related to this was the way in which the British government was prepared to disregard it when it suited them. The Buganda Agreement was not a treaty between equals, but to the Baganda that element was of merely theoretical importance. It established a system of administration later known as indirect rule by which Britain was to govern Buganda through Buganda's own institutions. The Kabaka, at least in theory, was to rule; in fact he was to be the instrument through which the British would rule Buganda. It was laid down that so long as the Kabaka, chiefs and people co-operated loyally with Her Majesty's Government, the existing structure of the Buganda native state would be maintained and the Kabaka would be its native ruler.

To reward the chiefs who negotiated the Agreement (the Kabaka was only four years old), the Agreement allocated several square miles of land to leading chiefs and other personages. This seriously altered land ownership in Buganda. In the past all the land belonged to the king, who held it in trust for the people. Even where it was held in perpetuity by the clan heads (*Bataka*), it was not owned personally but belonged to the clan as a whole. The Agreement changed all this when it granted vast amounts of land to chiefs personally. Chiefs in other kingdoms tried to secure this important concession too, but the British refused, driving home the point that Buganda was different from the rest of the Protectorate.

Although agreements were signed with the kingdoms of Ankole, Bunyoro and Toro, they were inferior to the one between the British and Buganda. The importance of the agreement with Buganda is amply demonstrated by the fact that when disagreements broke out in the 1950s between the British and the Baganda over the interpretation of the Buganda Agreement, it was not only the future of Buganda that was at stake, but also that of the entire Protectorate. Such a state of affairs could only underscore the fragility of the political institutions which Uganda inherited from the British at independence.

2

COLONIALISM IN OPERATION: DIVISIONS INCREASE AND HARDEN

The security forces

Once the initial conquests had been achieved and peaceful administration firmly established, the soldiers and agents from Buganda were no longer required. Once the Baganda had been disarmed, an exercise completed in 1905, they were told that they were too short in stature for the army and police. Recruitment was reserved for northerners and people from the east – who, it was argued, were naturally martial – lest the Baganda became too strong and colonial rule was endangered. The army became a despised profession, suitable only for uneducated people. The Baganda distinguished themselves in the Second World War when their services were needed, so one would have expected that when it came to recruiting Africans in the late 1940s and 1950s to take over positions of command when independence came, the British would have turned to those in the south who had not only shown their fighting abilities during the war, but had the education and ability to provide effective leadership for the army at the top. But it was not to be. Once again the consideration was security. Troublesome and educated southerners were to be encouraged to join the civil service and private businesses, but the top echelons of the army, police and prison service were to be recruited from societies which were backward in education and economic development. These recruits, even if they became army officers, would not be able to articulate their grievances and therefore would be easy to control. Not until just before independence did the British start sending educated young men from the south to military colleges such as Sandhurst.

This policy of recruiting the army from the less developed regions of the north had other unhappy side-effects. Both colonialists and post-independence leaders reminded the soldiers of the exploitation which their fathers had suffered earlier – especially at the hands of the Baganda, who therefore became enemies to be humiliated in their turn. The peoples of the north and east did not deliberately join the army in order to be avenged when the opportunity arose, but the colonial policy of dividing the people created an army composed of northerners which was later used by northern leaders to coerce the south.

6

Economic, educational and social policies

British economic, educational and social policies also helped to accentuate divisions in Uganda. At the time of East African independence, Uganda was hailed as a showpiece of British administration, far ahead of Kenya and Tanganyika. However, development was largely confined to the south and to Buganda in particular. It was assumed that Uganda's status as a protectorate rather than a colony placed it in a privileged position, held in trust for the African people, where settlers were not encouraged. But the facts suggest otherwise. By 1902, when the old Eastern Province was transferred to Kenya, there were over 450 whites in Uganda. White settlers established coffee, cotton and rubber farms from 1906 onwards, but they were outmatched by the indigenous producers of coffee and cotton, products on which the government relied for revenue; by the early 1920s African cultivators, mainly in Buganda, had done so well that the colonial government decided to support them rather than the settlers. The production of cotton and later coffee thus became the cornerstones of the administration's economic policy, and it was this which placed Buganda at the apex of Uganda's economic pyramid.

To ensure the steady and plentiful production of cotton, the administration forced the Buganda *Lukiiko* (parliament) to pass the Busulu and Nvujjo Act of 1927 which not only guaranteed the peasants the permanent use of their land, but also greatly reduced the tribute paid to the land-owning chiefs. This Act significantly altered the rural society of Buganda, with peasants now becoming independent producers of cotton and later coffee; they thus obtained an income which transformed their status. This process was encouraged by the administration at the expense of the economic interests of other regions. Colonial policy on labour recruitment assisted the Baganda by encouraging recruitment into Buganda rather than by expanding production to other regions. Labourers came from West Nile in particular, but also from Rwanda and Burundi and the Mwanza and Bukoba areas of Tanzania. Peasants who had themselves previously been exploited by their chiefs now joined the chiefs in exploiting immigrant labour, and sowed seeds of discontent. Among the immigrant labourers were Bahima, who came to herd cattle for the Baganda after losing their own cattle. Bonnie Lubega's book *The Outcasts* (London: Heinemann Educational Books, 1971) graphically describes the less than human treatment immigrant workers often received.

Yet a note of caution has to be sounded here. We must not ignore or underrate the benefits that Baganda sub-imperialism brought to those areas where it operated. To this day there are people in Kigezi, Teso and Mbale in particular, who still look back on the presence of Baganda in their midst as beneficial. The Baganda agents governed harshly, but their administration was not all negative, particularly with regard to education and the propagation of the Christian faith, and we must also mention the financial benefits of working on Baganda farms. Workers often sent home money for the education of their children: a Minister of Foreign Affairs in Burundi still speaks appreciatively of the benefits his family obtained from the labours of his father on a Muganda's farm in Masaka. But this does not alter the fundamental truth that the way the Baganda treated these workers was exploitative and increased division and hatred.

Other divisive policies concerned the Asians, who formed a privileged class acting as middlemen between Europeans and Africans. The ownership of big sugar estates at Lugazi and in Jinja, which were worked with immigrant (Asian) labour, was not something the indigenous people could have entered and exploited, so it did not attract their resentment, at least during the first decades of the twentieth century. It was rather the dominance by Asians of both rural and urban trade which angered local people, for it blocked their own efforts to run small businesses. It was to them that peasants pawned the whole of their crops in return for money for school fees and basic necessities such as sugar, salt, soap and paraffin. But it was the Asian control of the coffee-curing and cotton-ginning processes which first attracted the discontent of Africans, especially in Buganda, where riots in 1945 and 1949 were directed against Asian businessmen and chiefs. By the time of independence, Africans had won substantial gains in this area but Asians still dominated the wholesale and retail trade.

In concentrating on the economic disparities between the different regions of Uganda, we must not forget that the greatest benefits of colonialism went to the white colonialists and their agents the world over. The extent to which Uganda's natural resources were pillaged will take years to compute. Ill-educated men who were failures in their own countries presided over the exploitation of Uganda's wealth. We are still suffering from such policies, and their results are among the roots of Uganda's present agony.

Inevitably Buganda became the hub of the economic activity of the protectorate: after all, Kampala and Entebbe, respectively its commercial and administrative capitals, were located in Buganda. With the wealth obtained from cash crops the Baganda were able to build permanent houses, and to buy bicycles, motor-cycles and cars, all of which were non-existent in other parts of Uganda until the late 1950s. Buganda possessed the best communications, and whatever welfare services the colonial government provided were centred there. The first mobile cinemas, the best sports facilities and the best medical services were also in Buganda.

Nowhere was the disparity of development emphasised more than in education; it was the means by which southerners, particularly Baganda, came to dominate the affairs of the country. The education system had been started by missionaries, and the first schools were located in Buganda. When Makerere College was founded in Kampala in 1922, *all* the first students came from Buganda and some of the courses were actually conducted in Luganda. It was not till a decade after its foundation that non-Baganda students joined Makerere. Although schools were opened in other parts of the country, the people of the south generally had stolen a march on the rest. By 1920 there were 328 elementary schools in Buganda alone and practically none in the north. Wealthy Baganda and other southerners were in a position to educate their children, and the Buganda administration was determined to keep away people from other regions. The net result of this educational policy was further to divide the people into educated southerners and the uneducated, who were mainly from the north and east.

As a result the colonial period made Buganda into a citadel of the establishment and its people saw themselves as the natural leaders of the country. With their wealth and education and with the support of the colonial administration, they forgot that Buganda was not Uganda and they drifted into independence oblivious of the disadvantages under which non-Baganda had suffered during the time when Buganda's star was in the ascendant.

Administration

The policy of indirect rule was operated in Buganda but was only partially introduced elsewhere. In the 1930s District Commissioners were removed from Buganda, a major decision which followed an earlier one by which the title of Provincial Commissioner was changed to that of Resident. This meant that to all intents and purposes Buganda was ruled not by the British but by their Kabaka through his chiefs. Not until the mid-1940s was the system of provincial administration reintroduced; this move sparked off protests from chiefs and people, and was a factor in the riots of 1945 and 1949. Elsewhere in the protectorate, the Provincial Commissioners with their hierarchies of District Commissioners and District Officers were the real rulers of the colonised people. The chiefs were appointed, paid their meagre salaries, and told what to tell their people; if they did not, they would be sacked. But there was no mistaking where the power lay: British rule was *direct*, and it was directly that the ruled felt it. The different regions of Uganda were not encouraged to make contact with one another. This was disastrous for the functioning of national politics just before and just after independence.

The problems arising from policies that encouraged rather than removed differences were compounded by the fact that there was no central council in which people from different parts of Uganda could meet. In 1921 a Legislative Council (Legco) was set up to be the 'parliament' of Uganda, but it was a parliament of whites and Asians only. At first few Ugandans even knew of its existence. Yet it was not unimportant, and its decisions affected the colonised peoples in many ways. However, it was not their Legco; not till the 1940s were the first three Africans nominated to it. The Western Region was to be represented by the Prime Ministers of Ankole, Toro and Bunyoro (but not Kigezi) in turn; the Eastern Province was to be represented by the Secretaries-General of the districts in turn; Buganda, on the other hand, was to have its *Katikkiro* (Prime Minister) as a permanent representative; the Northern Province was completely ignored. The Baganda saw this special treatment as their right, and were blind to what was going on around them. It is against such policies, favouring one region over the rest, that we must view the political developments that led to the emergence of modern nationalism and independence. The contradictions arising from these policies spilled over into the arena in which Ugandan politicians were to fight for the political prizes before the British, now forced to act as unwilling umpires, departed in 1962.

3

POLITICAL DEVELOPMENTS TOWARDS INDEPENDENCE

The rise of nationalist movements

Right from the imposition of colonialism, nationalist movements that articulated African grievances were organised on a tribal rather than a national basis, largely because there was no such thing as a nation. It is easy to blame the British, but some of the blame should fall on the Ugandans themselves, particularly the politicians who emerged in the 1950s. The roots of this in fact go back to the early years of the twentieth century.

It was in Buganda that the first important political movements emerged. As the vagaries of colonialism began to hurt, movements emerged not so much to overthrow colonialism as to minimise it. The first was the Young Baganda Association, and a similar movement was started in Busoga. In the 1930s Baganda urban workers and peasants formed associations which, in addition to acting as welfare societies, were the precursors of the movements which would articulate their political views. The riots which broke out in Buganda in the 1940s against the Kabaka, the Buganda government and the colonial administration were the first signal of resistance. The torch of nationalism had been lit by the Baganda. Thus in politics as in the economic sphere the Baganda had stolen a march on the rest of the protectorate. This led to serious problems as the country moved towards independence.

First, it elevated the political importance of Buganda and made the Baganda proud and arrogant in their approach to political problems. Up till the 1960s they did not consider their political destiny as part of the country's as a whole. This situation influenced British policy, which saw the politics of Uganda through the lens of Buganda. It was Sir Andrew Cohen, that brilliant British administrator, who stated the obvious: namely, that Buganda was, and was to remain, a province of a united Uganda. The Buganda Agreement of 1900 had said so, but in practice all the Governors before Cohen had acted otherwise. As a result of Baganda attitudes and actions, the non-Baganda developed a sense of inferiority which, as the end of colonialism drew near, turned into suspicion and hatred. Were the Baganda not running too fast for the rest of the country? Would they not dominate the other peoples of the land?

The non-Baganda therefore called for caution and a breathing space in order for the rest of the country to catch up with Buganda. Perhaps this, rather than a dislike of independence, explains Milton Obote's political views in the early 1950s. In an article published in the *Uganda Herald* on 24 April 1952, the year in which the Buganda-based Uganda National Congress (UNC) was founded, Obote stated:

I shall be highly delighted if you would allow me space . . . to express the feelings of young enlightened Semi-Hamites and Nilotes about some of the aims of the Congress. Not long ago Mr Fenner Brockway, MP, came to Uganda and concentrated his activities in and around Kampala. He returned to England and gave his version of the 'Unification of all Tribes in Uganda'. . . . His version is a direct negation of the established traditions of the Semi-Hamites and Norsemen [Nilotes] and . . . we are worried about it. It will therefore be of great interest to us if the Uganda National Congress will point out exactly what they mean by the 'Unification of all Tribes of Uganda'. . . . Cooperation with the government is also recommended but we Semi-Hamites and Norsemen of Uganda feel that the Congress is aiming at 'Self-Government in Uganda', is hastening and therefore leaving us behind because of our present inability to aim so high . . . it must be pointed out to the Congress here and now that with us, the question of questions lies in education and rapid development of African Local Governments. . . . The height of folly [on the Congress's part] is the apparent omission . . . of a definite aim to the slogan of immediate Local Self-Government in Uganda.

Obote's letter was not a rejection of independence for Uganda, but a call by the non-Baganda for caution in moving towards independence while different regions of Uganda were clearly at different levels of political development.

The Young Baganda Association, soon to be followed by the Baganda Bataka Party, spearheaded the articulation of African grievances. In the early 1930s Baganda traders, taxi-drivers, farmers and teachers formed associations which voiced their grievances and the demands of the common man. But these were not truly national associations: both the members and the leaders were based in Buganda. Their grievances and demands coincided with those of Ugandans in general, but these associations did not succeed in uniting Ugandans. The same applies to the Uganda Farmers' Union organised in the 1940s to articulate the grievances of the farmers. It was based in Buganda and there is no firm evidence that it established any branches outside Buganda, although its concern with the protectorate's policies regarding the processing and marketing of cash crops was the concern of every farmer in Uganda.

This brings us to a related subject, the riots that occurred in

Buganda in 1945 and 1949. In the eyes of some Marxist scholars, these were the first proletarian risings against both the colonial administration at Entebbe and the feudal system of Buganda, mass movements determined to break the chains of capitalism and colonialism. Nothing could be further from the truth. The riots of the 1940s all occurred in Buganda. There was some sympathetic support in Jinja and Mbale, but only in Buganda did the King's African Rifles have to be deployed, at great cost in lives and property. The riots were directed against the ruling oligarchy in Mengo as well as against the Asian and European monopoly of crop-marketing and processing, and nowhere is this made more explicit than in the petition which the Baganda presented to the Kabaka of Buganda in 1949:

1. Your Highness should open the rule of democracy to start giving people power to choose their own chiefs.
2. We [Baganda] want the number of sixty unofficial representatives [in the Buganda *Lukiiko*] to be completed.
3. We demand the abolition of the present [Buganda] government.
4. We want to gin our cotton.
5. We want to sell our produce in outside countries, that is, free trade.

The first major uprisings against the colonial masters were tribally based, received little or no support from the rest of the population, and demonstrate the lack of political unity in the 1950s when it was no longer a matter of whether there would be independence, but when and how it would come.

The first political party

The first political party, the Uganda National Congress (UNC), was formed in 1952, and the way in which it came about was typical of the nature of politics in Uganda at the time. In addition to its being formed in Buganda with virtually an all-Baganda leadership, the party was also predominantly Protestant. The Protestants were in a minority, the Catholics being more numerous, but still constituted the dominant group in the country. Professor Karugire has aptly remarked that 'the first national party in Uganda started with two fundamental weaknesses: its Protestant-dominated leadership, and also its preponderance of the Baganda in the upper echelons of the party.' The UNC established a pattern which was to be repeated (with its weaknesses) when other political parties were formed later. Buganda also dominated the press in the 1950s when all sorts of local papers sprang up like mushrooms in the Katwe area of Kampala.

Before we proceed further we should look at an important political event of the 1950s which also contributed to division rather than to national unity. This was the deposition and deportation of Kabaka Mutesa II of Buganda in November 1953. The Kabaka's popularity had never been great, and during the Buganda riots of 1945 and 1949 he was the target of Baganda agitators. By 1952, when Sir Andrew Cohen arrived in Uganda as the new Governor, Mutesa was an unpopular ruler looking for a cause to espouse. His chance came in March 1953 when the British government announced the possibility of forming an East African Federation resembling the one then being formed in Central Africa. Not only did Mutesa demand assurances that such a federation would never be formed in East Africa; he also demanded that Buganda's affairs should be transferred from the Colonial Office to the Foreign Office and a timetable drawn up for its immediate independence. The British government rejected these demands, and when the Kabaka persisted and refused to sign a document that required his kingdom's acceptance that it was and would remain a province of Uganda, he was deposed and deported to Britain.

We should note first that the Kabaka's demands had the support of most Baganda, though there were reservations among some of the more educated. Secondly, the deportation was condemned by the rest of the protectorate, particularly by the western kingdoms and Busoga. Delegations were even sent from Lango and Acholi in support of Buganda, though there is no doubt that the true reasons leading to the Kabaka's downfall were not really understood. What Kabaka Mutesa should have done on his return from exile in 1955 was to tour Uganda expressing his gratitude to all who had contributed to his return, demonstrating that he realised that the cause of Buganda was the cause of Uganda as a whole, and that if all were to unite, the struggle against British colonialism would end in victory. Instead he chose to stay cocooned in Mengo, surrounded by conservatives and isolated from the mainstream of modern politics and popular nationalism. They promised to tell him which people had failed to support his return, and this added to division, not only in Uganda as a whole but even within Buganda itself. Mutesa missed the opportunity to unify Uganda behind his leadership and instead became the prisoner of a conservative oligarchy bent on secession. Politicians in the other regions of the country knew well that Buganda could not implement its decision to secede, a decision which was dead the moment the British decided to ignore it, but they were angered by Baganda arrogance, and no one forgot that they eventually returned to the fold not from choice but because they were forced by circumstances beyond their control.

It is interesting to compare Kabaka Mutesa's tactics with those of Jomo Kenyatta of Kenya. Kenyatta returned to Kenya in 1946 as the leader of his own tribe, the Kikuyu, but he was soon looking beyond his tribal frontier, saying that 'in order to win their freedom, the Kikuyu had to unite with other tribes.' Seretse Khama of Bechuanaland (Botswana) met Mutesa in exile and reminded him that the political situation in Africa was changing rapidly, and that in view of the rise of nationalism and pan-Africanism – of which Kwame Nkrumah's future Ghana was to be the symbol – there would soon be no monarchs left in Africa. Mutesa's response to this is not recorded.

Uganda was not unique in entering independence with divisions in the ranks of its politicians. This happened also in Zambia, Ghana, Kenya, Cameroon and Nigeria among others, but in Uganda the matter was more serious, because the country embarked upon independence without even a dominant political party.

Formation of more political parties

The Democratic Party (DP) was formed on 6 October 1954, and like the UNC it was Buganda-based. It was founded by eight Baganda, and all the other members of the first Executive Committee were both Baganda and Catholic. No wonder that the DP's political enemies later referred to it as *Dini ya Papa* (Religion of the Pope). Attempts have been made, unconvincingly, to deny that the DP was and is a Catholic party. We should remember that the Catholics have always been disadvantaged by the Protestant establishments of Entebbe and Mengo, and the formation of the DP must therefore be seen as a protest against Protestant privilege, aimed at reversing the trend of the preceding years of colonial rule. Karugire's comment clinches this point. He says: 'The fact that should surprise us is not that the DP was overwhelmingly Catholic in inception and following but that it took so long to be formed since the genuine grievances of the Catholics were of longstanding over the whole Protectorate.' In respect of Buganda, Yoweri Museveni has observed: 'Much of the trouble was caused by the Protestant clique of Mengo while they were trying to defend the colonial rewards for collaboration with colonialism according to the 1900 Agreement. Eventually,' he says, 'the Catholic elite elements of Buganda joined the DP to fight for "truth and justice" – i.e. "justice" for the *elite*, never for the masses.' We can understand the reasons for the Catholics founding a political party, but we must note that political parties founded on religious lines were a weak basis for building a united political system after independence was achieved.

A year after the DP was formed the Progressive Party (PP) was founded, and this too was not only Buganda-based but was also predominantly Protestant. According to Professor Anthony Low, an astute observer of Ugandan politics at that time, the Progressive Party 'represented in the main a largely Protestant group of school teachers, prosperous farmers and African entrepreneurs, who had not found a niche for themselves within the Buganda government hierarchy. . . . Many of them were old boys of the leading Protestant school, King's College, Budo, which had earlier replaced the Kabaka's own household as the main seminary for the country's elite.' From all this it is abundantly clear that the PP, too, could not contribute to the unity of the political movement. It was too conservative, too tribal and too parochial to survive the turbulence of the years that followed, and it soon fell into oblivion.

As if religion were not divisive enough, an element of anti-Bugandaism entered the political scene. In 1958 the first direct political elections took place, and the Baganda refused to participate. After this the Uganda People's Union (UPU) was formed by established leaders of the districts outside Buganda who sat in Legco, but, as one writer put it, the UPU had 'no existence outside the walls of the Legco'. The UPU was an anti-Buganda party, and it was little wonder that it later merged with the anti-Buganda wing of the UNC, led by Milton Obote, to form the Uganda People's Congress (UPC). Concerning the UPU, we should note first that it was formed to oppose the concessions which Buganda was demanding from the British government. Secondly, it was the first party to be formed and led by non-Baganda. Thirdly, its formation led to an inevitable confrontation between the Baganda leadership at Mengo and the non-Baganda politicians in Legco and later in central government. And lastly, it forced the Baganda to make a decision about their future which in turn led to the kingdom's decision to declare itself independent in December 1960 and, when this failed, to work out a compromise formula with one of the political parties so as to ensure its survival after independence.

Political life in Uganda became further polarised when the UNC split into three factions over the question of leadership, and these continued to wage war against each other until March 1960, when one wing of the UNC merged with the UPU to form the Uganda People's Congress with Apollo Milton Obote as its leader. Thus Obote, a man of humble beginnings, had successfully fought his way up the slippery ladder of politics to become the leader of a major political party. The supporters of the DP referred to the overwhelmingly Protestant UPC as the 'United Protestants of Canterbury'.

By the end of 1960 there were, then, two major parties, the DP and the UPC, who shared the view that Uganda should continue as a

Milton Obote receiving the instruments of independence from H.R.H. the Duke of Kent, October 1962.

Milton Obote on a military inspection in the 1960s with his Army commander, Major-General Idi Amin, and (*far right*) the Minister of Defence, Felix Onama.

united country and that Buganda's demands threatened that unity as Uganda moved towards independence. It was also appreciated that, however irresponsible Buganda's leaders were, there was an urgent need to establish a compromise with the Baganda to avoid delaying the country's independence. What the two parties disagreed on was how to bring that settlement about.

Mengo wakes up: formation of Kabaka Yekka

For Buganda, the year 1961 brought about a new realisation of the true position of Ugandan politics. Its bid to secede had failed lamentably; the rest of the country was more or less united against it; it faced renewed antagonism from Bunyoro over the lost counties; and, lastly, the future of the Kabaka in an independent Uganda was so obscured by recent events that there was a need to reappraise the whole of the kingdom's policies. It was because of such considerations that Buganda's leaders decided to work out a new policy. This included securing a position of supremacy in an independent Uganda for the Kabaka and the achievement of full federal status as a way of securing the kingdom's continued existence. To this end the leadership in Mengo decided to found its own political movement, Kabaka Yekka ('The King Alone', or KY, nicknamed by its opponents 'Kill Yourself').

The KY was formed with the specific intention of fighting the DP, believed by Mengo to be opposed to the Kabaka and therefore also to Buganda. It was generally believed that the DP had done nothing towards achieving the Kabaka's return from exile. In fact it had played a major role in the negotiations that had gone on in Britain and Uganda to bring this about, but this was soon forgotten. The second 'crime' that the DP had committed against Buganda was to have contested seats in Buganda in the general elections of March 1961 which led Uganda to internal self-government, thereby defying the Kabaka and the Buganda government which had called on the kingdom to boycott these elections. They had led to the appointment of Benedicto Kiwanuka, a Muganda, as Chief Minister after the DP victory, with the possibility that the DP, under his leadership, would come to power at independence. This was anathema to Buganda, and the Kabaka and his government saw it as their duty to prevent this eventuality. In short, therefore, the KY represented Buganda's nationalism at its worst, and it had no intention of advancing national interests unless they coincided with Buganda's own interests. Its leaders were prepared to delay independence or even prevent it, if they could, until their demands were met.

Nonetheless, Buganda was an important part of Uganda, a fact accepted by both its friends and foes alike, who realised that, because of the historical role it had played in the creation and development of the protectorate, it could not be ignored now that independence was approaching. Margery Perham referred to this dilemma in an article in the London *Times* of 10 February 1954, as 'the circumstances of Buganda's entry into British Protection [that] had a crystallizing effect'. Britain, she remarked, 'built up the Uganda Protectorate around and above Buganda, making it a heart that could never, without fatal result, be torn from the larger body politic and economic.' Buganda knew this well, which is why it conducted itself as it did when the independence constitution was being negotiated. Equally significantly, those who opposed Buganda and wanted to cut it down to size, knew they had to make a deal, however unpalatable it might be.

The DP was adamant about Buganda's demands, and it seems that Benedicto Kiwanuka, its leader, had formed a personal dislike of the Buganda leadership, a dislike strongly reciprocated. His arrogance when he became the first Chief Minister of Uganda in 1961 added to the acrimony between Buganda and the DP, a situation which the UPC was not slow to exploit. In this lies part of the explanation for the coming together of two parties that were diametrically opposed in their approach to the major political issues of the day. Obote's nationalist and seemingly progressive UPC joined hands with the traditionalist and conservative KY to form an alliance of convenience, entered into by each partner for personal gain. Obote was clearly a master of the art of the possible – something which the British-trained lawyer, Benedicto Kiwanuka, was not.

Debate over this issue remains as lively and rancorous today as it did at the time. But it was clear that the formation of the UPC-KY alliance in October 1961, which the British accepted, meant that the DP would not be able to lead the country to independence. In the elections of April 1962 the KY collected all the 21 seats nominated by the Buganda *Lukiiko* acting as an electoral college, the UPC winning 37 seats, and the DP 24. When the nine specially-elected MPs were added, the final make-up of Uganda's first National Assembly was 43 seats for the UPC; 24 for the KY and 24 for the DP. The DP leader, Benedicto Kiwanuka, was not even able to sit in this parliament.

Towards independence

In April 1962 Milton Obote became Prime Minister of Uganda and in October led the country into independence. He did so as leader of the UPC, but he could only form a government because of the

The Kabaka of Buganda with Sir Walter Coutts, the last Governor and first Governor-General of Uganda.

alliance with the KY, and it was the Buganda government, with the Kabaka at its head, which had made this alliance possible and thus enabled Obote to become Prime Minister. The fact that an alliance of mere convenience and of such fragility was the price the country had to pay for our independence is a sad commentary on the politics of the preceding decade.

We have maintained that the roots of Uganda's agony lie in the colonial era. We have seen the British government's deliberate policy of making Buganda into a state within the state and at the same time widening the historical division between the north and south of the country. The result was to make Buganda the pivot of the protectorate, with development in the north and the south proceeding at two different speeds. While the *pax britannica* ruled, the contradictions involved could be contained; after it ended, the motor had to be readjusted. The tensions created by colonialism were also apparent in Uganda's leadership, both political and military, for, as Mao Tse-tung has put it, 'power comes from the barrel of a gun'. The harvest of agony that Uganda reaped from the colonial era, and from the political and military leadership with which it emerged at the end of that period, will be the subject of the next chapters.

4

SHAKY START AT INDEPENDENCE: THE FIRST FOUR YEARS

Introduction

The events we have examined up to this point explain something of the roots of the agonies that were to beset Uganda after the achievement of independence. The three chapters that follow, starting as they do from the moment when the people of Uganda regained their sovereignty in October 1962, attempt to explain why and how these agonies began. They have an important place in the book in that they bring out into the open the contradictions and imbalances that had been smothered during colonialism. They highlight and bring into focus those problems which the leaders in Uganda were aware of but which they had hoped would not come to the surface and compromise the tranquillity and peace which independence was supposed to usher in. In short, the precedents of what was to become such a common feature in the body politic of Uganda of the 1970s and 1980s were clearly, and as it turned out irreversibly, laid and established during the nine years of Milton Obote's civilian regime from 23 April 1962 to 25 January 1971.

This point needs to be emphasised. The irony of Uganda's history is that its woes did not start with the arrival of the British *per se*; rather, it started with their departure. The main point at issue, therefore, is the way in which independence was entered into, particularly how the Independence Constitution was negotiated and drawn up. Related to this, of course, is the way in which different people (especially the leaders) and different regions of the country understood the meaning of Uganda's independence. For instance, it was too vague for those concerned with the administration of the country and therefore its future well-being to understand and appreciate clearly the true *locus* of political power in the new nation. The Baganda, smarting from the non-recognition of their unilateral declaration of independence of December 1960, entered an independent Uganda like a proud, well-dressed gentleman entering a semi-dark room full of hostile workers already angered by their employers.

On the other hand, the sons of those Langis, Acholis and Lugbaras who had worked as despised labourers on farms in southern Uganda, particularly in Buganda, were now among those at the helm of the new ship of state. They were the new leaders, in both the political and military establishments. The leaders from western Uganda, including the rulers of the kingdoms themselves, were somewhat unsure of where they really belonged and to whom they should give their loyalties. But they trusted the Buganda leadership, especially that of Kabaka Mutesa who, they believed, would take care of their interests (so closely linked with Buganda's) against any tide of those men from the north and the east who were now installed in Entebbe, Uganda's administrative capital. For the northerners as a whole, the new world was still unknown and vague. They were cautious but at the same time watchful. They were prepared to learn, and to put to good use any mistakes that their former superior brothers of the south and west might commit. Perhaps some of them, remembering their past experience, harboured a desire for revenge.

The position of Buganda and its monarchial institutions was central to the future relationship between the central government and the other regions of the country. Equally crucial was the fact that a satisfactory solution of this delicate issue depended not only on the views but perhaps above all on the personalities of the two most important players in this game, Milton Obote and Edward Mutesa. In examining the events of this period – which set the pattern for many that were to follow later – this personal factor cannot be ignored, although it is admittedly difficult to weigh up the significance of an individual's contribution against the prevailing pattern of the time.

The crisis of 1966 can be viewed as a definite watershed in the history of post-independence Uganda, however short the period that preceded it; some may see it as the beginning of the agonies of Uganda, when things started to fall apart. The period following the 1966 crisis is important for more than one reason. It saw not only the abolition of the old order of kings and hereditary rulers, and an attempt to construct a new order later to be seen in terms of the 'common man', but also the internationalisation of Uganda's internal policies, which brought the country and its policies into the mainstream of the pan-Africanist movement that was rapidly becoming radical and leftist. This was to compound the political problems.

Parallel to this development schisms began to emerge among the groups that had won the day in the 1966 crisis, schisms which assumed greater importance, as well as more animosity, as the protagonists resorted to military means to ensure their survival at the expense of their former allies. The ingredients for an armed confrontation were thus created, but at that time the pretext for one side to strike at the other was lacking. By the end of 1970, Obote, the over-confident President who once boasted that he was the only ruler in Africa who harboured no fear of a *coup d'état* against him, was now militarily lined up against Major-General Idi Amin, who had saved him from political extinction in 1966. The General now saw no reason why he should not combine the top position in the army with that of head of state; he was later to claim that he had once dreamed that this position would be his.

Inherited problems

When it achieved independence on 9 October 1962, Uganda inherited many problems. Apollo Milton Obote had the formidable and unenviable task of welding the various communities of the country into a modern nation-state called Uganda. On this point one writer has remarked: 'No other East African Commonwealth leader faced such an unenviable task at independence. That he survived as long as he did is a tribute to his political skill. That he fell when he did was a bitter irony.'[1]

The previous chapter showed how the political problems that had beset Uganda since the early 1950s were resolved. Because of the way in which independence came about in October 1962, and because it is our contention that many of the sufferings that befell Ugandans after independence resulted directly from these circumstances, we should seek to elucidate some of those points further.

To start with, there was the Independence Constitution itself, negotiated in London between many parties with differing interests a few months before independence. At independence, Uganda consisted of the kingdoms of Buganda, Ankole, Bunyoro and Toro; the territory of Busoga; and the districts of Acholi, Bugisu, Bukedi, Karamoja, Kigezi, Lango, Madi, Sebei, Teso and West Nile. The Independence Constitution granted – some would say over-generously – full federal status to Buganda and a semi-federal relationship to the other kingdoms, while the other districts were to be governed from the centre in a unitary fashion. Thus the federal aspect of the Constitution protected 'certain pockets of power . . . which were by law beyond the reach of the Central Government.'[2] The provisions of the Constitution were such that it could not easily be amended, thus entrenching and enhancing further the interests and the special position of the federal states – especially Buganda, home of Uganda's largest, best educated and wealthiest ethnic group. Indeed, in the country, particularly in Buganda, there was strong resistance to any changes that would put an end to pluralism and institute instead a centralised framework in politics or administration.

In view of the country's subsequent political, social and economic turmoil, it has been asked whether independent Uganda would not have fared better if, from the start, the form of government had been completely unitary rather than half-federal and half-unitary. This is an 'if' of history that is not easy to resolve, but it is crucial in examining or explaining the sources of our country's tragedies. We should remember that the British government, particularly Governor Sir Andrew Cohen, had planned to leave Uganda a unitary government, but in the end the quasi-federal construction was agreed upon. This was, first, because Buganda insisted on a federal government, with the full support of such influential politicians as Grace Ibingira; secondly, because Obote decided to accommodate – at all costs – Buganda's wishes which would clinch the UPC-KY alliance and therefore the rise to power of himself and his party at the centre; and, lastly, because the departing colonial power was no longer actively participating in events and was only keen to wash its hands of Ugandan politics, which had wearied it since the deportation of the Kabaka in the mid-1950s. In the end Uganda evolved on quasi-federal milieu, and the 1962 Independence Constitution was therefore, as Samwiri Lwanga-Lunyiigo has aptly put it, 'a composite one, consisting of elements of unitarism, federalism and semi-federalism, not the basis for successfully forging a peaceful and united nation.'[3]

The Independence Constitution of 1962 was a compromise document to meet political problems that had beset the country since the mid-1950s. Its complex nature was the natural result of the pre-eminent position Buganda enjoyed, *vis-à-vis* the country's other kingdoms and administrative units, in Uganda Protectorate since the turn of the century. This pre-eminence has been attributed both to the excessively pro-Buganda policy pursued by the British colonial government and vigorously implemented by the local administration, and to 'its historical authority and value structure'. This explanation, Martin Doornbos suggests, 'should at least be qualified by consideration of the government measures that promoted Buganda's political standing', namely the policy pursued by the British, after the Second World War, of encouraging and strengthening local and regional government units, which were now, unlike before, allowed to undertake more tasks. As Martin Doornbos has put it in his study, *Not all the King's Men: Inequality as a Political Instrument in Ankole, Uganda* (The Hague: Mouton, 1978, pp. 8–11):

The unit which fulfilled these requirements was Buganda; in the immediate post-war years, therefore, Governor Dundas initiated far-reaching reforms for devolution of administrative jurisdiction to the Kabaka's government. Thus Buganda was again treated as a single unit, administratively developed along separate lines from the rest of the country.

Doornbos adds that 'it was apparently theorised that Buganda would set an example of administrative proficiency that the other regions of Uganda would in time come to emulate.' Other regions of the protectorate envied the position of Buganda, which they tried to emulate. The result of this policy was that Buganda's status became enhanced as independence approached, which tended to alienate it from the rest of the protectorate. Buganda overplayed its new position, which even led it to declare secession from the protectorate in December 1960. Thus, when the Independence Constitution came to be written, the superiority of Buganda over the other three kingdoms (Ankole, Bunyoro and Toro) and the remaining administrative units of the protectorate was emphasised. Doornbos sums up the position well:

Uganda's 1962 independence was engineered on the basis of an unusually complex formula: a constitution which provided for the existence of four kingdoms within an independent state, one of which (Buganda) was to enjoy a federal relationship to the central government, the three others to have quasi-federal powers, while the rest of the country was to be administered through a form of district government which left a fair amount of discretion to the local administration. The delicate nature of this arrangement was indirectly suggested by the token declaration of independence by the Kingdom of Buganda on the eve of Uganda's independence [8 October 1962].*

But, leaving aside the nature of the Independence Constitution, Uganda started off its independence with a very shaky political base. This was largely because of the nature of the alliance which had been formed between the KY party of Buganda and the UPC led by Obote and consisting largely of non-Baganda. The alliance between a seemingly staunch conservative and monarchist party (KY) and a nationalist party (UPC) had been forged late in 1961 with the specific purpose of ousting from power the Democratic Party (DP), which formed the government when internal self-government was proclaimed in March 1962. After the failure of Buganda's bid to secede

---

*On 8 October 1962 there was a ceremony at Bulange marking the formal end of the treaties (particularly the 1955 Agreement) between the kingdom of Buganda and the British Crown. The Baganda attached – and still attach – great significance to this event, which suggests that Buganda entered independence as an independent nation itself, which, of its own free will, negotiated with fellow Ugandans to form the Ugandan state.

from the protectorate in December 1960, Mengo (the seat of power in Buganda) realised the urgent need to ally itself with a political party that shared Buganda's hatred of the DP. Hence the origin of the KY-UPC alliance, the initiative for which is said to have come from Mengo itself. The alliance was often referred to as one of convenience; indeed, as Samwiri Karugire has remarked, 'the coalition between the UPC and Mengo government was a cynic's delight because the two parties had divergent views on almost every conceivable subject.' Thus the means employed by the UPC to attain power 'were not justifiable because such political opportunism and unconstructive motivation could scarcely be a basis for political stability in the country.'[4] Indeed this proved to be the case. As Michael Twaddle reminds us, the foreign observers and Ugandan scholars who expressed surprise that the KY and the UPC led Uganda to independence in a coalition, 'since these parties had contradictory ethnic bases', should have remembered that 'both parties were defenders of the Protestant chiefly ascendancy in most part of Uganda, and the DP as a whole opposed this ascendancy.'

The other issue which would continue to be a matter of dispute was that of the so-called 'lost counties', which remained unresolved at independence. The 'lost counties' were territories of Bunyoro granted to Buganda at the end of the nineteenth century in recognition of the military support which the Baganda had given the British in the conquest of Bunyoro. The territories concerned were six which were of great cultural and historical importance to Bunyoro; within the counties of Buyaga and Bugangaizi were located most of the tombs of former Bunyoro kings. The counties had not been returned to Bunyoro at independence, as recommended by the Molson Commission, but provisions were made in the Constitution for holding a referendum later if parliament sanctioned it.[5]

As well as these major political and constitutional problems inherited at independence, there were other factors that portended future difficulties. To begin with, old religious differences and animosities had hung around Uganda's neck since the arrival of missionaries in the latter half of the nineteenth century. The rivalry and antagonism between the Protestants and the Catholics would not disappear merely because of independence; indeed, the way in which independence itself was achieved, and the first post-independence government formed, meant an intensification of ill-feelings between these two major branches of Christianity. Obote, as a Protestant, was not a neutral force in the religious squabbles that were to emerge. He could not take Catholic political support for granted, nor could he, after the devastating blow the KY–UPC alliance had delivered to the DP in the pre-independence elections,

expect Catholics easily to welcome and support his ideas and programmes as the years went by.

There were also the grave problems of ethnicity and of disparity in
development between the different regions of the country – already
touched on in previous chapters. When it came to nation-building,
Tanzania and Kenya, Uganda's sister-nations in East Africa, were
luckier than Uganda in many ways. Tanzania had tribes that were
mostly small and scattered widely round the arid centre of the country, and the country had the particular asset of a common African
language, Swahili. In Kenya the prolonged struggle for power and
independence with European settlers proved to be of immense
political advantage to Jomo Kenyatta in forging a united nation
despite the existence of many tribes. In Uganda things were different. Not only does the country contain numerous ethnic groups,
each with its unique cultural features and outlook, but in addition
the population is divided into three major linguistic groups: the
Bantu, the Nilotics and the Sudanic, from two major African language families – Nilo-Saharan and Congo-Kordofanian. These
divisions did not augur well for the new state.

The ethnic problems were compounded by the existence of a large
and advanced nationality – Buganda – that others believed to be
threatening to dominate the rest of the state. Largely because of
history – the fact that the Europeans first arrived in Buganda and
the south generally, and so the southerners were able to utilise
the new forms of economic production – the south, particularly
Buganda, had developed further educationally and economically
than the rest of the country by the time of independence. This factor
made the Baganda arrogant towards the rest of the country and
intensified their traditional and cultural separateness.

These differences were accentuated by the existence of monarchism in some regions of the country and of non-centralised societies
in others. Those from kingdom areas tended to regard themselves –
and to be seen by others – as superior to those from non-kingdom
areas. Obote, the Prime Minister and head of government, was from
Lango and a non-kingdom area, and could not be expected to have
much sympathy with the pretensions of believers in kingship and
hereditary leadership, although the woman he married – Miria
Kalule – came from this cultural group with which he was later to
trade punches. This partly explains the fact that soon after independence, in an attempt to achieve some sort of parity with the
kingdoms, most of the non-monarchical districts appointed district constitutional heads, and districts competed with each other
in their imagination to invent impressive titles for their constitutional heads. In the end, therefore, each district became a mini-

state with its constitutional non-hereditary monarch, something which made Uganda a quasi-federal milieu without being a fully federal state.

The existence of these kingdoms, particularly Buganda, weakened the central government for they represented poles of political and administrative power and authority that were in rivalry with the central government. Matters were made no easier when Buganda's leadership behaved as if it was interested in national unity; but all they wanted, as Karugire has remarked, was to get 'their things' and privileges 'at the expense of their own people and at the expense of the rest of Uganda' – at least, it appeared so at the time of independence. It would, however, be wrong and perhaps unfair to Obote simply to deduce from this that he would automatically work for the destruction of those kingdoms. As a politician – and politics is about capturing and retaining power – he would naturally grasp any opportunity if the kingdoms, to which he did not belong or feel sympathetic, were to challenge him or try to make independent Uganda ungovernable.

Besides, there was the personality and the position of Obote himself (the factor of personality emerges many times and in many forms in this story). Obote received power from the colonial government but did not inherit the authority that had previously gone with that power. There were other centres of power, such as Mengo, which commanded more authority and loyalty from its subjects than the African-led central government in Entebbe could enjoy. Secondly, Obote was a leader of a party of leaders. His own position within the party was not unassailable; he had rivals, some of them serious ones, within the UPC so that he was merely the first among equals. At independence, as Karugire has again remarked, 'the UPC had remained a coalition of powerful individuals and its leader [Obote] was by no means the most powerful individual in this lamentable set-up.'

Then, finally, Obote's own ideology and plans ran counter to those of the greater part of the country, particularly in the kingdom areas. Obote had, as an ideal, a one-party state,* a type which was not the ideal of the largest section of the Ugandan population. His ideology, as it unveiled itself or as he wanted to present it as the years went by, was a militant and pan-Africanist nationalism with a large dose of socialism, even if the latter was still vague in his mind at the time of independence. These clearly were not views or ideologies

---

*Professor Gingyera-Pinycwa has termed this 'the party-dominant system of the revolutionary centralising type'.

that would be welcome to those who controlled other centres of power, particularly Buganda and other kingdom areas.

However, whatever may be said about the way in which Obote ran his first government in the 1960s, it is indisputable that in April 1962, when he first formed the government which was to take the country into independence, he was extremely popular among Ugandans. And the region where Obote appears to have been most popular was Buganda itself, where a Muganda musician, Nsubuga, composed a calypso titled '*Tumukulisa Milton Obote*' ('We congratulate you Milton Obote'), which was to remain current for some time. He was popular particularly in Buganda and other kingdom areas at this time not because their people were naive or easily excited, as one *Musizi* editorial once implied; but because a seemingly peaceful transition to independence was being achieved with Obote as one of its architects. Uganda's political spectrum had been so difficult to focus as independence drew near, and the demands of the various regions so many and various, that it seemed almost miraculous that an independence constitution was agreed upon in London in 1962.

In particular, at a time when Buganda was threatening to secede from the protectorate, and the ultra-nationalist politicians within the UPC (the Nekyons) were determined to defy and even 'destroy' Buganda, any agreement that brought these two opposed sides together was to be welcomed. In this lies the jubilation of many Ugandans at the emergence of the UPC-KY alliance, even if this 'marriage of convenience' was to be a source of misery later. Notwithstanding the foregoing, it is important to note that in 1962, as in later years, the Baganda showed a remarkable capacity to embrace leaders or regimes which would later turn against them. It has become a significant part of the political culture of the Baganda that, when confronted with new political situations, they have embraced new regimes without adequately weighing the consequences.

Thus when Obote took over the leadership of Uganda at independence in 1962, his political brilliance and astuteness were widely acknowledged – buttressed, as we have seen, by the way in which he had outwitted the Mengo establishment by persuading it to enter into an alliance with his UPC. Yet as a statesman and conciliator he remained suspect and controversial, and it was Uganda's fate that it was this man who had the task of building a national consensus.

The period of caution and consolidation of the ruling group, 1962–5

Before the constitutional crisis of 1966, Obote pursued a policy of caution, for he was not yet in full control of either the UPC or the central government itself. Yet in those few years that followed independence, there was a slow but sure consolidation of power in the hands of the ruling party, the UPC, and of Obote himself in particular. It is a period which amply shows both the astuteness and ingenuity of Obote as a politician and his determination to deal devastating blows to his political adversaries by every means known in the game of politics. This period also shows how selfish interests and short-sightedness on the part of many Ugandan leaders – including those of the DP who defected in order to join the ruling party – caused democracy to be eroded until it disappeared, with the consequences that are all too clear today.

The first organs of state to suffer were the civil service and local government, which the Prime Minister manipulated to enhance his position and that of the central government. Because of the sharp divisions between the DP and the UPC, the functioning of local administrations was first hampered and later made impossible, especially in districts where the DP had more supporters than the ruling party. The independence of the judiciary was also undermined; laws were enacted not according to the dictates of justice but to promote the specific political interests of the ruling group. For example, William Nadiope was installed as the Kyabazinga of Busoga after a judicial decision had been taken barring him from that high office; such an action undermined the morale and stability of the judiciary.

Religious establishments and trade unions were also manipulated by the ruling group to consolidate its power. Largely in order to break down the strength of Catholicism in educational institutions, the government took over the denominational schools which, it was claimed, had produced or bred two cultures in Uganda. But it was with Islam that the government produced the greatest chaos. Up to independence the leadership of Ugandan Muslims had been in the hands of Prince Badru Kakungulu, an uncle of the Kabaka of Buganda, whose Uganda Muslim Community (UMC) embraced all the Muslims of the country. After independence, however, problems arose because in 1965 a rival Muslim organisation was founded with the government's support. This was the National Association for the Advancement of the Muslims (NAAM), which was founded by a group of Ugandan sheikhs meeting in Mecca, and whose ideas were articulated by Adoko Nekyon, a cousin and close confidant of Obote. The NAAM was seen as belonging to the Muslims outside Buganda; the UMC of Kakungulu continued to be active in Buganda, and its members were increasingly seen – and referred to by the government – as disloyal.

Government interference with a view to consolidating its

authority at the centre was also extended to the trade unions. In the 1950s and early 1960s, trade unions in Uganda were organised by Kenyan workers who had fled from the anti-Mau Mau state terror in their own country. These workers thus had organisational experience and 'a tradition of militant struggle', lacking in their Ugandan counterparts, so that not surprisingly they were in the forefront of trade union activity in Uganda. Soon after independence, Obote's regime came into a head-on collision with organised labour, with the result that, as Mamdani once remarked, the regime framed 'new and draconian labour laws that went further than colonial laws in curbing organised workers' activity.' One of the laws which the government enacted made it illegal for any non-Ugandan worker to hold any position as a union official – a clear move against the more experienced and militant Kenyan workers (they were not expelled from the country till later).

The government went further in manipulating the workers' organisations. In 1964 it sponsored the formation of the Federation of Uganda Trade Unions (FUTU) in opposition to the existing – although not very effective – Uganda Trade Unions Congress (UTUC), which had looked after the affairs of the workers since its formation in the 1950s. In 1966, FUTU and UTUC were both disbanded and a new body – the Uganda Labour Congress (ULC) – was formed by the government. The squabbles among the trade union leaders, not made easier by government interference, only played into the hands of those who wanted to use every division within the population to consolidate their power and thus realise their political ambitions.

Another important development from which Obote benefited was the ideological wrangle within the UPC itself, which led to a split in the party and to the constitutional crisis of 1966. The differences concerned the issues of a one-party state and of socialism. At independence, there had been three viable political parties – the UPC, KY and DP. All were determined to continue in existence and to play an active role in national politics. But a threat to the multi-party system appeared in January 1964, when Obote made a statement at Lira, his home-town, advocating a one-party state for Uganda. Opposition to this idea was voiced immediately, not least from some members of the UPC including Godfrey Binaisa, the Attorney-General. Although the issue was not raised again till about 1968, it had demonstrated the widening ideological differences among the ruling group.

However, it was the issue of socialism which provoked an open split. The most enthusiastic advocate for socialism within the UPC was John Kakonge, the party's Secretary-General. He was strongly supported by the UPC Youth League and some trade union leaders who wanted a more radical approach to national politics. Around 1964 Obote's views on socialism were vague and cautious; thus he did not support Kakonge on this issue, and at the UPC's annual conference, held at Gulu in April 1964, the issue of ideology was debated and Kakonge lost both the debate and his post as Secretary-General, which now went to Grace Ibingira. But the honeymoon between Obote and Ibingira did not last even a year, and as the months passed it became increasingly clear that the UPC was being split into two factions, led by Obote and Ibingira respectively.

The split soon polarised over ideology and ethnicity, for Obote's faction assumed the mantle of a nationalistic and socialist movement championing the interests of the so-called 'disadvantaged' of the north and east, while Ibingira's faction became identified with the conservative wing of the party which also served as an advocate for the position and interests of the Bantu people. Obote and Ibingira were both astute and ambitious politicians who, while remaining friendly, had vied with each other for power ever since the formation of the UPC in 1960. But as the years went by, the knives eventually had to come out in the open arena of national politics. The split between the UPC's two top men developed into an open challenge.

But we should first turn to what was happening within the KY-UPC alliance which formed the first independent government in 1962. The collapse of the alliance is closely connected with the decision, made by parliament in 1964, to hold a referendum in the 'lost counties' so that their inhabitants could decide whether to remain in Buganda or return to Bunyoro, as stipulated in the Independence Constitution. Also, between 1962 and 1965, the UPC had consolidated itself as a ruling party, and with the defection to the UPC of DP parliamentarians, including the DP Secretary-General Basil Bataringaya, it was soon able to command a majority in the legislature.

After parliament had decided on the referendum, the Kabaka's government too decided not necessarily to break the KY-UPC alliance, but to reassess its cooperation with Obote. But this did not prevent the implementation of the decision, and despite frantic attempts by the Kabaka and his government to influence the outcome of the referendum – for instance, by settling Baganda ex-servicemen in the disputed areas – the inhabitants of the two counties of Buyaga and Bugangaizi voted overwhelmingly to join Bunyoro. Buganda's prestige was shattered, as were Mengo's hopes of ever reconciling itself with Obote and the UPC. David Martin has observed that 'writers on Uganda generally paid far too little attention to the importance of the "lost counties" referendum as the crucial issue for Obote's showdown with the Baganda in 1966 and the new political phase which emerged after that until the *coup d'état* in January 1971.' Martin may well be right, because relations between Buganda and Obote's government not only went from bad to worse, but brought about fundamental changes in the politics of Mengo itself. With the loss of the referendum, the Buganda government faced the wrath of its citizens, who demanded the heads of their leaders. This led to the resignation of Michael Kintu as *Katikkiro* (Prime Minister) of Buganda and his replacement by Joshua Mayanja-Nkangi. These were developments which did not displease Obote and his associates – indeed it was said at the time that Obote's agents (in the *Lukiiko*) were instrumental in the choice and election of Mayanja-Nkangi as *Katikkiro* – events which strengthened the central government in relation to Buganda and hastened the confrontation between the two administrations in 1966.

In August 1964 the alliance was formally dissolved and Obote dismissed the KY members from the government side and from ministerial posts they had held up till then. He had used the KY parliamentarians to get his party into power and now that their presence tended to weaken rather than strengthen the government, it was time for them to be disposed of.

In retrospect, the issue of the 'lost counties' is another milestone on the road to Uganda's ruin. It was because of this issue, which required a referendum in the affected areas for its resolution, that an alliance and a whole government which had grown from that alliance collapsed, with disastrous consequences. After the inhabitants of two of the disputed counties had voted to leave Buganda and rejoin the Bunyoro kingdom, it is ironic that with the abolition of the kingdoms three years later, the whole matter became a non-issue. Today few people even know, let alone care, in which districts the affected counties are located!

There is, however, one point which we should mention here in connection with Obote's dismissal of the KY's ministers from the central government in particular and the dismantling of the KY-UPC alliance in general. This is the conduct of the KY parliamentarians themselves, which was far from commendable. Thus while we may attribute the UPC's increasing strength within the National Assembly, before the 'lost counties' issue came into the open, to the defection of the DP parliamentarians to the UPC, we should not ignore the even more irresponsible – and some would say more sinister – defection of the KY parliamentarians to Obote's party which then made the KY-UPC alliance increasingly irrelevant. In this, both the KY and the DP clearly contributed to the breakdown

of multi-party government which, in turn, led to the virtual establishment of a one-party state and the consequent extinction of
democracy.

That is why, when we apportion responsibilities for bringing
about the tragedies of the past two-and-a-half decades, the behaviour of the Baganda parliamentarians, who always talked as if they
would never abandon their kingdom's interests, must be seen in
their true perspective. They are not without blemish. Buganda's
MPs who crossed over to the UPC might have argued, following
Edmund Burke, that they were not delegates of Buganda but its
representatives, and therefore not bound to follow the dictates of
those who elected them. But, nevertheless, it is a sad commentary on
Uganda's politics at that time that men were prepared to abandon
their original loyalties and join the party in power for the sake of
money, office and influence. With these defections from the KY, the
alliance was bound to die a natural death sooner or later, which
makes it seem as if the dispute over the referendum on the 'lost counties' was the last straw – the official pretext for the dissolution of
the KY-UPC alliance.

The significance of these events was twofold. There occurred, first
of all, the joining of hands between Mengo and Ibingira's wing of
the UPC; and, secondly, an open attempt on the part of this group
to challenge Obote's leadership and remove him and his faction of
the UPC from power. The first thing that happened after the break-
up of the alliance was that the KY itself broke up as a party and
instructed its members to join the UPC in an attempt to consolidate
the conservative faction of the party, with Ibingira now its head,
with the avowed aim of ousting Obote from the party and the government. When new UPC Buganda Branch elections were held in
1965, they were won by the ex-KY parliamentarians. 'The KY now
masqueraded as the Buganda UPC', Mahmood Mamdani has aptly
commented. Ibingira's group was now ranged against Obote's
group, and the strength of the former was demonstrated in a parliamentary debate late in 1965 in which the Prime Minister and a few of
his close associates, including the Deputy Army Commander
(Colonel Idi Amin), Adoko Nekyon and Felix Onama were accused
of embezzling money, gold and ivory obtained from Uganda's
involvement with the rebels in the Congo-Leopoldville (now Zaire).
In this debate, a vote of censure against Obote and his government, introduced by Daudi Ochieng, a KY parliamentarian now in
Ibingira's UPC faction, in alliance with the ex-KY-cum-UPC members, was carried by an overwhelming majority. Parliament decided
that a commission should be appointed to study the charges against
Obote and Colonel Idi Amin, in connection with the Congo

operations. Significantly, Ibingira's group had the full support of
the few remaining DP members. The message was clear to all: it was
possible for Obote to be overthrown by his opponents.

There now emerged a new component in the field: the army. Since
January 1964, when the Uganda Rifles mutinied in pursuit of a
demand for higher pay, better conditions of service and africanisa-
tion – all of which the government granted – the army had gained
increasing prestige, particularly after its involvement in the Congo
rebellion when it displayed a high degree of efficiency against Moise
Tshombe's Katangan soldiers, among whom were mercenaries.
When the Congo operations were mounted in 1964, Obote entrusted
this task to Colonel Idi Amin, the Deputy Army Commander and
the officer commanding the 1st Battalion. They operated in Zaire
territory near the border with West Nile, Amin's home area. Iain
Grahame, who had been Amin's commanding officer in the King's
African Rifles, tells us that Amin 'enlisted a large number of dissident Sudanese Nubians and operated with them in the territory
which they all knew well, thus forming the nucleus of a ruthless
force who owed allegiance to none but himself.'[6]

Apart from giving Amin and his soldiers much-needed battle
experience in their fight against Tshombe's rebels, the Congo
operation, which spilled into Uganda, also led to the enlargement of
the Uganda army and the purchase of better and more sophisticated
weapons, and to the creation of a Ugandan air force. As mentioned
above, the success the army achieved fighting the Katangan rebels
raised its morale and improved not only its own image but that of the
government as well. It was to this 'new' army that all those involved
in the political intrigues of 1965 – Obote, Ibingira and Mutesa II of
Buganda, who was also the state President – turned for support in
the desperate bid to outmanoeuvre and eliminate each other. All
those involved realised that in their in-fightings the army would be
their last card. Ibingira and Mutesa II turned to the Army Commander, Brigadier Shaban Opolot, who had married the daughter
of a prominent minister in the Kabaka's government, and whose
support for Obote could therefore be discounted. Obote and his
group, on the other hand, counted on the support of Opolot's
deputy, Colonel Idi Amin, who, like the Prime Minister himself,
came from the north. The political problems were compounded, as
weeks went by, by a personal confrontation between Opolot and
Amin in which each claimed that the other wanted to kill him. Thus
the setting for the 1966 crisis was already in place – although of
course there might have been constitutional remedies such as a dissolution of parliament followed by a fresh election.

The crisis of 1966 and the triumph of Obote's group

Essentially, the constitutional crisis of 1966 was a conflict between, on one side, Obote and the central government and, on the other, Ibingira, Sir Edward Mutesa and the Buganda kingdom.

As we have seen, the in-fighting within the ruling UPC reached a climax with a motion of censure in the National Assembly against Obote and his close associates. The motion was passed on 4 February 1966 by an overwhelming majority; the only dissenting voice was that of John Kakonge. This was the greatest challenge Obote had ever had to face, and his reaction to it was characteristic. On 22 February, when the cabinet met to appoint the proposed Commission of Inquiry and study the charges in connection with the Congo affair that had been debated in parliament, five of its members were arrested, including Grace Ibingira, thus destroying the leadership of the anti-Obote faction within the UPC.[7] On the following day, Amin, who had been Deputy Army Commander, was promoted to be Army Chief of Staff, and Brigadier Opolot, the Army Commander, was made Chief of the Defence Forces, a demotion. This placed the command of the army in the hands of Idi Amin, who a few weeks before had been in danger of suspension from the army by parliament – a remarkable escape!

The political dispute between Obote and Ibingira and his supporters centred around the control of the UPC and ultimately the very leadership of the country in terms of the political and economic ideologies to be followed. Obote claimed – not without justification – that Ibingira's group, which included President Sir Edward Mutesa and the Buganda government at Mengo and counted on the support and assistance of the Army Commander Brigadier Opolot, wanted to remove him from power, and that plans to this end were in an advanced stage by the end of 1965. No one, let alone Ibingira and his supporters, has denied that they wanted to see Obote and those who believed in socialist and autocratic philosophies removed. Their only regret is that they failed.

Ibingira's group seems to have been too cautious and hesitant to act in time against such a cunning and ambitious opponent as Milton Obote. The group's problems were compounded by the apparent naivety and the incredible indecision of Sir Edward Mutesa, who, had he been resolute and tactful as the situation warranted, could easily have tipped the scales in favour of Ibingira's faction. If he had wanted to survive Obote's well-calculated manoeuvres, Sir Edward should have acceded to the pleas of those ministers, politicians and army officers who supported the cause of Ibingira's group, which was also his own cause, and had Obote and Amin immediately arrested and placed 'in safe custody'. As it turned out, Sir Edward, perhaps falling prey to notions of fair play and acting the gentleman which he had picked up in his days at Cambridge University, merely thought of how the United Nations and the rest of the world would react to such abrupt and unconstitutional steps! Apparently having more confidence in the British than in his own people, Mutesa now muddied the waters by approaching their High Commissioner in Kampala for military assistance. While the Ibingira-Opolot group was still confused and debating its course of action, Obote struck, as we have seen, arresting the five ministers who were plotting against him and making Opolot powerless. This effectively removed the anti-Obote faction from within the UPC, the government and, to some extent, from the army. These developments led the Buganda government at Mengo, where Sir Edward Mutesa now returned after leaving the State House at Entebbe, to assume the leadership of opposition against Obote and his central government. This brought into focus the awaited confrontation between Obote and Mutesa.

The conflict now assumed greater proportions, in both political and economic terms. It was clear that this confrontation between Obote and Mutesa, now in his capacity as the Kabaka of Buganda, was no more than a repetition in the 1960s of that between Buganda and Governor Sir Andrew Cohen in the early 1950s. The issue on both occasions was Buganda's relationship with the central government – in other words, Buganda's bid to secede from the rest of the country. The Baganda would again claim that it was never their intention to cut themselves off from the rest of the country, and that all they sought was a meaningful relationship between Buganda and the central government that would safeguard their kingdom and their traditions. But the realities of Ugandan politics demonstrated otherwise. Buganda could not tolerate what it saw as the arrogance of power of Obote's government in Entebbe; Obote and his UPC, for their part, could not remain silent and impotent when the unity of the government was being challenged and flouted by Mengo, which in turn was being manipulated by Sir Edward Mutesa from the State House at Entebbe. Thus Obote's difficulties in the 1960s were the same as Cohen's in the 1950s – i.e. how to bring home to Buganda the needs of a united and independent Uganda.

The conflict turned partly on who controlled the economic surplus in Buganda. The central government reduced its annual grant to Buganda's government 'by the amount of the non-African tax collected by the latter'. Buganda responded by taking the matter to the Privy Council in London, and won its case. But Mengo, as always, had failed to read the political barometer correctly and lacked the maturity necessary to appreciate the true import of these events. As a result of these developments – Obote's clashes with Ibingira's faction, the wrangles over the Congo affair and the open confrontation with Buganda over constitutional and financial matters – Obote took decisions which led to a major constitutional crisis and to a fundamental change in the country. On 22 February 1966 Obote took over the powers of the government 'in the interest of national unity and public security and tranquillity', as he put it. Two days later he suspended the 1962 Independence Constitution, and the post of President was one of its provisions that were not preserved.

It was now Mengo's turn to react to Obote's moves over the Constitution. The Kabaka, in his capacity as President of Uganda, made an appeal to the Secretary-General of the United Nations Organisation, while the Buganda *Lukiiko* passed a resolution calling on the central government to remove itself from Bugandan soil. In short, Buganda wanted to secede, a move which immediately precipitated a confrontation and led to the 'battle of Mengo' of May 1966 when the central government troops, led by none other than Idi Amin, attacked the Kabaka's palace. Although Mutesa, assisted by his lieutenants equipped with Lee-Enfield rifles, put up a stiff resistance and Amin's forces were obliged to call in large contingents of reinforcements, it was not to be expected that Mengo could hold out for long against the Ugandan army. Obote's lieutenant, Amin, won the day, but the Kabaka eluded his attackers by climbing over the wall of his palace and escaping to safety, eventually taking refuge in England.

The battle of Mengo was the first major bloodbath in independent Uganda. It is true that in 1964 there was a disturbance at Nakulabye, Kampala, in which innocent civilians were killed following a quarrel between a Congolese and a Ugandan over a woman, but this could not be compared with the tragic slaughter in Mengo and its environs in May 1966. Following the flight of the Kabaka and the capture of his palace, Amin's men – and Amin, it must be remembered, acted on Obote's orders – unleashed a savage and unprecedented slaughter of Baganda who, in conformity with their traditional requirement to fight and die for their king, had put up a determined resistance against the regular army. Scores of these civilians were loaded on to army trucks and disposed of, many of them while still alive, either by being thrown into Murchison Falls or by being buried alive in common graves. After the coup in January 1971, in his anxiety to please and court the support of the Baganda, Amin said that ten truckloads of bodies were taken from Mengo, thereby confirming Sir Edward Mutesa's own estimate that the death toll of the battle had been as high as 2,000. Thus a precedent had been set for violence, murders and atrocities, which occurred on an even greater scale later. Violence appeared to become institutionalised in Ugandan society.

With Edward Mutesa's flight from his palace, the official battle of Mengo was over, although that was not the end of the massacre of the Baganda at the hands of Obote's soldiers. Throughout Buganda, especially at county and sub-county headquarters, harassment of people who had gathered there was inflicted and in many cases there was much loss of life. Indeed, the security forces traversed many parts of the kingdom, suppressing whatever resistance to Obote's regime they encountered. In a way, however, the ease with which Buganda's resistance in the countryside was crushed by Obote's army was something of an anti-climax. For several weeks before the showdown, there was frenzied excitement in Buganda and almost everywhere the semblance of a clear determination to put up a stiff fight against Obote's soldiers. At that time it appeared as if the latter were not invincible; at least, the messages which Mutesa and his government received made it seem that the Baganda were prepared to defend him and his kingdom. For instance, big holes were dug in some roads and tree-trunks were felled and laid across others to prevent trucks ferrying government troops from reaching the rural areas. The Kampala-Entebbe road was one of those which was damaged when deep holes were dug in many places, especially at or near Kajjansi, some 8 miles from Kampala.

But, as it turned out, all these preparations proved futile when the hour of reckoning arrived. Mutesa was failed by his chiefs and, to a certain extent, by his people. It is true that those who were with him in the palace at Mengo put up a determined fight, but there was no meaningful armed support outside. There was hardly any rising within the capital – not even in the traditionally volatile suburbs such as Katwe, Kasubi or Bwayise. Buganda's cabinet ministers, with the *Katikkiro*, Joshua Mayanja-Nkangi, at their head, took refuge in their own houses in fear of being arrested and detained. The chiefs in the countryside did not live up to their vows to defend the 'Lion' of Buganda, and with their leadership disorganised or paralysed, the people were hardly in a position to rise against the government, which would have meant marching on the capital where the military scores were being settled. Thus, in the end, Kabaka Edward Mutesa II was failed and abandoned by the people of Buganda who proved to be talkers rather than actors when the chips were down.

This, in essence, was the constitutional crisis of 1966 which changed the course of Ugandan history. It was a momentous event which transformed people's views of liberation from colonial servitude to independence as a member of the comity of nations. In the words of a government statement on 11 April 1986, marking the day on which Uganda was liberated from the dictatorship of Idi Amin, 'When political independence was won from Britain in 1962, the people had hoped for a better future. Little did the people know that colonial domination would be replaced with indigenous dictatorship and ruthless administration under the first Obote regime.' And in a television interview on 16 April 1986, the veteran Buganda states-man, Paulo Kavuma, said that what Ugandans got from independence, under Obote's regime, 'was to be killed, to be detained and to be tortured'. Joshua Nkomo of Zimbabwe likewise said that he had come to learn late in his life 'that a nation can win freedom without its people becoming free'.

We now turn to some general points arising from the constitu-tional crisis of 1966 before considering its aftermath.

NOTES

1. D. Martin, *General Amin*, London: Sphere Books, 1978 edition, p. 105. See also James H. Mittelman, 'The State of Research on African Politics: Contribution on Uganda', *Journal of Asian and African Studies*, XI, 3–4 (1976).
2. This is discussed well in A.G.G. Gingyera-Pinycwa, *Apollo Milton Obote and His Times*, New York: Nok, 1978, pp. 80 ff., to which some of the discussion here is indebted.
3. See S. Lwanga-Lunyiigo, 'The Colonial Roots of Internal Conflicts in Uganda', paper given at an international seminar on internal conflict in Uganda, Kampala, 21–25 Sept. 1987.
4. S. R. Karugire, *A Political History of Uganda*, London: Heinemann, 1980, p. 183. See also A.G.G. Gingyera-Pinycwa, *op. cit.*, p. 225.
5. We should, however, point out that the 'lost counties' issue between Buganda and Bunyoro was not the only boundary dispute in Uganda at that time. There were, as Professor Karugire reminds us, 'the dispute between Bukedi and Bugisu over the ownership of the town of Mbale and the surrounding areas of Lwanjusi and Nakaloke; the demands for Sebei to be made a separate district from Bugisu; and the Bamba and Bakonjo rebellion against the rule of the Batoro which led to a civil war after independence.' All this only goes to show how tenuous the political stability of the newly independent nation was. See S. Karugire, *The Roots of Instability in Uganda*, Kampala: The New Vision Printing Corporation, 1988, p. 37.
6. I. Grahame, *Amin and Uganda: A Personal Memoir*, London: Granada, 1980, p. 81. This gives a useful portrait of Idi Amin.
7. The other four ministers were Balaki Kirya, Dr Lumu, Mathias Ngobi and George Magezi. Balaki Kirya, at the time of writing, is Minister of State in the Office of the President responsible for security.

5

THE CONSTITUTIONAL CRISIS OF 1966

Much has been said and written on the 1966 constitutional crisis, and responsibility has naturally been apportioned for the circumstances that led to these events and thus to the destruction of traditional institutions which had been the bedrock of our culture for several centuries. The most conspicuous protagonists were Milton Obote, the Prime Minister; Sir Edward Mutesa, Kabaka of Buganda and President of Uganda; and Grace Ibingira, Secretary-General of the UPC. These men were supported by men and women who sincerely believed they were supporting a cause whose objective was to consolidate and enhance the true interests of their motherland. Let us, therefore, begin with these three personalities.

In 1980 Grace Ibingira published a book entitled *African Upheavals since Independence*,[1] which dealt, among other things, with the events preceding the constitutional crisis and the subsequent violence and upheavals. This book is invaluable since Ibingira was not only one of those closest to Obote in the years before and immediately after independence, but also a shrewd and articulate observer of those events. But the book has a major flaw: Ibingira seems to attribute all the blame for the 1966 crisis to Obote. No one inside or outside Uganda with knowledge of these events can be in any doubt about Obote's role in, and responsibility for, the political tragedy that befell Uganda in the 1960s – nor can they forget the crimes committed by those on his side in the struggle, for Obote was not the only culprit – there were many others.

This is where Ugandans tend to go wrong. We always point our fingers at others and forget our own role in bringing about the events which others, perhaps more shrewd or with sinister motives, were able to manipulate to the benefit of a few and at the expense of the many. Surely many other politicians – of the UPC, KY and DP – share the blame for the political chaos of the 1960s from which we still suffer. Who, for instance, is not aware of the role which Grace Ibingira, William Nadiope and their friends played in creating the UPC-KY alliance which brought Obote to the premiership at the time of independence? Was it not Ibingira who, accompanied by Balaki Kirya, William Nadiope and Abu Mayanja, led Obote by the hand to the Kabaka of Buganda to whom Obote, on his knees, paid homage and pledged his support before the UPC-KY alliance was clinched, which enabled Obote to be catapulted into power? Had it not been for these people who introduced him to Mutesa II at Mengo in 1961, it is conceivable that Obote, a lonely man from Lango, unemployed and perhaps unemployable at the time when he returned to Uganda from Kenya in the 1950s, would have remained in obscurity. That is why many Ugandans, particularly in Buganda, believe that those who brought Obote, a man who had earlier vowed to crush Buganda and other kingdoms, to Mengo share responsibility for the agonies of Uganda today with Obote and his henchmen such as Idi Amin.

Besides, who does not know of Ibingira's bitter fight against John Kakonge for the post of Secretary-General of the UPC in Gulu in April 1964? Ibingira was as ambitious a politician as Obote and others were; he and his group wanted to wrest the leadership of the UPC and the government from Obote and his group. Obote won and Ibingira lost – and that is politics. Grace Ibingira's contribution to the erosion of democracy in Uganda during the period preceding the 1966 crisis is further demonstrated by the fact that he was among the first leading politicians to call for the introduction of a Detention Act. This was apparently done when his relationship with the leader of his party, Milton Obote, was still warm and strong. It was Senteza-Kajubi who, at a rally at Naguru, near Kampala, reminded Ibingira of what had happened to democracy in Ghana when Nkrumah introduced a Detention Act. Senteza-Kajubi went on to warn Ibingira that if he was not careful and he persisted in his hankering for a Detention Act in Uganda, he might well fall into police hands and be detained, even before Senteza-Kajubi himself. And so it was.

Yet many people, particularly in Buganda, supported the Ibingira group, and today many regret that it was not successful, believing that Uganda would have been spared much suffering if it had won the political contest with Obote. Here we wish to underline our main theme, namely that the blame for what went wrong in our country in the 1960s and subsequently cannot and should not be seen in a narrow perspective. Above all, it should not be attributed solely to one person or to a few individuals who happened to be at the helm of the government. There are many others, particularly those who were at one time Obote's comrades-in-arms, who were equally responsible for atrocities committed then and since. Perhaps it would be even truer to say that *all* Ugandans – including those of us who either through ignorance or backwardness allowed ourselves to be mere onlookers, indifferent observers of the games which the politicians and soldiers played – have a share in the responsibility for our country's agony. For too long, Ugandans have been mere observers rather than participants in the planning of our destinies.

Criticism alone says nothing of how the politicians should have conducted themselves or what solutions should have been reached at that time. But if we examine those events of the past frankly and objectively, we may be better able to understand the present and perhaps even throw up a thought or two that could be useful for the future.

The Baganda as a nationality have tended to ignore the role that they and their Kabaka played, which led to the destruction of their kingdom. As already noted, they have *en masse* – and not without reason – placed all the blame for their woes on Milton Obote, and their curse will for ever rest on his head, in whatever foreign land he may reside. But however much the Baganda may attract and even deserve the world's sympathy, there is much more to be reckoned with than Buganda's anguish. In his book *The Desecration of my Kingdom*,[2] Sir Edward Mutesa has left his own testimony on the events that led to his own and Buganda's downfall. No full biography of Mutesa II has so far been written, and a detailed and authoritative account of these events is still awaited. When it comes to be written, his role will certainly emerge as one among the most important – fatally so, because in many ways Buganda's disaster and indeed that of Uganda as a whole can be traced to the misguided leadership and unfortunate activities of Sir Edward himself and his lieutenants in Mengo.

The personality and character of Sir Edward Mutesa were a crucial factor in the events that brought about the 1966 crisis. Those who knew him, particularly his contemporaries at King's College, Budo and Makerere University, have described the kind of man he was. That he was intelligent, able and modern is beyond dispute; that he was also conceited and arrogant, and at times conservative, many will also concede. As Sir Andrew Cohen and other British officials in Entebbe and Whitehall found when dealing with him in the 1950s, Mutesa II was obstinate, extremely proud and full of ambitions. Many of his contemporaries at Makerere recall that he showed a lack of seriousness and a penchant for frivolous things (such as wearing big watches); he was lax over important matters, including his studies. These, admittedly, were the sort of weaknesses that might have been expected of any 'king-student'; but there is a consensus that he gave the impression of being a lightweight extravert, whom his colleagues did not believe to be able and serious enough to handle affairs of state, particularly at a time, like the 1940s and 1950s, when politics were becoming so much more complicated. Mutesa was a perfect 'black Englishman' of the public school and Oxbridge variety, but the English must have been uneasy if they looked upon him as the best product of their civilising mission in Black Africa.

The personality of Sir Edward Mutesa amply demonstrates the importance of individuals in the welfare of nations. At the time of independence, Buganda and Uganda needed a ruler at Mengo with a clear vision of how to balance the strong aspirations of the monarchistic institution over which he presided with the wider interests and demands of a unified Uganda led by a man from a non-kingdom area. But at the time when crucial decisions affecting the future of Uganda were to be taken, the Buganda establishment at Mengo appeared disunited. There was in-fighting, suspicion and open rivalry for office and for the ear of the Kabaka. There was, it is true, a semblance of Protestant solidarity within the establishment but this rested on the shaky basis of a collective hatred of the DP and the Catholic establishment at Rubaga. In these circumstances other ambitious politicians were ready and able to take advantage of the confusion and lack of professionalism at Mengo to reap what they certainly had not sown. Mengo's naivety was only made worse by Mutesa's controversial character, and by the Baganda tradition that made little allowance for the Kabaka's servants and ministers to clash with him openly on important issues. Mutesa was surrounded by counsellors who told him not what he should have heard but what they believed he wished to hear. Statesmanlike advice was not to have been expected from people like Ssebanakita, James Lutaya and Sempa, representatives of the old guard who were always at Mutesa's elbow. He detested and no doubt avoided younger men who felt they had nothing to lose in offering frank counsel on how matters affecting Uganda as a whole as well as Buganda should be handled. That Mutesa's shortcomings became the source of Buganda's and Uganda's tragedies may be unpalatable to many Baganda, but has to be understood. This needs further elucidation.

Mutesa's ambitions, which were influenced by his naive perception of modern African politics, were clearly demonstrated when he succumbed to Obote's charm tactics in the formation of the UPC-KY alliance. Mutesa's eyes were riveted on the state presidency which Obote threw into the bargain. Although his advisers, headed by Michael Kintu, the *Katikkiro*, pointed out the incompatibility of combining the Kabakaship of Buganda with the presidency of Uganda, Mutesa's vanity and stubbornness carried the day. His hatred of the DP – due mainly to religion and perhaps to his personal animosity towards Benedicto Kiwanuka – had fateful consequences because it was partly these factors that pushed Mutesa over to the side of the UPC (of Ibingira, Kirya, *et al.*) and ultimately of Milton Obote himself. Mutesa trusted the Ibingiras, Kiryas and Nadiopes who took Obote to him, and was certain that those who accompanied him to Twekobe in Mengo would 'control' Obote and his northerners (such as Nekyon Adoko) who were anti-Buganda. It was a serious miscalculation. To clinch our point, let us quote Kabaka Mutesa's own testimony of how and why he welcomed and embraced Obote and agreed to work with him in a coalition which he believed would not only block the hated DP under Kiwanuka but also safeguard the interests of Buganda and his kingdom:

An alliance between Buganda and UPC was suggested, with innumerable promises of respect for our position after independence. He [Obote] would step down, and I should choose whoever I wished to be Prime Minister. Though I did not particularly like him, for he is not a particularly likeable man, I agreed to the alliance without misgivings. He understood our fears for the position of Buganda; we shared his hopes for a united, prosperous and free Uganda. Kintu [Buganda's *Katikkiro*] was the only one who objected. Obote had said that he meant to crush the Baganda, and Kintu would not forgive or trust him. We waved it aside as an impetuous remark made to please crowds. Now we thought him reformed, the obvious and best ally against Kiwanuka and the hated DP. . . .

Obote assured us that all the details would be ironed out later in discussions between the relevant Ministers of the Lukiiko and of the National Assembly. We could count on him. 'Trust me,' he said and smiled reassuringly. With only faint misgivings, we did.

Mutesa's arrogance is evident here, but the point is clearly made. When other ambitious and self-seeking people – their eyes fixed on ministerial posts to be filled in the central government – such as Amos Sempa, Lumu and Mayanja-Nkangi, nodded their approval, Mutesa fell into Obote's net. Obote was later even to tell parliament, in April 1966, that when Mutesa agreed to become President of Uganda he knew he had him. We shall never know what plans Mutesa really had for Buganda and the country as a whole in assuming the presidency, but, judging from the way he bungled and confused the issues during the 1966 crisis and certainly from his obvious failure to provide leadership at that critical time, it is not unreasonable to conclude that he had no plans for either Buganda or Uganda, the two constituencies for whose welfare and survival he had been born and elected respectively. He should also have been well aware of the difficulties of serving in a purely ceremonial office (as President) when all effective powers are in the hands of your would-be adversary. One may sympathise with Mutesa, understand his motives, and agree that Milton Obote perhaps gave him no chance to defend himself and his kingdom; but these things cannot mitigate the fact that Mutesa II failed in the task for which his whole life had been a preparation. He was a good man and king who sincerely meant all his actions to be for the good of his people, but if the path to hell is paved with good intentions, the private hell in which he passed the rest of his life in exile in London had at least some paving-stones of his own quarrying.

We have dealt almost exclusively with Sir Edward Mutesa, the Kabaka of Buganda, as one of the main protagonists in the 1966 constitutional crisis. But it is difficult to separate his actions from those of the Mengo government and indeed of the Baganda themselves over whom he reigned; indeed, it would be unfair to do so. So we should mention briefly the role of the Mengo establishment itself (meaning the Buganda government and *Lukiiko*, both quietly supported by the Church of Uganda of Namirembe), and that of the Baganda as represented by the KY movement which was founded in 1961 to espouse the cause of the kingdom of Buganda. Buganda's position, as represented by the Mengo establishment, was centred on one philosophy: their hatred of the DP and the Catholic establishment at Rubaga.

In so far as Mengo's hatred of the DP was the central factor in the reconciliation of Kabaka Mutesa and Mengo with Obote and his UPC, which enabled the UPC-KY alliance to be struck, this must be considered as a factor that contributed to the later problems of the country. However, there is one important point that should be made. When we talk of Mengo's hatred of the DP, we of course include the attitude of Mutesa himself. Yet in the early 1950s, particularly when they were in Britain, Benedicto Kiwanuka and Mutesa were great friends. Only after Mutesa returned to Buganda from exile in 1955 did their friendship cool. Many observers attribute Mutesa's change of attitude towards Kiwanuka to the influence of the Mengo establishment, particularly such people as Amos Sempa, Ssebanakita and even Michael Kintu who had an unbounded hatred of the Catholics. Mengo's hatred of the DP and the Catholic establishment perhaps needs emphasising, for it was central in the overall policy which Buganda pursued, both in its own affairs and also in relation to the central government, from about 1955 when Kabaka Mutesa returned from exile. This policy centred on the two-fold stratagem of preventing the DP both from having any effective say in the political affairs of Buganda, and from assuming political leadership of the central government at independence.

The stratagem of blocking the DP from political participation in the Mengo establishment was manifested in three instances. The first was in 1955 when the DP sponsored Matayo Mugwanya, a former Minister of Justice in Buganda, as a candidate for *Katikkiro* of Buganda. This post had always been reserved for Protestants, and Matayo Mugwanya, a Catholic, found his campaign thwarted from all directions, and when in the end it looked as if he had support among many chiefs, some of the latter were retired from public service. As a result Mugwanya lost to Michael Kintu, but by only three votes. The second incident concerned the same man – Matayo Mugwanya – who, having won a *Lukiiko* seat in a by-election in Mawokota county in 1956, was not allowed to take his seat, even when the High Court in Kampala had ordered that he should do so. The Kabaka refused to confirm his election, thereby depriving his electors of their representation. It is noteworthy that the British government, so keen to espouse democratic institutions and procedures, did not intervene against Mengo to have Mugwanya's constitutional rights upheld.

The third incident was in 1959, when the DP sponsored another candidate, Yusuf Lule, at that time a minister in the colonial government, as *Katikkiro* of Buganda. The same anti-DP forces were once again mobilised to defeat Lule's candidature. One reason that the Buganda establishment advanced against him was that he was in fact a Muslim who had converted to Protestantism; thus he was not a 'true' Protestant and so could not become *Katikkiro* of Buganda. In the end Lule, a highly educated man and a proven administrator, was defeated by Michael Kintu – to widespread astonishment. Certainly the history of Buganda – and no doubt that of Uganda as a whole – would have been different if men such as Matayo Mugwanya or Yusuf Lule, particularly the latter, had been at the helm of the Buganda leadership at Mengo instead of the narrowly conservative Michael Kintu, during the crucial period (1955–64) when the most important decisions affecting the future of Buganda and Uganda as a whole were under consideration. It now appears as a lost opportunity, along with all those disappointed hopes and aspirations that were supposed to have been ushered in with independence in 1962.

The second stratagem of the Mengo establishment was the campaign to keep the DP out of power in the central government, especially at independence. This was partly why Buganda boycotted the 1961 elections, which nevertheless sent the DP to power at the centre early in 1961, and why Buganda made an alliance with the UPC in order that the DP would be defeated in the elections preceding independence. This hatred was shown not only in the way the supporters of the KY and the Mengo establishment treated the DP supporters as enemies of Uganda whose coffee trees and *bitooke* (banana trees) deserved to be cut down and destroyed; but, even more seriously, in Buganda's narrow-minded conviction that the position of 'superiority' it had enjoyed under colonial rule would continue in an independent Uganda. As a *Musizi* editorial later put it:

Those who attempted to warn Ugandans on such a policy which was imposing a one-way of thinking on all the people depriving them of their freedom to unite with others in other political parties, and which had even generated disaffection and hatred for the Kabakaship itself, were thwarted and demoralized by ourselves [the Buganda government]. But what was the outcome?

Perhaps the Baganda and other Ugandans now know the answer.

And what of Milton Obote himself? We are told that he came from a chiefly family, and that he spent many of his youthful years herding goats in his home area, Lango. He was not unintelligent, and shone academically; thus despite all the disadvantages that always beset people from his background, he was able to go to Busoga College, Mwiri, one of the 'Etons' of Uganda, and ultimately to Makerere University. Why he did not complete his scheduled studies at Makerere has been explained in a variety of ways. According to his own testimony, he was in exile in Kenya during the 1940s and it was there that he learned the game of politics which he was to pursue with vigour on returning to Uganda early in the 1950s.

As a man Obote is difficult to assess. However, during my two years' spell as a Foreign Service Officer in the Ministry of Foreign Affairs in the early 1960s, I myself was impressed by his frank and sincere approach towards his civil servants, whom he was prepared to defend against some of his crude and irresponsible ministers. I was also impressed by his wide knowledge of national and international affairs. I found in him a politician with a clear mind, intelligent and shrewd, conscientious and even obsessed with detail.

Obote's political views and ambitions are easier to describe than his personality. He was a follower of Kwame Nkrumah, a man who believed in the dismantling of all those traditional institutions which had been fostered by the British and which, in his view, would not favour the creation of a united and dynamic African state or the united and dynamic African continental government which he also held dear. Perhaps he harboured deep in his heart a sort of love-hate feeling for the traditional institutions such as the kingdom of Buganda, the importance of which Ugandans could not really ignore however much they might dislike them; but there is no evidence that Obote openly favoured them or was prepared to work for their survival. The creation of the UPC-KY alliance in 1962 should not therefore lead us to believe that he wanted to perpetuate the existence of kingdoms in Uganda, although this does not necessarily mean that he would not have allowed them to continue if other factors had not been present. For him, the removal of the Ugandan kingdoms was not an end in itself; it was a means to achieve a republican African state on the model that the neo-nationalist and pan-Africanist politicians such as Nkrumah, Sekou Touré and Modibo Keita wanted to create in Africa.* He was not so much a socialist in the ordinary sense as a radical nationalist, bent on creating a united republic. He later referred to this as 'One Nation, One People, One Parliament', and perhaps he saw himself as the predestined messiah of this creation.

Like so many radical reformers and revolutionaries, Obote believed not only in his own destiny but also in the rightness of every course of action he undertook. He knew what was good for Uganda; those who did not see things his way were enemies of the state who should, if necessary, be eliminated. I have said that as an official in the Ugandan Foreign Service I was impressed by Obote's humility and gentleness towards his civil servants and the way he conducted government business. But that was in the early 1960s; the apparent change in Obote's personality later (or perhaps it was his true personality revealing itself), especially after he became President in 1966, is a stark example of what I see as the evil forces that move the world, and particularly young states, to a destiny of chaos and destruction. Moreover, the 1966 crisis which raised Obote to the pinnacle of power was brought about by hatred, particularly of Mengo and the Kabaka. He should have remembered that 'what is obtained by hatred proves a burden in reality, for it increases hatred.'

Thus, considering the personalities of Obote and Mutesa, it is difficult to find a more unnatural and incompatible alliance; what is amazing is not that the two men drifted apart after three years' collaboration, but that two men from such differing worlds and with such different conceptions of Uganda and its future should ever have become friends and allies.

We have considered three of the protagonists in the political struggle that rocked Uganda barely four years after its independence. We should now look beyond them to others on whom some of the responsibility for the country's traumas should be placed. Take, first, the Democratic Party itself, and before looking at the debit side of its record, we should record that in some important respects the DP appeared a more democratic party than the UPC. Throughout the turbulent years preceding independence, the DP had been prominent in waging a bitter fight against the Buganda

---

*Although Obote was Nkrumah's disciple in his nationalistic outlook, Nkrumah spared the chiefs in Ghana. For example, the Asantehene is still in his palace in Kumasi today.

establishment on issues involving Buganda's domestic politics as well as the whole protectorate. For instance, the DP was certainly more 'democratic' and principled than the UPC when it decided to contest all the seats in Buganda during the general elections of March 1961, thus defying the Kabaka and the Buganda government who were calling for a boycott from all Baganda, although those elections were part of the constitutional process leading to Uganda's independence. The UPC, led by Obote, contested only one seat in Buganda in these elections, thus colluding with the Mengo establishment to defeat the ends of democracy. The only seat the UPC contested (successfully) was East Kyaggwe, won by John Kakonge.

Secondly, the DP also deserves credit for having once again insisted, even to the point of disrupting the independence negotiations at Lancaster House in London in 1961, that Buganda's twenty-one National Assembly members should be *directly* elected, and not *nominated* by the Buganda *Lukiiko* acting as an electoral college as Buganda was demanding. The UPC, it will be recalled, supported Mengo in rejecting the DP's stand on this issue. Thus although the DP appeared at its inception to have been established with a narrow religious base, in the end and particularly in the years preceding Uganda's independence when the difficult negotiations were taking place that led to the drawing up of the Independence Constitution, it strongly resisted the high-handed feudalist and conservative aristocracy of Buganda centred on the Mengo establishment, who were at that time supported by the UPC.

An important question to consider in assessing the DP's record is whether the tactics adopted by the DP, and notably by its leader Benedicto Kiwanuka, at the time of the transfer of power from Britain in 1962 were appropriate. The first point at issue is the DP's attitude to kingship in an independent Uganda, especially in Buganda. At the time when independence was being negotiated, the DP announced loud and clear that it supported the institution of kingship and would preserve it at all costs. However, there were many people, most of all in Buganda, who doubted the seriousness of the DP leaders' commitment to the Kabakaship of Buganda. Many will recall the arrogant and almost contemptuous way in which, after winning the elections of March 1961 and becoming the first Chief Minister of Uganda, Kiwanuka summoned the Kabaka to discuss with him the future of Buganda and the Kabaka's own position in an independent Uganda. Although, as Chief Minister, Kiwanuka ranked higher, constitutionally speaking, than the Kabaka, many of the Baganda were not amused by his lack of tact in trying to tell the world that it was he and not Mutesa who would solve Buganda's problems. Kiwanuka should have remembered

King Solomon's saying, 'Thoughtless words can wound as deeply as any sword.'

The DP leader's behaviour was criticised by the Committee of Inquiry set up by the party when it lost the elections of April 1962. The committee observed 'that some members of the party regarded Kiwanuka as shortsighted, stubborn and incorrigible and argued that his military experience had made him unnecessarily insensitive to public opinion and highhanded in dealing with his subordinates. These members felt strongly *that Kiwanuka should relinquish the leadership of the party* [emphasis added].'[3]

Here we should go back a little and mention that the DP appeared somewhat unclear – or just did not want to be specific – on the issue of what precise form of government Uganda should have when it achieved independence; the party's manifesto issued in April 1960 for the general elections of March 1961 made no specific commitment either way. On whether Uganda's constitution should be federal or unitary, the manifesto posed the question how, if federalism was the form of government that safeguarded kingship, the United States of America, the Soviet Union, West Germany and other countries were both federal and republican without kings, whereas Britain, a unitary state, was able to retain its monarchy? Statements such as this left many doubts in the minds of the Baganda and others as to the DP's real intentions.

It is therefore not unreasonable to ask whether the DP under the leadership of Kiwanuka would have run into a constitutional tangle with Mengo, which would have landed Buganda in a similar situation to that in which it found itself with Obote. For in the final analysis, the issue between Mengo and the central government was the basic constitutional one of where power actually resided: in a local unit (Buganda) or with the central authority (Obote's UPC government). Personalities came into the story merely as catalysts. Considering the gravity of Uganda's problems at the time of independence and in view of Buganda's obduracy in meeting the wishes of the other parts of the protectorate, it is questionable whether the DP under Kiwanuka could have found a formula whereby the central government would have coexisted with Buganda, a somewhat feudalistic and arrogant kingdom that had respected no one but the British for as long as colonialism lasted. With Kiwanuka's known personal antagonism towards the Kabaka, and on the evidence of the anti-Buganda attitude he displayed at the Lancaster House constitutional talks, one wonders whether the DP could have really formed an inclusive and secure basis for a strong post-independence government.

Above all, the way in which, from mid-1964, the DP Members of

Parliament, led by no less a figure than the party Secretary-General
Basil Bataringaya, crossed the floor and joined the ruling UPC
could in no way be considered as helping to strengthen and preserve
democracy in Uganda. It was argued at the time that Uganda needed
a strong central government, which could only be achieved by the
DP joining with the UPC to deal with the country's problems. But if
that was intended, the results were very different: the defection of
DP MPs to the UPC only strengthened the latter party's position
and gave Obote the strength and confidence which enabled him to
stage the coup of 1966.

Finally, should we accept the verdict of some Ugandans, including
the leaders, that it was the British who were partly responsible for
the events that led to the constitutional crisis of 1966 and the chaos
and tragedy that resulted from it? The issue deserves consideration
not least because Ugandans, like many other ex-colonial Africans,
have persisted in attributing all their woes and tragedies to their
former colonial masters. The central issues here are the scrapping of
the Independence Constitution, the abolition of the kingship and
the eventual introduction of republican government. The thrust of
the argument, so it is said, is that the people to whom the British
handed over power and therefore the destiny of Ugandans at independence were from the north, a region which, due to historical
circumstances, had lagged far behind in political, educational and
economic development compared with the south and west. Hence
those to whom power was surrendered did not possess the skills and
experience necessary to run a modern state.

The second consideration is that the region from which Obote
and those who later came to dominate the UPC government and the
military came did not have kingdoms and therefore could not be
expected to nurture love or respect for monarchial institutions.
Obote and his associates from the north – such as Nekyon Adoko,
who had openly declared at Bwayise that they would abolish the
Kabakaship – could *show* respect for Mutesa, Rukidi, Winyi and
other monarchs, but it was believed that in their hearts they harboured a strong and unshakable distrust, tinged with hatred, for
kingship and all that it stood for. Thus, in a nutshell, political and
military power passed at independence to the 'northmen' who,
coming from non-kingdom areas, were unsympathetic to the survival of monarchial institutions on which the culture of the majority
of Ugandans was based. The people of the south, whom tradition
and culture coupled with education and training had fitted to lead
the country at independence, were passed over, and they naturally
ask whether it is to be wondered at that things fell apart almost as
soon as the British left Uganda.

It is true, as we saw in the previous chapters, that the British did all they could to solve the peculiar political problems that faced Uganda before independence and did their best to secure a constitution in which the position of the Kabaka of Buganda and the other traditional rulers would be guaranteed within an independent state. However, all those efforts proved abortive in the face of the wind of nationalism that was sweeping Africa and now engulfed Uganda in the 1960s. The Baganda and the people of the other kingdom areas were abandoned by the British and left at the mercy of the northerners, and they have wondered whether the British did not plan all along to leave political power and the military in the hands of people whom they knew were relatively unsophisticated and would therefore be pliable and unresistant to their machinations.

To blame the British for the constitutional crisis of 1966 is persuasive and evokes sympathy from many Ugandans, especially those in the former kingdoms. But this argument merits little consideration. Take the points concerning the relative 'backwardness' of the northerners, on the one hand, and the abolition of kingship in Uganda on the other. It is absurd that the British should be blamed for these factors. It is true that Obote came from the north, but to what extent was he the *dominant* figure in the UPC-KY government that ushered in independence? We have already noted that, at independence, he was merely leader of a party of leaders so that his own position within the UPC was not unassailable. He had rivals in his party, some of whom were very powerful. There were such politicians as John Kakonge, the party's Secretary-General; Grace Ibingira, the UPC's legal adviser, Magezi, Nadiope and others – all from the south and west, the so-called 'advanced and modern' regions of Uganda. When one remembers that at independence Obote's UPC was in coalition with the KY from Buganda, it becomes clear that the 'northern element' within the UPC-KY government was considerably diluted. Indeed, with so many powerful UPC members from the south and west and with the KY members, all of whom came from Buganda itself, the *dominant* elements of Obote's government in the first two or three years of independence – the crucial period of post-independence Uganda – were from the south and therefore from the so-called 'experienced, trained, educated, modern and advanced' part of the country. If Ibingira, Magezi, Kakonge, Sempa, Lumu, Nadiope and other Bantu-speaking politicians from the south and west failed to maintain their dominant position and were outsmarted and outmanoeuvred by Obote, they only had themselves to blame.

The same argument applies to the second issue, the abolition of kingship. As already noted, Uganda's first government at independence, though led by a northerner, was very much dominated by Bantu-speaking politicians from the south. Not only were they supposed to possess expertise and natural gifts of leadership, but they all came from kingdoms or areas which accepted and respected kingship. It was therefore to be expected that such a government would be the greatest supporter and safeguard for the monarchy in Uganda. That the Ibingiras, the Sempas, Lumus, Magezis and their fellow devotees of kingship failed to save it when they were at one time in a position to do so will always remain a bitter irony.

The last point to consider which has been mentioned in criticism of the British is their attitude to the DP in particular and the Catholics in general as independence approached. This is worth examination. It is said that right from the early 1950s, when it became clear that Uganda, like other British colonies in Africa, would get independence, the British pursued policies which tended not only to support the Mengo establishment and the UPC but also deliberately to thwart the political programmes of the DP in order to prevent that party and the Catholics from taking power at independence. This view is popular among the DP and their supporters and is naturally rejected by the Baganda Protestants and other non-DP Ugandans.

First, it is pointed out that the colonial establishment in Entebbe watched with unease and misgivings as the DP attempted to seize power in Mengo itself. This was when the DP tried to have one of its members elected *Katikkiro* of Buganda, something which, had they succeeded, would surely have brought about fundamental changes in the political working of Buganda and consequently in Uganda as a whole. It is further claimed that when the DP won the elections of 1961 and Kiwanuka became Chief Minister of Uganda, the British government became alarmed. They were certainly perturbed at the prospect of leaving an independent Uganda in the hands of a Catholic party which many believed, and some still believe, takes its orders from the Vatican. As DP writers Simon Mwebe and Anthony Sserubiri put it, 'Consternation fell upon the officials heading the British colonial party [in Whitehall] that always discriminated against Catholics and thwarted their efforts to get power so that urgent steps were taken to fight the DP.'[4]

The British are also accused of having had a hand in the formation of the UPC-KY alliance. One of those thus accused was Dr Geoffrey Fisher, then Archbishop of Canterbury, who visited Uganda in 1961. It has also been seriously suggested that the British assisted the UPC in the decisive general elections of 1962 which preceded independence. Certainly some of these insinuations may not be unfounded, but there is little evidence that British officials deliberately rigged the 1962 elections, so that beaten UPC candidates could nonetheless gain seats. For example, it was said that a prominent UPC official from a western kingdom was thus saved by a colonial official. In a political tract purporting to explain how the DP was kept out of power at the time of independence, the author wrote:

The colonialists now used the situation of the Baganda question to postpone the granting of independence. They argued that if we did not resolve our conflicts politically then independence would be delayed. But among other reasons was the British fear of leaving power in the hands of a Catholic [Ben Kiwanuka] who would most likely antagonise their interests by bringing in either Germany or France because those were the patrons of DP.

Here again, like in many other cases, we Ugandans are trying to turn to outside factors in order to explain the sources of our agonies. It is true that the British had their own preferences as to whom they should leave in control of Uganda – and why should they not when they were anxious to safeguard their interests? – but it is we Ugandans who were largely to blame, since we allowed ourselves to be outmanoeuvred by others, including particularly the very colonialists from whom we were wresting our independence and sovereignty.

In this consideration of the crisis of 1966, we have finally to look at the fundamental constitutional question. Whoever might have ended up as Prime Minister of Uganda after independence – the Muganda Benedicto Kiwanuka or (as it turned out) the Langi Milton Obote, the crucial issue was where the focus of power actually lay: in Entebbe or in Mengo. Who was the real master of the country – the constitutional head of state (the Kabaka) or the Prime Minister as executive head of government? Mutesa and Obote were not fools, and knew the relative importance of their positions. A crisis was inevitable.

Of the two men, Obote and Mutesa, it is instructive to ask which gained more at independence. The Baganda will readily argue that Obote was the one who gained more. Obote was a former herdsboy from Lango who had spent a few years working on sugar-cane farms in Kenya; he was a 'nobody' who, because of the UPC-KY alliance forged largely by his Bantu friends (e.g. Ibingira and Abu Mayanja), nevertheless outwitted the possibly more deserving Democratic Party leader, Ben Kiwanuka, and emerged as the national leader at independence. Mutesa, on the other hand, was already the 'Lion' of Buganda, with great power and prestige in his realm. He had little to gain from independence.

And yet this is the rub. If Mutesa II had undisputed power in his centuries-old kingdom, why did he then aspire to the new presidency of Uganda? Why abandon his seat at Mengo, where he had no rival and his word was law, and venture into the unknown at State House, Entebbe, where he became like a prisoner in the enemy's camp? The answer is simple and complex at the same time. He did so because of the one certain truth he had grasped, namely that power resided not in Mengo but in Entebbe. Mutesa was an astute politician, at least of a sort. Soon, both Obote and Mutesa started to move towards the same goal, the control of Uganda. They were bound to clash. A test came for Mutesa in mid-1964 when the Non-Aligned Conference was to be held in Cairo. Mutesa wanted to attend it as Ugandan head of state, where he would naturally consort with such fellow rulers as Emperor Haile Sellassie of Ethiopia. Obote told him he could not go because he was not the head of government, but merely a constitutional head. We do not know what Mutesa II thought of this, but it is not difficult to imagine: he wanted to reverse the *status quo*, while Obote naturally sought to strengthen it – for good. It was not an issue of republicanism versus monarchism but of where political power should lie.

NOTES

1. G. S. Ibingira, *African Upheavals since Independence*, Boulder, CO.: Westview Press, 1980.
2. Edward Mutesa, Kabaka of Buganda, *The Desecration of my Kingdom*, London: Constable, 1967.
3. Richard Muscat (ed.), *A Short History of the Democratic Party, 1954–1984*, Kampala: Foundation for African Development, 1984, p. 73. The real author of this work is Samwiri Lwanga-Lunyiigo.
4. S. Mwebe and A. Sserubiri, *Ebyafaayo bya D.P (1954–1984)*, Kampala: Foundation for African Development, 1984, p. 26.

6

AFTERMATH OF THE
CONSTITUTIONAL CRISIS

Towards the Republican Constitution

After the battle of Mengo in May 1966 and the flight of the Kabaka to London, Obote could have remarked, if he had known the adage, 'Burn your Greek and Roman books, histories of little people', for the battle of Mengo had something of the significance for Obote and the history of Uganda as its victories over the French in Canada and India in 1763 did for Britain.

Obote was a changed man, and he now emerged in his true colours. He lost no time in tightening his hold on the country, and proceeded to enhance the powers of the centre at the expense of the kingdoms, particularly Buganda. Earlier, on 15 April 1966, he had introduced the 1966 Constitution in parliament – while the building was surrounded by armed soldiers; the Members of Parliament were advised that they would find copies of the Constitution in their pigeon-holes after the meeting. Gingyera-Pinycwa has called the spirit of the 1966 Constitution one of 'anger and unitarism', as opposed to the spirit of 'compromise, tolerance and pluralism' which infused the 1962 Constitution. 'We suggest that this element of anger was an important factor that made possible the boldness Obote showed in his speech to the emergency meeting of parliament and in the actual constitutional provisions, especially as they affected Buganda.'[1]

The 1966 constitutional proposals attacked federalism and monarchism, though without specifically removing them, but the move to centralism was strengthened because local governments were henceforward to have only insignificant subjects to deal with. Changes were introduced which greatly curtailed the powers of the Kabaka of Buganda and the *Lukiiko*. The most important feature of the Constitution was the abolition of the post of Prime Minister and the placing of all executive powers formerly exercised by him in the hands of the President, who now happened to be Obote himself. By one stroke, Obote had triumphed over his adversaries and, in the process, elevated himself to the presidency. He was now the most powerful man in the land:

He was at once: the head of state and commander-in-chief of Uganda. . . . the repository of the executive authority of Uganda . . . the leader of the

58

dominant party controlling the national assembly. . . . As Chairman of the cabinet of ministers . . . he was also the head of government and was responsible for diverse important appointments in the country.[2]

The road along which democracy, as envisaged in the Independence Constitution of 1962, had tenaciously proceeded was now at a junction; the country – or rather the leaders – now took the turning that could only lead to one destination: dictatorship.

In September 1967, a new constitution was enacted by parliament which brought to an end the constitutional changes – always craved by the government – aimed at permanently strengthening the centre at the expense of the periphery. This time there was no caution or shyness, as in 1962 or 1966. 'The 1967 Constitution was thorough and bold in as far as centralisation of power was concerned', says one observer, 'in that unitarism remained the sole guiding spirit. . . .' One interesting thing about the Constitution, unlike that of 1966, is that it was widely discussed by the National Assembly and the public after being published in June 1967. It was debated for three months before its adoption on 8 September, including a month of discussions by a Constituent Assembly of Members of Parliament, and the government accepted a substantial number of amendments. The most notable change introduced was the abolition of kingship and the establishment of a republic. Thus Obote erased the kingdoms of Buganda, Ankole, Bunyoro and Toro from the map of Uganda, thereby fulfilling his ambition to remove any centres of loyalty and authority other than his own emanating from the central government in Entebbe. With the exception of the Kabaka of Buganda, the traditional rulers were merely pensioned off – another reminder to the Baganda that Obote still harboured a grudge against them.

The 1967 Constitution conferred wide-ranging powers on the central government in diverse spheres, and greatly enhanced the executive and legislative powers of the President at the expense of the cabinet, judiciary and legislature. The 1966 crisis, which had occasioned these changes, had given Obote and those who believed in and worked for revolutionary-centralisation the opportunity to remove all these impendiments to the achievement of centralism. The worst victims were Buganda and its government at Mengo, which had stood behind the 1962 Independence Constitution as well as political pluralism in Uganda. That Constitution had been based on negotiations which had succeeded because of mutual trust among different regions and different personalities from different religions, cultures and traditions. Now Ugandans were offered a virtually dictated constitution, although there was some semblance of democracy when the draft constitution could be debated and amended by the National Assembly.

But all this had been achieved at the sacrifice of national unity as this was seen by a large section of the population, especially those from the kingdom areas. It was true, for instance, that the Baganda had acquiesced, but acquiescence is not acceptance. Indeed, it remained to be seen whether this Constitution would be not only acceptable to the majority and give power to the people, but also durable, given the new circumstances created by the events surrounding the crisis of 1966.

Up to this day, the Baganda and the people of the other kingdom areas have never forgiven Obote (this does not apply to Amin who, they knew, acted only as Obote's instrument) for the destruction and abolition of their kingdoms which had existed for some five centuries. In particular, the Baganda have never forgiven Obote for forcing their Kabaka to flee as an exile to England, where he died in poverty three years later.

The anguish of the Baganda at the desecration of their kingdom that was the symbol of their culture and tradition is aptly captured in the following:

No one, however brilliant or well informed can come to such fullness of understanding as safely to judge and dismiss the customs or institutions of his society; for these are the Wisdom of generations after centuries of experiment in the laboratory of history. The sanity of a group lies in continuity of its traditions. To break sharply with the past is to court madness that may follow the shock of sudden blows or mutilations.[3]

Having moulded Uganda into a nation-state at the expense of Buganda, Obote went on to weaken it still further by dividing the former kingdom into four districts – West Mengo, East Mengo, Masaka and Kampala – with the same status as other districts elsewhere in Uganda. The term 'Buganda' was thus removed from the political language of Uganda. To rub salt into the wound, Obote turned the former Buganda parliament building (*Bulange*) into the headquarters of the Ministry of Defence; the Kabaka's palace at Mengo (*Twekobe*) was turned into Malire army barracks; and his palace at Bamunanika, some 30 miles north of Kampala, was occupied by Obote's soldiers and later used by Amin to train his own army from southern Sudan. All these actions exacerbated the Baganda's bitterness. Indeed, as President Yoweri Museveni told the people of Lira in March 1986, the massacre by Obote of innocent Baganda at the battle of Mengo in 1966 and the great humiliations he subsequently inflicted on these people and their kingdom 'drew to Obote the wrath, hatred and curse of the Baganda which are still haunting and following him up to now wherever he goes'. Thus a permanent enmity was created between Obote, the leader striving to create a united polity out of the many ethnic groups of Uganda, and Buganda, the country's most populous region which happened also to be its richest and most productive region and contain some of the most talented people.

The 1967 Constitution: general considerations

Although there are many other highly important provisions of the 1967 Constitution, the most fundamental changes that have remained intact are the abolition of kingship and the introduction of republicanism in Uganda, and the Detention Bill. And it is remark-able that while subsequent leaders of Uganda have condemned the 1967 Constitution, they have not only sworn to it on taking office but have used those dictatorial provisions (such as the Preventive Detention Decree) whenever it has suited them. But the other two issues mentioned above have remained open to debate.

The central issue addressed by the 1967 Constitution was, as has already been mentioned, to do away with the quasi-federal arrange-ments that had maintained the powers of the kingdoms of Buganda, Ankole, Bunyoro and Toro and the district of Busoga. Although not stated in so many words, it was clear that the one region the constitution-framers had in mind was Buganda, a region that had always been a thorn in the flesh of the central government. Thus although the official explanation for bringing in republicanism was to achieve national unity – Obote always played on this sentiment whenever he had the opportunity or was in trouble – it was being said and not just implied that Buganda had always had separatist or sectarian tendencies and was therefore an obstacle to the national unity that was so necessary for development.

But was this really so? The Baganda argue that no other region in the country had been more Ugandan than Buganda itself, and fur-thermore that, throughout the history of what was now Uganda, no kingdom or state was as accommodating towards people from for-eign lands as Buganda. The very nation of Buganda was born of the assimilation of people from other nationalities, and it had expanded and built a viable nation, even before the Europeans arrived, by incorporating many of the non-Baganda elements surrounding it. Assimilation thus had deep historical roots in Buganda, and the kingdom had been built through that process. As an anonymous political analyst has said,

Nubians sat in the Buganda Lukiiko in the 1950s as *bona fide* representa-tives of the Baganda. Non-Baganda Ugandans living outside Buganda were

awarded Buganda government scholarships to study abroad when there
were many Baganda who would have been offered these scholarships. The
late Daudi Ochieng had his constituency in Buganda and so did Visram and
Simpson. . . .

The Baganda welcome other people in their midst and proceed to assimi-
late them and when they have fully integrated them they accept them and
allow them to play all sorts of roles without any discrimination whatsoever.[4]

The Baganda of the mid-1960s could well have asked if any other
kingdom or nationality in Uganda had done even half as much
towards national unity. Was the abolition of their Kabakaship and
the other punishments meted out to them by the Republican Constitution in the name of unity the best way of acknowledging the services they had rendered to the rest of the nation?

In a wider context it began to be debated whether or not kingship
in Uganda should have been abolished outright. Many, especially
outside Buganda, concede that the 1966 crisis between the central
government and Buganda was perhaps inevitable, although it should
be remembered that it was not exclusively concerned with Buganda.
The question is therefore why, after defeating those seeking to oust
him from the leadership of both the UPC and the government (that
is, Ibingira's faction in the UPC and Kabaka Mutesa), Obote should
not only have continued to treat Buganda as an enemy deserving the
ultimate punishment of having its kingdom abolished, but have
gone further and abolished the other three kingdoms, which had had
no quarrel whatever with Obote and the UPC. National unity was a
pre-requisite for development and there was no disagreement over
that; but had it to be bought at the price of so many lives and of
traditions and cultures that had existed for centuries? In other
words, could a compromise not have been struck, leaving the kings
with their traditional powers over those they ruled, positions that
could have been incorporated even into a republican constitution?
Inevitable comparisons were made with African republics such as
Nigeria and Ghana, where kings once reigned, and it was naturally
asked whether the abolition of kingship in Uganda had really been
inevitable.

It takes two, however, to make a compromise leading to a deal. In
this case, the two sides were the Baganda (that is the Mengo establishment) and Milton Obote and his now reinforced and powerful
UPC, and the compromise in question would have been over the
events that followed, rather than preceded, the 1966 crisis – that is,
after the battle of Mengo and the Kabaka's flight to Britain and
before the abolition of the Kabakaship and other kingships in
Uganda a year later. That the Baganda had cause to be angry at their
humiliation by Obote no one could deny, but should that alone have

prevented them, in the face of political realities, from seeking a compromise with their adversary?

Politics being the art of the possible, it became imperative after the battle of Mengo that if the Baganda were to salvage anything of their 'Bugandaism', they had to come to terms with those they disagreed with, but this they adamantly refused to do. Is it to be wondered at that Obote behaved as he did? Is it impossible to imagine that after the 1966 crisis Obote, as a shrewd and astute politician, might have treated the Baganda (his brothers-in-law) less harshly and more humanely if they had extended an olive branch to him? However, there is no evidence that the Mengo establishment ever sought such a compromise, or even considered the possibility. Buganda's *Katikkiro*, Joshua Mayanja-Nkangi, had fled the country (clutching the *Damula*, his symbol of office) to Britain to join his master, and the rest of what had once formed the formidable voice of Mengo were all scattered and subdued like the Lord's disciples after his arrest and crucifixion.

And what of Obote himself? Did he, for his part, seek a compromise with those he had vanquished? Again there is no evidence that he did, and it is not difficult to see why. He had emerged victorious in what had started as a dangerous and intractable political game. But this is not to say that he should not have sought to come to terms with Mengo after winning the first round of the encounter. There were, and still are, many Baganda, especially the more educated and enlightened who have influence in Buganda politics, who did not regret the removal of Mutesa II personally so much as they regretted the abolition of his office; it was that, and not its incumbent, which struck chords deep in the heart of every Muganda. Edward Mutesa was not a popular Kabaka and there are many, despite the circumstances of his flight from Mengo, who did not mourn his departure from the *Namulondo* (Buganda's royal throne). Indeed, when rumours started circulating a few months after his departure that Obote was considering recommending the election of another prince as king, many influential Baganda were known to have been sympathetic towards the idea. Had this idea materialised, Obote could have pulled off a magnificent coup against his many Baganda enemies, and perhaps the country could have been saved much of the misery it has suffered since the 1966 crisis.

As it turned out, Obote and his 'victorious' clique in the UPC were determined to press ahead in complete disregard of the views and wishes of the people of Buganda, who constituted over 20 per cent of the entire population of the country. To Obote peace, tranquillity and, hence, development depended on the total abolition of kingship, the concentration of all political and administrative powers at the centre under his direct control and, later, placing the destiny of Uganda and Ugandans in the sole hands of the single party that had brought these changes about.

One important organ of state – the army – emerged from the 1966 crisis with flying colours. It had been central to all the events that had taken place, and saw itself, and was seen by others, as a factor that could no longer be ignored in the reconstruction of the politics of the country. It had supported Obote and he had won; it had not backed Ibingira's faction and Buganda and they had lost. Obote rewarded the army accordingly: its size, quality and equipment were improved, and its personnel were afforded training opportunities outside Africa. The 1966 crisis also gave Obote an opportunity to purge the army of any dissident elements. All officers who had not supported his cause were purged, leaving a seemingly loyal body committed to his cause. As we have already seen, the army was almost exclusively from the north, as was Obote himself. As such, he and the army saw themselves as united in a common cause of survival against the rest. But although Obote and the army needed each other, because of Buganda's resistance to Obote's rule, the government needed the army for its survival and security more than the army needed the government. This enhanced the army's status and image. Thus after the 1966 crisis, Uganda had a quasi-military government, and in the uneasy period between May 1966 and January 1971 the country had a civilian administration which used military means to implement its policies.

But a crucial factor at that time was the elevation of Idi Amin – now promoted to Major-General – to heights of power he had never dreamt of. By giving him power that went beyond the ability to provide military support, such as Obote needed to contain Mengo and the Baganda, Obote had let a genie out of the bottle. As it turned out, it was a genie which grew so much that by about 1969 it was much too big to be forced back; Amin had acquired a political as well as a military base, which he would use without qualms and with sophistication. The result was the January 1971 coup against the government.

Consolidation of 'state hegemony'

After the 1966 crisis, the way appeared clear for consolidating further the political and administrative control of the country by the UPC group. In particular, the proposals for establishing a one-party state, first hinted at by Obote in Lira in January 1964, could now be made a reality; likewise, the introduction of socialism. The greatest obstacles to the realisation of these ideas – Mengo, the DP and

Ibingira's faction within the UPC – had been eliminated. By 1968 all opposition to the ruling group had been swept aside; indeed, with only six DP members in parliament, the UPC was virtually the only party in the country.

The climax appeared to have been the UPC annual conference held in June 1968 which was attended by, among others, Nyerere of Tanzania, Kaunda of Zambia, Moi of Kenya and a representative of President Mobutu of Zaire. For the first time, top civil servants and the heads of the security forces appeared at a political conference, with both Idi Amin, Commander of the Army, and Erunayo Oryema, Inspector General of Police, addressing the cheering audience. The conference re-elected Obote to a seven-year term of office as president of the party and gave him sweeping powers in the choice of his lieutenants and the organisation of the party. There were, it is true, dissenting voices within the UPC (and, of course, from the small Opposition band of DP parliamentarians), but it was clear that effectively the UPC was the only party in the country. In December 1969, at a UPC delegates' conference summoned to consider *The Common Man's Charter* and *National Service Proposals*, a resolution was also passed 'urging the government to amend the republican constitution so as to establish a one-party system in Uganda'. On 22 December, after an attempt on President Obote's life, parliament banned the DP and other opposition parties and societies in the country, which were declared to be 'dangerous to peace and order'. The UPC was now the only *legal* party in Uganda.

The way in which Uganda drifted into a state of dictatorship should be emphasised. Although Obote wreaked most of his fury on Buganda, the major obstacle in his political designs, almost the entire country felt the force of the dictatorial measures deployed to ensure the centralisation of power. The state of emergency, first declared in Buganda early in 1966, was extended in 1969 to other parts of the country. Indeed, the former kingdom was placed under a permanent state of emergency which was not lifted till after Obote's overthrow in 1971.

Under the draconian laws and conditions that followed, the liberty of the individual became eroded, and for the first time in Uganda's history accusations of human rights violations began to be heard. As state power began to be used against those considered dissidents, leaders of political parties, religious organisations or any group or community suspected of not having fallen into line with the government's thinking were arrested and thrown into prisons – not to be seen again until Obote himself was thrown out of office. Those detained included such leading politicians as Benedicto Kiwanuka, the leader of the DP, Jolly 'Joe' Kiwanuka, and of course the five

UPC ministers who had been arrested and detained in February 1966. Still haunted by the spectre of Buganda's kingdom, Obote persecuted the most prominent remnants of the Buganda royal family. For example, he detained Princess Nnalinya Mpologoma, sister of the former Kabaka, who had become a central figure in Buganda's opposition to Obote's regime, and among the religious leaders thrown into jail was the veteran Muslim leader, Prince Badru Kakungulu, who was not only the leader of Uganda's Muslim community (the rival faction to the NAAM, which supported the government) but an uncle of Edward Mutesa and the rallying point of many Baganda elders and others who regretted the passing of the kingdom. In addition, many businessmen, lawyers, teachers, doctors and others from all walks of life (including students) were detained from time to time. Late in 1967 occurred the *Transition* affair, in which Abu Mayanja and Rajat Neogy were detained. The August–September issue of the periodical (vol. 7, no. 32), of which Neogy was editor, contained an article by Mayanja entitled 'Government's Proposals on the Constitution' at the time when the 1967 Constitution was being debated. It displeased President Obote. The shooting of Obote on 19 December 1969 as he left Lugogo sports stadium after the closing of the UPC delegates' conference can now be seen as a natural culmination of the mounting feelings of anger, frustration and despondency in the country.

Still, although many people died in Buganda during the 1966 crisis and there continued to be many violent incidents that caused loss of life in the years following those events, it must be conceded that during these years of Obote's dictatorial and barbaric regime there was not what was later called 'state-inspired terrorism'. People were terrorised, harassed and threatened, and many were detained and tortured, but there was no state-inspired extermination of citizens such as became the hallmark of the regimes that followed. Violence had been introduced and institutionalised, but mass-murder, indiscriminate and efficient destruction of human lives, ordered and supervised by the state and especially by the President personally, had not yet begun. Indeed, in many ways, despite the political and economic hardship experienced at the time, many Ugandans feel today that some important economic infrastructures were established by Obote's regime in the 1960s which, had they been maintained and nurtured instead of being disrupted under the regime that followed, would have made Uganda a leading, if not *the* leading, economic power in East Africa. Paradoxically, while Obote pursued and persecuted those who opposed him with vigour and utter ruthlessness, he left alone those who were prepared to 'live and let live' within the political perimeter he had circumscribed for them, and it happened that those who derived most economic benefits during this period of political violence were the Baganda themselves.

Yet there is no doubt that with the open harassment of the populace by the notorious General Service Unit headed by Obote's cousin Akena Adoko, the five years that preceded the coup of 1971 will always be seen, especially by those who remember the nightmare, as the lasting testimony to Obote's misuse of power and his cruel disregard of democratic principles, fair play and decency. It was an agonising period in the Ugandan people's history – the beginning, as it turned out, of the consolidation of 'state hegemony' that brought continued suffering to the country.

State hegemony was extended to trade unions and religious organisations, as had been attempted before 1966. Between 1966 and 1968, relations between the Uganda Labour Congress, which the government had set up early in 1966, and the ruling group deteriorated; a Commission of Inquiry into trade unions was set up, and went a long way to establish state hegemony over the trade union movement. In 1965 the government had barred militant Kenyans from leadership positions in the movement, and in 1969 it proceeded to expel Kenyan workers *en masse* from Uganda 'on grounds of improving the conditions of national labour'. As one writer sadly commented, 'This was the first mass expulsion in Uganda's history.' At the same time the government declared all strikes illegal; so, at a time when the cost of living was rising, workers found themselves with no means of making their voices heard to redress their economic plight. No wonder that by 1970 the workers too 'were ready to support any other class or action of society that might lead the opposition to the bureaucratic state'.[5]

In the religious bodies, government intervention tended to divide rather than unite Muslims and adherents of the Anglican Church of Uganda. Division within the Church of Uganda appeared in 1965, when Archbishop Leslie Brown retired and Eric Sabiiti, a non-Muganda, was chosen as his successor. The Baganda, perhaps in one of their rare parochial moments, were angered by the choice of Sabiiti which, they claimed, had been influenced or even dictated by Obote. They felt, not without reason, that they were the Church's 'natural' leaders and therefore natural successors to the English religious leaders who had brought the Englishman's religion to Uganda. Had it not been Kabaka Mutesa I of Buganda who invited the first British Protestant missionaries, and did Christianity not spread into other parts of Uganda from Buganda? Thus the Baganda questioned, and wagged their fingers at the non-Baganda Christians. Here we see an anticipation of Uganda's later tragedies when a matter of such importance as the election of the Archbishop

of Uganda was being considered in terms not of his merits and qualifications but of the region from which he came. The two Buganda
dioceses of Namirembe and West Buganda decided to secede from
the province, and the government, instead of taking a neutral position in the dispute, decided to give full support to Sabiiti's faction.
This only exacerbated matters.

As for Islam, we have seen how the creation, with government
backing, of the NAAM led to schisms among the Muslim community. By 1968, the government's support for this body had gone to
the extent of regarding those who did not support it as 'disloyal to
the state'. There were ugly scenes whenever supporters of the two
rival groups met, which often led to killings. One interesting
development, however, was that just before the coup in 1971, Idi
Amin had ceased attending NAAM meetings but was attending
UMC meetings instead. He was even speaking publicly against the
'intrusion of politics into religion'.

The establishment of state hegemony over economic affairs
involved placing the ruling bureaucracy in control of the economic
surplus, which in effect meant squeezing out the Indian commercial
group. The second component to this was the so-called 'Move to
the Left strategy', declared at the end of 1969, which was intended
to involve the ruling group in sharing the economic surplus with
multinational organisations. The Move to the Left strategy was
intended as the culmination of Obote's philosophy of socialism,
which he hoped would place him on the same socialist platform as
his friends Julius Nyerere of Tanzania and, to a certain extent,
Kenneth Kaunda of Zambia. But Obote's commitment to socialism
remained questionable, and the coup coming as it did so soon after
the socialist strategy was launched, spared Obote the ordeal of
having to demonstrate it. Commenting on Obote's ideological stand
as well as leadership, Ali Mazrui wrote:

> Obote was a sincere socialist in my estimation, but did not have the right
> skills of leadership for socialism. He was also less tolerant of his opponents
> than he should have been, and more tolerant of his Cabinet Ministers and
> their self-aggrandisement than he should have permitted himself to be. The
> tragedy of Obote was that he had the conciliatory skills of a great liberal
> leader but chose instead to be authoritarian and socialist.[6]

To destroy the economic base of the Indian commercial bourgeoisie, the government intensified its earlier efforts to create an
African commercial bourgeoisie. But in effect those who stood to
benefit from this policy were the ruling group themselves – the
ministers, party officials, top civil servants and senior army officers.
Cooperative movements, which hitherto had handled the marketing

of a large variety of produce in the country, were accused of corruption (which was true), and the government created parastatal bodies to take over their activities. This was the origin of such organisations as the National Trading Corporation (NTC) and the Produce Marketing Board (PMB), both created in 1968. However, neither was in the end any better than the cooperatives and other organisations they replaced.

The move to elbow out the Indian traders only led to economic difficulties: food shortages sent prices through the ceiling, which led to political discontent among the most exploited classes in the country – the urban workers and the working peasants. All this contributed to the economic crisis which appeared in mid-1969, for there was less surplus to share out and yet there were many mouths to feed. The government had counted on increased exports of primary commodities and on obtaining foreign assistance, but neither was achieved and the country experienced a serious problem with its balance of payments. From 1969, because of the rising prices we have already mentioned – especially of food – and the clampdown on car loans, wages and salaries announced in April 1970 by the President in *The Communication from the Chair* as part of the Move to the Left strategy, there was much hardship. There was no clearer manifestation of the economic crisis and the economic plight of the people than the rise and expansion of *kondoism* (armed robbery by professional thugs called *kondos*). Its prevalence and the apparent inability of the authorities to stamp it out caused general frustration and a sense of grievance against Obote's government.

It was evident by 1969 that economic difficulties were leading to, and in turn being exacerbated by, political strife. The government lacked a mass political base; its policies had alienated the small Indian traders, and the small African traders, in whose name those policies were being instituted, fared no better. It was these factors which led the governing group to take political measures that it believed would further strengthen its control of the country. On the economic plan, as we have seen, they led to the Move to the Left strategy. In November 1968 Obote had informed the country that he was adopting a socialist strategy, but it was not till October 1969 that the publication of the 'Common Man's Charter' was announced. It was the basic document of the proposed Move to the Left strategy, and was adopted at a delegates' conference in Kampala on 19 December 1969. Its adoption was followed by the publication of three companion documents. However, it was the 1970 Labour Day Pronouncements – known as the 'Nakivubo Pronouncements' because they were announced at Nakivubo stadium in Kampala – which were meant to implement the Move to the Left strategy. Basically these Nakivubo Pronouncements placed over 60% ownership 'in all means of production' in the hands of the government, a move which affected about eighty-five companies operating in Uganda. Government entered into negotiations with the various companies affected over the terms of partnership, but these were not yet completed by January 1971 when Obote was overthrown.

The Move to the Left was received with considerable cynicism by a large section of the population, especially those who had been squeezed out of commercial enterprises and the ordinary workers and peasants who were struggling to cope with the ever-increasing economic difficulties. Also, it was clear that those who were preaching socialism were far from being socialists themselves: ministers, party functionaries and top civil servants were enjoying a life-style that could only be attained by corruption. The class of *Wamabenzi* ('Mercedes Benz owners') had emerged and the gap between the rulers and the common man, in whose name socialism was being introduced, was widening every month. The forces representing the 'right' now posed as the guardians of public virtue in opposition to the governing bureaucracy, and voices began to be heard more frequently inside and outside parliament against the flagrant and widespread corruption among ministers and top civil servants. Thus the Move to the Left, particularly the 1970 Navikubo Pronouncements, were received with alarm by commercial circles in the country; the whole strategy was vague and people interpreted it in different ways, to the detriment of the ruling group which, as already noted, lacked any political mass base and at the same time enjoyed the distinction of being widely hated in Buganda, the country's most populous region. No wonder it was Buganda, where political and economic hardships combined to produce unprecedented discontent among the majority, where the change of leadership in January 1971 was most eagerly welcomed and celebrated.[7]

Finally, although there was growing discontent by 1970 among some sections of the population, and most of all in Buganda where such political unrest was most easily manifested and encouraged, it was not expected that this could lead to Obote being ousted from power. Those events were momentous; opposition to him appeared strong in some areas but he was still widely popular, especially within the UPC and in the regions outside Buganda. Obote was vulnerable but still powerful; he had enemies around him but he had all along been a master at staging coups to extricate himself from the many tight corners in which he had been since the 1950s. In January 1971, he attempted to do this but this time he failed. Obote and

Amin had fallen out, and in the process things fell apart, first for Obote and then for the rest of Uganda.

Drift to the coup of 1971

The army – notably Amin – had remained outstandingly loyal to Obote in the 1966 crisis and in the years immediately after that event. Eventually, however, while still enjoying support in parts of the army, Obote became estranged from that section led by Amin. To return to the army's origins, Nubians – the men with whom Captain Frederick Lugard had come to Buganda from the north – had monopolised the force from the creation of the King's African Rifles 4th Battalion in 1901. However, when the First World War broke out in 1914, there was a need for its expansion, and Acholi then became the main recruiting area. Soldiers were also recruited from other areas such as Lango and West Nile, and by the time of the coup in 1971, in an army almost 9,000 strong, more than a third were Acholi.

However, from the beginning of 1969, Obote had divided the army into two factions along ethnic lines. As President and the Chairman of the Defence Council, he relied on the Nilotic soldiers, largely from Acholi and Lango, while for his part Amin built his support on his fellow West Nilers, especially those who happened to be Sudanic people like himself. Felix Onama, the Minister of Defence, was also a West Niler, and as time went on, he drew closer to Amin. It has been suggested that Onama, then Secretary-General of the UPC, was working, along with others in the ruling party, to oust Obote from the presidency with the possible aim of replacing him. It is possible that what sparked off disagreement among the leading members of the UPC was that in December 1969 the party passed a resolution to the effect that its president would automatically be President of Uganda, thereby ensuring that in the general election scheduled for early in 1971 Obote would be returned unopposed. This, according to observers, explains the wrangle over how the country's President should be elected, a protracted and acrimonious debate throughout 1970 which almost split the party. In the end, Obote won the contest, with great astuteness and audacity, but at the cost of alienating a large section of the 'old guard' within the UPC National Council.[8]

Although the Acholi were *against* the West Nilers' faction led by Amin, not all of them supported Obote. There were divisions even among them, particularly as Acholi district was believed to be predominantly DP. 'Only a portion of Acholis therefore could have supported him [Obote]', Ibingira has suggested. Obote overcame the well-known hatred and mistrust between the Acholi and Langi by presenting the presence in the army of the Sudanic people, headed by Amin, as the 'external threat' to all the Nilotics. Present-day Acholi is the result of an ordinance of 1937 amalgamating both Chua to the east and Gulu to the west; before that date, the people in the region knew themselves in terms of their clans rather than of a collective Acholi identity. This factor of two different though closely connected peoples having been amalgamated further under-mined the concept of a united Acholi people who, as a group, would overwhelmingly support Obote in his conflict with Amin and the West Nilers. This point becomes particularly crucial in that the Acholis were among the army personnel who were grumbling over promotion delays. However, although the majority of the soldiers were from Lango and Acholi districts, the professionals – who in the end turned out to be the true backbone of the army – were the men from Koboko (Amin's territory), generally referred to as Nubians. It was they – and all Kakwas or West Nilers who became Muslims were usually referred to as Nubians – who saw the army as their natural calling and themselves as a distinct entity, in contrast to the Langi and Acholi, for instance, despite the Acholis' numerical superiority within the army.

In a series of moves Obote threatened the existence of the regular army by attempting to create armed organisations that were seen to be acting in rivalry to it. The army perceived the Special Force, a paramilitary wing of the civilian police, and the General Service Unit (GSU), whose head was Obote's cousin Akena Adoko, as a design to create, as they put it later in their famous eighteen points, an army in the cabinet office; and there was a complaint that Obote was favouring his own tribesmen, the Langi, in promotions. The Special Force and the GSU appeared to have been favoured by the President in terms of arms, equipment and budgetary allotments, which further angered the regular army, and because of the coun-try's economic difficulties the largesse which the army had been used to enjoying in the past was no longer forthcoming. To the soldiers, with their imperfect understanding of economic problems, some of which are anyway outside the control of African govern-ments, the loss of privileges and surpluses appeared as a deliberate policy of neglect of the military by the politicians. The military could not be expected, either, to feel enthusiasm for Obote's Move to the Left, implying, as it did, equalisation of the country's resources and thus less for the military.

But the most important cause for the parting of the ways between Obote and the army was the personal estrangement between the President and Major-General Idi Amin. Why this happened we are not yet able to tell exactly, but by early 1970 it was clear to all that Obote wished first to isolate and later to remove Amin from the army. During his absence – Obote had sent him to Cairo to attend the funeral of President Nasser – the army was reorganised in such a way that Amin's grip on the command was weakened. The reshuffle of the army's hierarchy was significant: Brigadier Hussein was appointed as Chief of Staff (and therefore effectively the army's commander) and Colonel Juma Musa as Chief of the Air Force, which left Amin, who was now named as Chief of Defence Forces, appearing to be little more than a figurehead. He was angered by this, and remarked as much on a number of occasions after the reshuffle, which took place on 1 November 1970. Amin must surely have recalled how, after the 1966 crisis, Obote had 'promoted' Brigadier Shaban Opolot to the post of Chief of the Defence Forces, a sideways promotion which led to Opolot's removal from the army, and deduced that Obote must have a similar fate in mind for him, whether or not this was the case. These changes in the army command came on top of Obote's increasing tendency to by-pass normal channels when dealing with army affairs, and the two incidents gave Amin and his supporters in the army a growing feeling of ominous political demotion.

On his return from Cairo, Amin started identifying himself with the Uganda Muslim community, which now represented Buganda's opposition to the regime, thereby bringing about a coalition between his group within the army and the civilian groups, especially in Buganda, opposed to Obote. Mistakenly or not, in the open rift between Obote and Amin, the ordinary people, particularly in Buganda where the final act of the drama was being played, now saw Amin as the 'lone soldier' who represented the official opposition and therefore the would-be saviour of the country from impending catastrophe. Indeed Idi Amin's pose and behaviour at that time worked greatly to his advantage in the eyes of the public at large; he appeared to be an urbane, jovial yet serious personality, which was both a welcome contrast to Obote's menacing look (especially where the Baganda were concerned) and a reassurance to all who hoped for a decisive move from him against Obote. These events, small at first, began to be transformed into great forces of revolution for a decisive change. External factors too were not lacking. Obote had alienated the Israelis, who had been training the army and the police, when his government withdrew support from the southern Sudanese Anyanya who were locked in a civil war with the Arab regime in Khartoum, and whom the Israelis had been providing with arms. The Israelis were particularly angered, as was Amin, when Obote's government arrested a German mercenary called Steiner and handed him over to the regime in Khartoum for trial.[9.]

By October 1970 Obote and Amin were no longer on speaking terms, and each camp was working out plans for the elimination of the other. Scenes of open quarrelling between the two men became more frequent; Obote blamed Amin for not disciplining his unruly soldiers, and Amin blamed Obote for the hardship the ordinary people, including soldiers, were experiencing when he and his close associates were enjoying the rich booty of corruption. There is an incident, seemingly unimportant at the time, which shows that as much as two years before the coup that brought Amin to power, there was awareness of the growing rift between him and Obote. At the celebrations marking the consecration at Gulu of the Rev Janani Luwum as Anglican Bishop of northern Uganda, in February 1969, someone asked Judith Countess of Listowel if she had ever met General Amin. When she replied that she had indeed met the General, her questioner replied: 'Then have another look at him – you will hear a lot more about him.' A more significant foretaste of things to come occurred at the inauguration of Makerere as a full-fledged university in October 1970. The occasion was attended by important dignitaries from East and Central Africa, such as Jomo Kenyatta of Kenya (who very rarely travelled outside his own country), Julius Nyerere of Tanzania and Kenneth Kaunda of Zambia. Amin, of whom it was rumoured at the time that he had been placed under house arrest, arrived uninvited and strolled into the packed arena like a lion, several minutes after all the important guests, including Obote and the three visiting heads of state, had taken their seats. Amin was given what almost amounted to a standing ovation by the students and some other guests gathered for the occasion, which he acknowledged with his habitual huge smile and a salute. The meaning of this 'show' by Amin cannot have been lost on the three Presidents, and the embarrassment of President Obote must have been acute. No wonder that in his speech as the new Chancellor of Makerere University and in an attempt to put matters on an even keel, he announced the intention of his government to take drastic measures against corrupt army officers; the reference was clear.

Before leaving for Singapore on 11 January 1971 to attend a summit conference of Commonwealth leaders at which the sale of arms by Britain to South Africa was to be discussed, Obote left for Amin a memorandum in which there were two important matters to attend to and explain. One concerned the report of the police investigations into the murder of Brigadier Pierino Yere Okoya, the Deputy Army Commander, and his wife in Gulu in January 1970, which connected Amin with that murder. Equally important, Amin was requested to account for a large sum of money (believed to be £2.5 million) which the Ministry of Defence (or rather the army) had spent and which had not been accounted for. It was implied that Obote expected clear explanations to be ready on his return from Singapore.

Obote's accusation that Amin had misappropriated defence funds and his directive that they should be accounted for had a ring of irony, but all the same this must have hurt Amin in a special way; to him it was a dishonest accusation. For eight years, as Grace Ibingira has indicated, Obote had lavished money and privileges on Amin and the army, and encouraged his misuse of defence appropriations, despite criticism from his close colleagues.[10] Why, therefore, should Obote now turn about and make this accusation? It was clear to Amin, though less so to those ignorant of the inside story, that the accusation was a pretext, a trick intended to tarnish the General's name and reputation in the eyes of those likely to support him in the coming power struggle. Amin took the cue. It has been suggested that before leaving for Singapore Obote instructed a committee of his close associates to have Amin arrested before his return. The committee included Basil Bataringaya, Minister of Internal Affairs; Erinayo Oryema, Inspector-General of Police; Brigadier Hussein, and Lt.-Col. Oyite Ojok of the army.

Obote was never to receive the information he sought from Amin, for instead of attending to the President's queries, Amin attended to other, more urgent matters. When President Obote was on the point of returning to Uganda from Singapore, the storm broke. It is not clear who struck first, but Amin for his part has stuck to his story that he initiated a counter-coup aimed at foiling one that had been mounted by Obote himself from Singapore. The other and perhaps more plausible version is that Amin, aware of what Obote's memorandum really signified, decided to strike while his adversary was away and his lieutenants in the army and the General Service Unit were without their commander.

As Obote stated in a handwritten commentary on these events addressed to George Ivan Smith, the immediate cause of Amin's coup was the fact that two trials were about to take place, in Khartoum and Kampala respectively, which might affect Amin personally. The trial in Khartoum was of Steiner, the German mercenary who had assisted the Anyanya in the Southern Sudan and been arrested by Ugandan authorities and handed over to the Khartoum regime; that in Kampala was of those accused of murdering Brigadier and Mrs Okoya. According to Obote, Amin was involved in the affairs that had led to both trials, and had to act to protect himself.[11]

Obote should in fact have added the British to the list of those wanting to see his downfall. Ever since, early in 1970, Obote's government resolved that all Asians holding British passports should leave Uganda, there had been considerable anxiety in government circles in London. This was one reason – additional ones were Obote's socialist posture and his foreign policy which ran counter to Britain's interests.

It now seems incomprehensible that Obote should have decided to go to Singapore – and to do so, furthermore, while leaving his back undefended – at a time when Kampala was full of rumours of an impending coup attempt. He should not have underestimated Amin's capacity for action, his supporters later lamented; a prudent man would have made arrangements to combat any opposition, even if they had later proved unnecessary. Obote had not originally intended to go to Singapore because, apart from the persistent rumours of a coup, general elections were due in April 1971 and preparations for them were already under way. In the end, however, Obote decided to go because of the importance which he, like other African leaders, attached to the liberation of Southern Africa. Julius Nyerere and Kenneth Kaunda, in particular, strongly urged him to go because the British government's decision to sell arms to South Africa was the main topic on the conference agenda. This, incidentally, would also explain why people like Julius Nyerere took Obote's downfall personally. But the details of why and how the coup was staged and how it might have been foiled need not occupy us here. On 25 January 1971 the die was cast, and in the ensuing struggle Idi Amin won and Milton Obote lost.

Unlike Sir Edward Mutesa, Uganda's first and only truly elected President, Amin burst into the presidency, like Obote before him, through the barrel of the gun, stumbling on to the pages of history, muttering gloomily about his unwillingness to take charge of the country and wondering why he had been sent for. It was the opinion of many, both in Uganda and outside, that he would not be around for long. It was generally believed that after a year or two he would escape through a window and return to the obscurity of the barracks from which he should never have emerged in the first place. But this was not to be.

NOTES

1. A.G.G. Gingyera-Pinycwa, *Apollo Milton Obote and His Times*, New York: Nok, 1978, p. 93.
2. ibid.
3. Quoted from V. Kyobe *et al.*, *Proposed Federal States of Uganda*, Kampala, Jan. 1986.
4. From Benedicto Kiwanuka papers, privately held at Kiwanuka residence, Rubaga, near Kampala.
5. M. Mamdani, *Politics and Class Formation in Uganda*, London: Heinemann, 1976, for this analysis, p. 285.
6. Ali A. Mazrui, 'Political Science and Social Commitment in the First Republic of Uganda: A Personal Interpretation', *Kenya Historical Review*, vol. 6, nos. 1 and 2, 1978, pp. 63–83.
7. I am indebted to M. Mamdani (see note 5) for this analysis.
8. See P. Willetts, 'The Politics of Uganda as a One-Party State, 1969–70', *African Affairs*, 74, 296 (1975).
9. Steiner was subsequently put on trial in Khartoum and given a death sentence in late 1971, which President Nimeiri of Sudan commuted to twenty years' imprisonment.
10. G.S. Ibingira, *African Upheaval since Independence*, Boulder, CO: Westview Press, 1980, pp. 291–3.
11. See G.I. Smith, *Ghosts of Kampala*, London: Weidenfeld and Nicolson, p. 79; and A.M. Obote, 'Amin, Onama, Anyanya and Israelis conspired', *The Nationalist*, July 1980.

7

AMIN TAKES OVER: THE 'HONEYMOON YEARS', JANUARY 1971–JANUARY 1973

Introduction

At about 3.45 p.m. on Monday, 25 January 1971, a hesitant voice announced on Radio Uganda that the armed forces of Uganda had overthrown A. Milton Obote and his government. About half an hour later, the same voice returned to the air and announced that the armed forces had given power to their fellow-soldier, Major-General Idi Amin. The reader of the announcements was later identified as Warrant Officer (Class II) Samuel Aswa – fated to die three years later at the hands of Amin. But at that historic moment, when he was struggling through the text which listed the famous eighteen reasons why Obote had been toppled, Aswa must have shared the excitement of some of his countrymen at what was happening.

The period between the military take-over and the beginning of 1973 was one that witnessed great events in the country, which in turn became the springboard for many others that marked the rule of Amin in Uganda over a period of eight years. These events, although seemingly varied, were in an important sense connected, so that they need to be looked at and thought of as a single chain. First there was the great jubilation among some sections of the population at the birth of the new regime; the statesmanlike policies pursued by Amin soon after the coup which made him appear a 'man of peace'; then the slaughter of both civilians and members of the armed forces, mostly Acholi and Langi; the pursuit of a foreign policy that abandoned traditional friends and embraced new allies; the expulsion of citizens as well as non-citizens of Asian origin; and, finally, the invasion of the country by those ousted from power in the coup of January 1971. But before we proceed to the events themselves we should consider the new ruler himself: what kind of man was he? What was his background?

Idi Amin Dada: the man

According to his own testimony, Amin was born on 1 January 1928 on the very site where Kampala's International Conference Centre now stands. While we may accept the first part of this statement, all accounts agree that he was born hundreds of miles from Kampala, at Koboko, virtually on the border with Zaire and Sudan. However, as George Ivan Smith has observed, 'there is no way of proving whether he was born in a hut in Zaire, in Uganda or in the southern Sudan'.[1] His father was a Muslim of the small West Nile Kakwa tribe, consisting of some 60,000 people; his mother was a Christian Lugbara. Both the Kakwa and the Lugbara are Sudanic peoples, but the Kakwa are more frequently described as Sudanic Nubian. Amin is thus, by all accounts, a Muslim and a Kakwa-Nubian, these people being identified by the tribal marks – intended as a form of ornament to increase beauty – of three parallel longitudinal cuts on the cheeks (later in the regime, they were generally referred to as 'one-eleven').

Idi Amin's parents separated when he was still small, and he followed his mother to Buganda where she lived first at Lugazi and then at Buikwe, before finally settling permanently at Jinja in neighbouring Busoga. Amin received at least two years of primary education, probably at Semuto primary school, some 30 miles north of Kampala. At the very best, he was semi-literate and although he could later speak, read and write English, which showed an ability to learn, he lacked, as Grace Ibingira has commented, 'the sound foundation upon which to build and it was too much to expect an absolute head of state to have sufficient time to catch up on what has taken others decades of training and education'.[2] Besides this, Amin's whole background is in the rural peasantry, a factor which had a major influence on events in Uganda:

If President Amin has charisma, it would seem to appeal to Uganda's peasant-oriented peoples [rather] than to any of its elite groups. Amin is the embodiment of a man who has made it big from humble, peasant beginnings without having to submit himself to the frustration of formal education's elite acculturation process. He is a man who has combined the social mannerisms and survival instincts of peasant life with the thorough training and experience of a military leader.[3]

It is not true, as Amin used to claim and as others have suggested, that he fought in the Second World War, since he did not join the King's African Rifles (KAR) till 1946, after the war was over. But he possessed, in abundant measure, the qualities that appealed to the British when recruiting Africans into the army. They did not care for intellect or academic performance; 'a thumbprint was the accepted signature for pay and equipment, and what the officers were looking for was a strong physique, stamina, speed of reaction and an upright bearing.' Amin fitted the bill exactly, and was recruited. He served in Company 'E' of the KAR, and in 1953-4 fought loyally for the British in Kenya against Mau Mau, although he was later to claim

that he assisted the Kenyans, and especially Kenyatta, in their liberation struggle. In 1954, by now a corporal, Amin went to a special
training school at Nakuru where he acquired his basic knowledge of
English. His lack of education might have impeded his progress, but
as Iain Grahame, under whom he later served, tells us, 'on the
ground that he stood head and shoulders above all the other students
in every respect apart from education, an exception was made. He
was promoted to Sergeant.'[4]

As what has been referred to as the 'stampede towards independence' gathered pace in the East African countries, there was an
urgent need to create an African officer corps in the army to take
over from the British. It was largely for this reason that men like
Amin were promoted to positions that they would never have
reached in normal circumstances. Thus in 1958 he was already a
sergeant-major, serving under Iain Grahame at Jinja, and all his
supervisors were then agreed that Idi Amin 'had reached his ceiling',
but who would replace the British officers at independence? The
dilemma for the British was what should prevail: the traditional
martial qualities or education. Although some educated young men
were being sent to Britain for training, there was no alternative but
to promote Amin and Shaban Opolot on the spot as the first
Ugandans to be given the Queen's Commission as lieutenants. But
Amin's anxiety to show efficiency and please his British superiors
nearly cost him his army career. Early in 1962, now a platoon commander, he led an operation to the Northern Frontier District where
he brutally beat up an entire Turkana village community, killing
three tribesmen. The Kenya authorities demanded that Amin be
tried for this atrocity, but Sir Walter Coutts, the Governor of
Uganda, took the advice of the Prime Minister, Milton Obote in
deciding not to prosecute him since he was one of the only two commissioned officers then available, and especially since independence
was only six months away.

With the arrival of independence, Amin was a captain and was
now sent to England to undertake a commanding officers' course at
the School of Infantry in Wiltshire, but he returned to Uganda in
1964 without having completed the course. He was then sent to
Israel for a parachute course, which he did not complete either, but
in order not to create embarrassment the Israelis gave him his wings
just the same. Amin did not have any part in staging the mutiny of
1964, but he played an important role in suppressing it, which
earned him the admiration and support of both the soldiers and the
British officers. After the mutiny Shaban Opolot was made Commander of the Army and Idi Amin Deputy Commander. From here
the story is familiar. As the political alignments among the different

protagonists emerged, so did Amin's fortunes rise, particularly as he was on the side of the Prime Minister. As we saw in the last chapter, the 1966 crisis raised him to the highest place he had yet attained; it made him a kingmaker, an indispensable ally of any politician who subsequently aspired to become ruler of Uganda. Amin was not without personal ambition, and his chance came in January 1971 when he was swept to power by a group dominated by the Kakwa-Nubians, all NCOs, whom he had recruited and trained during the previous few years. Amin's background – being a Kakwa-Nubian and a Muslim, and coming from West Nile – was to be crucial in the events that followed. One writer has aptly observed that 'as he became older and acquired power, he considered himself first and foremost a Nubian/Kakwa, secondly a Muslim, thirdly a West Niler and fourthly a Ugandan. Consequently the closest people around him came in this order which was later repeated in his choice of senior operatives and agents.'

Welcome for the coup: the people's jubilation

The coup that unseated Obote has received much attention and attracted a considerable body of literature.[5] Of course, it was not bloodless, and there was strong resistance from soldiers loyal to Obote and the civilian government. Outside Uganda there were plans, worked out in Dar es Salaam, for Tanzania, Somalia and possibly other countries in the region (though not Kenya) to mount an attack on Uganda 'to put down what was regarded as a mutiny by sections of the army led by Amin'. Indeed the coup could have been resisted, and at any time in the first week Amin could have been toppled. But inside Uganda, any resistance would have foundered on the obvious popularity of the coup among the civilians, particularly the Baganda in whose territory lay Kampala, the capital. Indeed, what saved Amin and his collaborators, at least in the early period after the coup, was the geographical factor: the capital, where power was seized and held and where the international press were concentrated, lay in Buganda, the former kingdom where feelings towards Obote were not friendly.

Needless to say, praise for the army's action against Obote was not confined to Buganda, although it was the Baganda's reaction which could be monitored by the international media since they were at the centre of all activities during the first few months of the coup. The people of Uganda, particularly the Baganda and Basoga, who welcomed Amin in January 1971 did not do so out of love for a man whom they hardly knew but more because they sincerely believed that a new era had opened for their country; in it, at least, those

Idi Amin at the time of his military take-over, January 1971.

Idi Amin being sworn in as President.

values which they believed had been trampled on and buried would be resurrected and reasserted for the prosperity of all. We have to re-emphasise the fact that the rejoicing of the Baganda was given so much publicity partly because the international press were based in Kampala, in Buganda, and it was not till six weeks or so after the coup that President Amin toured up-country areas so that their reactions too received some publicity. Morever, because Obote had been a leading critic of British policies in Southern Africa, the British journalists who swarmed in Kampala after the coup naturally wanted to give the impression that his views had not been representative even of those elements in the population who were unhappy at his departure.

Many of those who welcomed Amin's coup and sent him messages of congratulation and praise for his 'timely' action were to suffer later at his hands. These people seemed to be vying with each other in the extravagance of their praise. Writing on behalf of the members of the royal clan of Buganda, Prince George Mawanda-Cwa, elder brother of Sir Edward Mutesa, congratulated Amin and the officers and men of the Uganda Army 'for the successful bloodless coup which has saved our country from corruption and inconsiderate government.' It was their fervent prayer, he added, 'that Almighty God may grant your Excellency the light to lead our country to peace and prosperity and that under the inspiration of your rule the people of Uganda may enjoy the blessings of security, unity, liberty and justice which the protection of your Excellency and the Uganda Army and Air Force has brought to us all.' Amos Sempa, who had been prominent in Buganda politics since the 1950s and been detained by Obote, paid tribute to Amin who had delivered the citizens and residents of Uganda from 'Dictator Obote's regime'. He continued, 'We are all grateful to the new Military Head of State for the salvation he has brought to this country! In fact, he has cut his name on the memorial tablet of the Uganda braves by sheer courage and unselfishness.' Abu Mayanja's message to Amin was even more fulsome: 'You and our brave officers and men of the Uganda Army have saved the honour, integrity and freedom of our country. Uganda, Africa and humanity owe you a deep and irreparable debt of gratitude. The whole country is behind you, our redeemer.' To Joseph Kiwanuka, who had recently been released from detention by Amin and was to be extradited from Kenya and killed two years later, the General should be awarded the same title as Churchill: 'saviour' of his country.

On his first return to Uganda since fleeing into exile in London in 1966, Joshua Mayanja-Nkangi, the last *Katikkiro* (Prime Minister) of Buganda, said: 'The new revolution of the coup is the country's resurrection. My pleasure is beyond words and is really not express-able, just leave it at jubilation.' Mayanja-Nkangi said that the coun-try had been redeemed from tyranny and oppression, and the second revolution 'deserves celebration as it has brought new life to most of the citizens of Uganda'. From Masaka, Alderman Francis Walugembe, who was later to fall victim to Major Maliyamungu and Abdul Nasur, sent this message to Idi Amin:

No doubt all the people lived under fear during the former regime and could not express their views freely. You have freed us now. Thank you for having freed our fellow citizens from detention to enable them to take part in the development and growth of our dear nation. . . . We will work hand in hand with you to fulfil the objectives which prompted your wise decision to take over the control of the Government of Uganda.[6]

Praise of Amin was not confined to the Baganda or indeed to the African population; even some important members of the Asian community added their voices to the general euphoria at Amin's emergence. In his true colours as a staunch capitalist, multi-millionaire Jayanti Madhvani spoke of the commercial opportuni-ties opening up under the new regime after 'the dwindling scope for private enterprise under the former Government of Obote'. Even those who had served as ministers in Obote's government turned against their former leader and started praising Amin. But Amin condemned these tactics and, at a press conference, wondered why the former ministers had not given good advice to Obote but waited until he was deposed. He warned them to stop trying to clear their names by trying to show that they were good people now that Obote had gone.

Many foreign newspapers, particularly *The Times,* the *Daily Telegraph* and the *Guardian* of London, hailed the event as some-thing which would herald a new era in Uganda. But we should not be unduly harsh on foreigners for doing what we ourselves were only too anxious to do without realising the true import of our actions.

The purpose of quoting these messages of congratulation and support for Amin is not to depict them as wrong or insincere; they represented the situation as it was at the time and reflect the euphoria and excitement in the country, particularly in Buganda, after the coup. Most of the messages we have cited were from those who had been in detention or in exile. But their importance lies in the fact that they were the pillars that propped up the fragile framework of Amin's regime during its first twelve months or so. They enabled Amin to convince and win over the doubting Thomases within the country, civilian and military; on the other hand, because they were communicated publicly and appeared in the local press, they convinced the international media that the military government was supported among the population. This show of support was also crucial in achieving recognition for the new regime from the Organisation of African Unity (OAU), whose Council of Ministers was meeting at that time in Addis Ababa, and from countries and organisations outside Africa. Essentially, however, this adulation and excessive praise gave Amin a confidence he had previously lacked, arousing ambition and a sense of destiny which he probably did not have at the time of the coup. In the words of Iain Grahame, one of the few military officers who can justifiably claim to know Idi Amin well,

Had the new President had the wisdom to hand over power to a civilian government in the spring of 1971, and concentrate his own energies on restoring peace and discipline within the army, much of the tragedy which was to befall Uganda might have been avoided. Encouraged, however, by adulation and euphoria, and quite unable to transcend the severe limits imposed by his lack of formal education, Idi Amin chose a course that was to take his country back down the dark tunnel to an era of barbarism and internicine slaughter.[7]

Ugandans should desist from piling all the blame for the agony of the country on to those who happened to be in power. It has often been we, the citizens, who have enabled those bad leaders to thrive. The people who supported Obote in 1962 and Amin in 1971 bear some responsibility for the chaos of our politics. Also, it is worth noting that some of the Ugandans who embraced Idi Amin in January 1971 had earlier helped Obote to attain power (particularly the Baganda and the old DP politicians), and saw Amin as the springboard to their political resurrection. Uppermost in their minds was not the true welfare of Uganda but the removal of their political adversary and the field day they would have in this new era. They fell for Amin's sweet promises of a speedy return to civilian rule and the holding of elections within a year. Who, they felt, would challenge Benedicto Kiwanuka's revamped DP now that the UPC was discredited and in confusion?

Amin: the 'man of peace'

Amin's behaviour in the first few months after the coup, at least in the eyes of Ugandan civilians and the international media, was that of the man of peace, concerned above all with reconciliation and the securing of national unity, peace and prosperity. Three days after the coup, he released all detainees, some of whom had been in prison for five years. In all fifty-five people (most of them Baganda) were released – a small number, admittedly, compared with what prison doors disgorge following coups in other Third World countries.

Amin's actions, for which many enthusiastic Ugandans dubbed him 'Man of Peace', 'Redeemer' and 'Saviour', were extended to religious affairs, and he made efforts to reunite Muslims and bring together the factions that had emerged in the Protestant Church. To demonstrate his concern, he announced the setting-up of a Ministry of Religious Affairs in which every religious leader would have an office where he could be contacted. Although this ministry never came into being, a Permanent Secretary for Religious Affairs in the Office of the President was appointed.

Nowhere did Amin more clearly demonstrate his concern for reconciliation, as a mark of a new era, than in his decision to have the body of Edward Mutesa, first President of Uganda and former Kabaka of Buganda, brought back to Uganda for a state funeral. This pleased not only Baganda but all Ugandans, including those in non-kingdom regions, who considered that although the events of the mid-1960s had been inevitable, as indeed they were, a way should be found to heal the wounds that had been created. There is no need to impute sinister reasons for Amin's decision to return the Kabaka's body, while also acknowledging that he saw clearly that political capital was to be gained from the gesture, particularly as this would win him the overwhelming support of the Baganda, who were important geographically if for no other reason, at a time when his regime was far from being firmly established. So the decision to return the Kabaka's body for burial in the land of his fathers was a political one, intended mainly to win popular favour. Certainly to Amin, at least in the early days of his regime, the Kabaka's funeral was of great importance and soon his personal prestige depended not only on its taking place but also on its being done well. The announcement that the body would be returned was made on the day following the coup. As one who knew Amin well observed, 'it was a remarkably shrewd move, which enhanced people's adulation of him still further. To many of them, it seemed that a saviour had arrived.'[8]

The body arrived at Entebbe on 31 March 1971 and was buried at Kasubi, near Kampala, the traditional royal burial-place, on 4 April. Amin had achieved, with this gesture to the Baganda, a political initiation, which strengthened his still fragile leadership. A group of Baganda mourners were specific. They told him, according to the *Uganda Argus* of 1 April 1971:

We are grateful for what you have done for us. . . . We have nothing to give you except to give you our love and loyalty. We pledge to continue to be always obedient to your Government. The Government has returned our beloved Kabaka who died destitute for the greed of one man, the man who never suffered for the independence we are enjoying today.

But while Amin appeared to be the 'saviour' with a new message of salvation for the nation, and the outside world watched a 'man of peace' on a crusade to achieve reconciliation in a country that had been torn by factions and hatred, a vicious revenge was being wreaked on some sections of the military. These killings were totally hidden from the civilian population, and known only to a few people outside the country with access to information supplied by exiles from the affected barracks or areas. Most were confined to the army, where tribal conflicts existed and plots were hatched to overthrow the new regime.

Killings in the army

Amin and his military men, the West Nilers and particularly the Nubians, who had taken over power against the predominantly Acholi and Langi supporters of Obote within the army, were filled with a desire for vengeance, and we should look at the factors which had led to this.

Amin and his supporters, having seized power, found themselves in a hostile world where international politics were concerned. First and foremost, President Nyerere of Tanzania refused to recognise Amin's regime and offered sanctuary to Obote, his arch-enemy. Coupled with this, his delegation, led by his Foreign Minister Wanume Kibedi, failed to be seated at the OAU Council of Ministers that was sitting in Addis Ababa in February 1971. The non-recognition of the delegation was an affront and a blow to Amin's prestige, and was pregnant with repercussions at home. Amin's pride was also hurt when the venue for the OAU summit conference, which had been planned for Kampala and for which he had ordered the completion of an international conference centre, was shifted to Addis Ababa. For several months the Sudanese leader, General Nimeiri, was strongly anti-Amin, and this produced security problems for the new regime in Kampala. For instance, in the middle of February 1971, Obote went to Sudan, where the Sudanese government allowed him to lay on training facilities at Owiny-Ki-Bul, in the South, so that he could plan to regain power. From there he contacted soldiers and civilians in Uganda, who wanted to fight, to go and join him in Sudan. Thus the circumstances in which the Second Republic of Uganda was launched were grave. Amin had a strong sense of insecurity, and the predominance of the Acholi in the army worried him especially, for at the time of the coup one-third of the army were Acholi and Amin was not sure of their loyalty to him. The activities of Obote and his supporters to oust him from power only increased his killer instinct and his determination to strike a blow against the Acholi and Langi soldiers as well as civilian leaders.

In one important sense, it was unfortunate that Amin should have automatically singled out the Acholi as his enemies. As we have seen, not all Acholis in the army were pro-Obote, and certainly there was ample evidence that not all Acholis supported efforts to frustrate the success of the coup. The first radio announcement of the coup gave the impression that it had been pro-Acholi and anti-Langi; for one of the eighteen points read out accused Obote of enhancing the interests of the Langi at the expense of the Acholi and other tribes in the north. Only later – perhaps unconvinced that the Acholi would remain loyal to the new regime and not maintain a prior loyalty to Obote – did Amin start to explain the coup by saying that the Acholi, in alliance with Obote's tribe, the Langi, had plotted to disarm all other soldiers and institute a complete ethnic monopoly of military power in the country.

Most of the killings in the army during the first twenty months took place in four phases or incidents. The first was when a coup was attempted in July 1971 and Acholi and Langi soldiers were massacred at Jinja, Moroto and Mbarara barracks; the second was at Mutukula on the Uganda-Tanzania border in February 1972; the third was during another attempted coup in June 1972; and the fourth, which we shall discuss separately, occurred after the invasion in September 1972 which coincided with the departure of the Asians from Uganda.

There is no need to describe these attempted coups in detail. But as these troubles arose, Amin took the opportunity to eliminate his enemies, who happened to be from Acholi, Lango and Teso, the three groups which dominated the security forces. Thus, although the public did not know it, this early period of the Amin regime witnessed unprecedented organised violence. During most of 1971, the up-country areas, where the majority of the killings took place, were sealed off from foreign journalists and those daring few (such as Nicholas Stroh and his colleague Siedle, representing the *Philadelphia Bulletin*) who attempted to find out the truth from Mbarara barracks, fell victim to Amin's wrath. Foreigners as well as Ugandan civilians tended to see these killings as no more than the normal 'mopping up operations' that follow a coup. But the murders of the military officers and men were never reported, nor were they believed by Western diplomats based in Kampala, the British and Israelis openly ridiculing suggestions of mass killings. Eventually, however, the truth began to leak out and Amin, needing to suppress news of the atrocities which would remind the world of the internal instability and vulnerability of his regime, decided on certain initiatives that would divert both domestic and international attention. This at least partly explains the hitherto unthinkable expulsion of, first, the Israelis and then the Asians from Uganda.

Expulsion of the Israelis

These two events set the stage for much of Uganda's subsequent history. First, expelling the Israelis turned Uganda towards the Arab world, a foreign policy position with important results. As for the expulsion of the Asians, this has been the prime cause of the dismantling of the Ugandan economy from the mid-1970s onwards.

The Israelis came to Uganda in the mid-1960s, and their relations with the civilian government were close and friendly. At first they were mainly involved in the army and police training, and many army officers, including Amin himself, received part of their training in Israel. In the late 1960s, the Israelis became involved in construction projects, including the building of roads and of housing units in Kampala, Arua and Tororo – the latter in particular are a living testimony to their admirable assistance. They were also involved in education and medical services. Their role in the coup and the reasons why they supported Amin have already been mentioned. In the first press conference he gave in Dar es Salaam after the coup, Obote explicitly blamed the Israelis for the success of the coup, a charge which was dismissed in Jerusalem as fantasy. The Israeli Foreign Minister saw Obote's accusations as designed to dissuade Arab states from recognising the new regime in Kampala. However, there is no doubt that the Israelis were instrumental in planning the logistics for the coup, particularly in the deployment of the mechanised equipment, and afterwards they had a high profile in the capital and its environs. They were to be seen everywhere. For example, they manned roadblocks in Kampala, and a friend of the present author was badly roughed up by them at a roadblock in Kololo.

Uganda's friendship with Israel continued for some more months; more Ugandans were offered scholarships for study there, and Ugandan air force personnel continued to receive training from the Israelis, for which Amin expressed gratitude. Then, in February 1972, Amin completely fell out with them. His own explanation for the expulsion of his erstwhile friends was simple: they were sabotaging the economy and the security of the country.

The reasons for the expulsion are, however, somewhat more complex. It seems that Amin found the Israelis high-handed, especially since they knew they had played a significant part in his rise to power and continued to believe that his survival depended on their support. Certainly, during the first few months of the coup, they behaved as if Amin was 'in their pocket', an attitude which awoke all Amin's resentment against 'white racist arrogance'. To make matters worse, Israel demanded to be paid for its construction projects in the country, and a figure of 70 million shillings was mentioned. Amin had no money to pay them. There was also the issue of the civil war in Sudan, between the Anyanya in the south and the Arab regime in Khartoum. So long as the war continued, Amin could not turn against the Israelis because they were supporting the Anyanya, his relatives and allies, some of whom he had recruited into his own army. In February 1972, however, a peace agreement was signed in Addis Ababa and the civil war came to an end. Israel's support was no longer indispensable. In the words of Ali Mazrui, 'The causes of Amin's rejection of the Israelis did not lie in the Arab world. They lay in the history of Southern Sudan.'[9]

It would appear, however, that the most important reason for the breach between Amin and the Israeilis was their refusal, together with the Western powers, to sell him arms. Israel was the first country which Amin visited after the coup, on 11 July 1971, and in his talks with the government there, he sought armaments. Prime Minister Golda Meir was shocked by Amin's 'shopping list' and would not oblige. He was given the executive jet he asked for and a small quantity of arms that were already in the pipeline, but that was all.

From Tel Aviv Amin went on to London, where he was received as a hero and dined with both the then Prime Minister, Edward Heath, and the Queen. In his talks with the British officials, Amin again requested arms. But they declined to give him aircraft, as he wanted, although they agreed to the supply of some light arms and promised him a grant of £10 million. Thus Amin failed to secure from Jerusalem or London the arms he wanted to deal with Tanzania and others outside the country who wanted to overthrow his regime. As for other possible sources, the Chinese were cooler now than they had even been towards Obote, and he expected little from that quarter. The Soviets, for their part, were cautious about Amin's pro-Western policies, and were unlikely to commit themselves so soon to a regime that had received such a grand reception in Western capitals. In view of all this, Amin felt seriously let down by Israel and Britain.

However, his break with the Israelis did not immediately follow these visits. The immediate cause of the breach seems to have been Amin's visit to West Germany in February 1972. In Bonn he met all the figures who mattered, and there were some promises of aid, but he obtained no firm offer of credit or of any sophisticated armaments. The writing was now on the wall: the West would not supply him with the kind of arms and the amounts of money that he wanted. The only people to whom he could now turn were the Arabs who, being Muslims, were natural allies. He turned first to President Sadat of Egypt, but Sadat could not supply Amin's needs because he had no military equipment himself and was also shopping around. However, Sadat was sympathetic to his fellow Muslim, who also happened to rule the country that contained the source of the Nile. Sadat, like Nimeiri of Sudan a few months before, told Amin that the best solution to his financial problems would be to turn to the oil-rich Gaddafi, who had few people on whom to spend his country's wealth.[10]

According to G.I. Smith,[11] it was while Amin was visiting the German city of Essen that agents of Colonel Gaddafi contacted him – he was negotiating at the time with a British company to explore for and exploit oil at Lake Albert in western Uganda. Amin was invited to visit Tripoli, and did so on his return journey to Uganda. The visit was for one day only, 12–13 February 1972, but its results were far-reaching. Seven days later, a ten-man Libyan delegation arrived in Uganda for top-level discussions (it was the first Libyan delegation to visit Uganda since Gaddafi's assumption of power in Libya in 1969). Soon after its departure, Amin began his accusations that the Israelis were sabotaging the economy and security of the country, although he had earlier on assured the Israeli ambassador, who called on him to find out what had transpired in Tripoli, that Uganda's relations with Israel would remain unchanged. The anti-Israeli campaign continued until Amin was forced to come out into the open and declare his true sentiments towards the Israelis. Amin expelled them from the country and by 1 April 1972 they had all left. The breach between the two countries was total and final.

The departure of the Israelis brought Amin's Uganda and the Arab world into a close embrace. Aid started to flow into Uganda from Arab countries – Amin denying Israeli accusations that he had thrown them out on advice given to him by the Arabs and because of the offers of financial assistance that would result. He insisted that Libya had had nothing to do with their expulsion and that the decision had been arrived at in January 1972 before his visit to West Germany and Libya. He refuted the Israelis' claim that they would be replaced by Libya; however, he did turn to the Arab world in general and he did in fact replace the Israelis with the Libyans.

The expulsion of the Israelis turned out to be a dress rehearsal for that of the Asians a few months later; this time, the victims were not mere visitors but people for whom Uganda was home. More than half of the Asians who were expelled were in fact of Ugandan nationality.

Expulsion of the Asians

The expulsion of the Asians from Uganda[12] was perhaps the single event in Uganda's modern history that has wrought the greatest change. It received great publicity around the world – perhaps even more than the coup itself – largely because it affected Britain and other Western countries, to which most of the expelled Asians fled.

Indians originally came to East Africa in substantial numbers at the end of the nineteenth century as indentured labourers to construct the Uganda Railway. With the termination of the contract in 1901, most of the workers returned to India, while 6,724 stayed in Uganda. However, the former spread news of the immense opportunities in East Africa, and this caused a further Asian influx. The British used the Indians to establish and later consolidate their rule, using them as middlemen – political as well as economic – between themselves and their African subjects. As such they became an essential part of the colonial infrastructure.

The economic activities of the Asians prospered. As to whether Asians developed or exploited East African states, the answer is 'both'. 'The Asians did invest both resources and themselves in East Africa; they did feed as well as milk the cow. However, the milk and the cream were worth far more than the cost of the feed.'[13] In Uganda they were involved first in trade, and then successively in manufacturing, agriculture and finally in public service, including the administration. However, at the time of the expulsion, few were engaged in agriculture except for the two giants Madhavani and Metha, who owned large sugar industries at Kakira and Kawolo respectively.

Why did Amin decide to expel the Asians from Uganda? It has even been suggested that it was because an Asian girl spurned him. This claim would hardly appear serious until one recalls that the shape of Cleopatra's nose changed the history of the Roman Empire, and what sort of ruler Amin was. Economic considerations have been given much weight. At the time of the coup that brought him to power, Amin had promised heaven to everyone, and certainly an impression was created that the new (or Second) Republic would make the economic situation of the population easier. The eighteen points given as the reasons for overthrowing Obote had stressed the economic hardships which the people had suffered under his regime; but after a year and more, Amin had nothing to show to justify his coup. Taxes had not been reduced, and the people were called on to make the sacrifices necessary to make development possible. The prices of basic foodstuffs and the general cost of living were rising; *kondoism* was still rampant; there were ever fewer jobs for school-leavers; and violence and murder, far from being eradicated, were virtually institutionalised. Not only the civilians were complaining; even army personnel were looking to Amin for a solution.

So it was not surprising that, unable to deliver the goods, Amin should have turned upon the only community with money and property that he could plunder to give to his people. There is a tendency in reconstructing historical developments to emphasise economic factors but here they can hardly be over-stressed. The expulsion of 50,000 Asians, many of whom were millionaires in Ugandan shillings at the time and who together owned and controlled perhaps half of the country's wealth, opened the way for the state to acquire their assets, without payment, for Amin to dispose of as he saw fit. It was Amin's answer to the plight of the masses and the greed of his soldiers. Those who benefited most from the expulsion were those, military and civilians, who would not have made it to the top under Obote or any other civilian ruler.

There were other considerations that made this an easy step for Amin to take. He knew that he could capitalise on what had become the traditional hatred of the Asians by the African population. This did not emanate only from their wealth, although that was a major factor; the Asians also kept themselves within their own community, refusing to integrate with the Africans, and hardly ever intermarrying with them. Although some had taken Ugandan citizenship, the Asians remained – and were seen to be – foreigners in their own country. The Asians' failure to integrate within Ugandan society was a theme to which Amin always returned, right from the time of the coup. He knew that any measures taken against Asians would find favour with Uganda's black population.

Amin also knew that by expelling the Asians from Uganda, he would indirectly be punishing Britain, the country where most of them would go to. Although the British had welcomed the coup and hailed Amin as the 'Good Big Guy', their actions towards him had not been reassuring, as had been all too clearly shown on his visit to London in July 1971. In expelling British citizens from Uganda, he would, as he later put it, 'be teaching the British a lesson they would never forget'.

A parallel has been drawn between this expulsion and that of the Italians from Libya in 1969. The two events could be seen 'as part of the process of decolonisation' and in both cases, as Ali Mazrui has noted, 'could only have been done under a military regime, with all the relative insensitivity to the diplomatic and humanitarian implications of those measures.'[14] Amin got away with it, as Gaddafi had done with the Italians, largely because the British genuinely feared that Uganda, being in the hands of a soldier and an undisciplined army, was capable 'of taking physical action against British Asians and even British Europeans in Uganda in a manner which would have been inconceivable under Milton Obote'.[15] It is more than possible that Gaddafi had urged Amin to emulate his own action against the Italians, a move which would both strike another blow against imperialism and colonialism and solve some of his financial problems.

According to Amin, the final decision to expel the Asians came to him as a directive from God in a dream[16] which he had early in August. However, the campaign against the Asians had started right from the time of the coup. In the tours of the country which he made a few months after taking power, he made the accusation, already referred to, that the Asians kept to themselves and failed to integrate in Ugandan society, mentioning that on Sundays every town in Uganda was turned into a little Bombay.

The first statement on the expulsion affected only those Asians who held British passports; but Amin soon changed his mind and announced that all, including those with Ugandan passports, had to go. He had also originally exempted professionals, but in the end he said that they too would have to leave since they could not serve the country with a good spirit after the departure of other Asians. Despite what may have been said later to the contrary, the move received wide support among the indigenous population. Amin had judged their reaction correctly. Several letters were published in both the English and the vernacular press, all praising the action of Amin, whom they called 'the saviour of Uganda'. As far as we know, not a single editorial expressed any criticism of Amin's decision, although at this time there was still freedom of expression in Uganda. The only dissenting voice came from Makerere University Students' Guild, whose president, Tumusiime Mutebire, told Amin in a speech at Kampala City Square on 8 August 1972 that Makerere students supported his decision 'to uproot Israelis from Uganda and Asians with British passports', but strongly appealed to him to reconsider his decision to expel Asians who were Ugandan citizens.[17]

The British reaction, as expected, was that of a wounded buffalo. During his visit to London in July 1971, Amin had discussed the Asian issue with ministers who had received the impression that an agreement could be reached with Uganda, as had been the case with the Kenyan government on the Asian intake rate. Amin's bombshell therefore caused utter dismay. In retaliation, the Foreign and Commonwealth Secretary, Sir Alec Douglas-Home, announced in parliament that Britain would have to review all its economic arrangements with Uganda if Amin went ahead with his professed intention to expel Asians holding British passports. Sir Alec added that the action would be highly irresponsible, and while admitting that Britain accepted 'a special obligation for those people who are British passport holders', there was no way of dealing with the problem humanely 'other than by the kind of scheme we have which is an orderly quota arrangement'. He concluded by saying that Britain would use all the diplomatic arts 'to try to get General Amin to alter his mind, supposing he really meant what he said'.[18]

However, Amin was adamant, and when it became clear that he would not rescind the decision, the British government sent a minister, Geoffrey Rippon, to Kampala to plead with Amin. Iain Grahame, who had once been Amin's commanding officer in East Africa, offered to accompany Mr Rippon. The two men arrived in Uganda on 10 August 1972 but it was not till 15 August that Amin found time to receive the minister. The encounter between the British gentleman and Uganda's ex-heavyweight champion turned politician cannot have been easy. As Amin himself later confessed to Iain Grahame, he had an 'awful time': 'I found Mr Rippon very hard to understand. I think he is a good minister, but he does not speak Swahili.'[19] Grahame spoke good Swahili, but in spite of apparently being on good terms with Amin, he could do nothing to change his mind. Geoffrey Rippon returned to Britain, soon to be followed by the Asians whose fate he had vainly tried to avert.

It has been estimated that as a result of their expulsion the Asians lost no less than 4.5 billion shillings,* and that a more realistic figure would be 6–7 billion.* Apart from the financial loss, they suffered brutal and inhuman treatment at the hands of soldiers as they went through roadblocks on their way to Entebbe airport. Such personal belongings as jewellery, watches and cameras were seized as they proceeded to the various points of departures from Uganda. The Asians' sufferings, including beatings, were all witnessed by black Ugandans, many of whom showed little sympathy or concern. Their luggage, which they left at the airport with the promise that it would be air-freighted to their destinations, never left Uganda, but was appropriated by the army. Sadly, the economic expectations which

---

*The equivalents of these figures in late 1991 are, respectively, 643 and 857–1,000 billion shillings.

Ugandans then entertained debased human values. 'Your turn will come,' some of the Asians warned the jubilant Ugandans, a prophecy which soon became true as thousands were forced to flee into exile from Amin's terror.

The expulsion of Asians was almost effected within the specified period of three months from the day it was announced. Indeed, most were out of the country well before the deadline.[20] There then followed the sharing of the booty by the jubilant Ugandans, and many of them, including top officials in the civil service and professors and lecturers at Makerere University, joined the scramble for the allocation of Asian businesses; for some it was a horrifying experience. Amin had delivered the goods to his hungry people and for this he was decorated by the Defence Council on 9 September with the country's eight highest honours and medals for expelling the Asians. The army pledged its support for him in any difficulties that might arise as a result of his action.[21] With the expulsion of the Asians, a new term – 'Economic War' – came into use in Ugandan society; this was after a speech by Amin to the students of Makerere University on 12 August 1972. The Economic War was soon extended to British interests.

On 17 December, in a midnight radio and TV broadcast to the nation, Amin announced major decisions affecting the lives and property of British citizens in Uganda. The Ugandan government was to take over all tea estates, BAT, Ugandan Transport Company, Brooke Bond, Chillington Tool Company, Consolidated Printers, Securicor, British Metal Corporation, Uganda Television and the Kampala Club, which till then had been exclusively British. At the same time he announced several other drastic decisions mainly affecting the British community. Certain categories of trading licence would not be renewable for non-Ugandans; British personnel who had indicated a wish to leave Uganda had to do so by 31 December 1972; those Britons who chose to stay were warned not to act as spies for Britain or any other power, otherwise they 'will be in trouble'; places bearing 'meaningless imperialist names' were renamed, e.g. Queen Elizabeth National Park and the Murchison Falls became Ruwenzori National Park and Kabalega Falls respectively; all blocked accounts would be transferred to the Uganda Commercial Bank with effect from 1 January 1973; and finally, all government and parastatal bodies were to switch their insurances to the National Insurance Corporation (NIC), and all Ugandans were to do likewise.[22]

Amin promised that, as with the departed Asians, the government would pay compensation for the British property which had been taken over. Thus, despite his earlier assurances that Uganda would not nationalise British or any other foreign property, Amin had gone ahead and nationalised British businesses, a move described by Sir Alec Douglas-Home as 'outrageous by any standards'. Britain retaliated by cancelling all aid to Uganda, including the £10 million grant promised in July 1971. It is noteworthy that Tanzania, despite its strained relations with Uganda, welcomed Amin's take-over of foreign, particularly British, companies and offered Uganda its assistance in case of difficulty in view of its own experience in running such enterprises.

Amin was over-optimistic when he declared the Economic War. In his broadcast of 17 December 1972, just referred to, he gave several reasons why he had taken those decisions in particular and why he had declared the Economic War in general. The latter was intended 'to make the ordinary Ugandan master of his own destiny and above all to see that he enjoys the wealth of his country. When the future generations look back in history decades and hundreds of years to 1972/73,' he declared, 'if they do not remember us for any other good thing, they will at least remember us for having given Uganda her economic independence.'[23] The effects of the Economic War will be discussed in the following chapters. Meanwhile, on the very day of the first airlift of Asians to Britain, 17 September, Obote's guerrillas, with fighters belonging to other anti-Amin movements, crossed the Ugandan border from Tanzania.

The invasion of September 1972

Plans to remove Amin were mounted right from the time of the coup. An invasion of Uganda from Tanzania was considered in August 1971, but the plan was vetoed by Tanzania's military leaders who did not consider the chances of success good enough. Apart from spasmodic cross-border exchanges of fire between Ugandan and Tanzanian soldiers, no serious invasion was mounted from Tanzania till September 1972. This time was chosen because it was believed that, with the Asian exodus from Uganda beginning, the chances of success were high. The international community, particularly the Western powers, was hostile to Amin, and it was not expected that he could count on assistance from outside. Indeed, it was expected that Britain and Israel, the two countries Amin had particularly offended in the past few months, could make things rough for him. Also, the guerrillas who had been trained in the Southern Sudan since February 1971 were itching for some action and above all wanted to return home. In July 1972 they had been transferred to Tanzania, where Obote himself had returned in June after being away from Dar es Salaam for sixteen months. In contrast to the previous occasion in August 1971, the Tanzanian army command did not give close scrutiny to the plans of the September invasion, which was only revealed to very few Tanzanians and to Obote's most trusted associates.

President Nyerere and the Tanzanian military were also anxious for some action to be taken against Amin. They welcomed this opportunity to topple him particularly because in August 1972 he had threatened to invade Tanzania and capture the 100-square-mile triangle of the country in the extreme north-west bounded by the Uganda border, the Kagera river and Lake Victoria. Amin claimed that the Kagera river should be the natural boundary between the two countries, and said that if Tanzania did not give up the 'Kagera Salient' he would take it by force. The Tanzanians had taken these threats very seriously, and moved up close to the frontier the infantry battalion from Tabora and the heavy mortar and artillery support unit from Musoma.[24] Indeed, on 15 September 1972, a story appeared in the *Daily Express* in London in which Major Ian Walsworth-Bell, a former British army officer, claimed that he had drawn up plans for Amin to invade Tanzania from Uganda. The Tanzanians were seriously alarmed, and glad that the Ugandan exiles were now ready to strike at their arch-enemy.

The invading force, amounting to a little over 1,000 men, belonged mainly to Obote's fighting forces, although other groups – such as Yoweri Museveni's guerrillas who later formed Fronasa (the Front of National Salvation) – also participated and Museveni himself fought at Mbarara. The overall command of the invading forces was placed under Colonel Tito Okello, with Lt.-Col. Oyite-Ojok as second in command. The plan was that seven truckloads of men would cross the frontier at Nsongezi and head for Mbarara. The main force, consisting of twenty truckloads of men, would cross at Mutukula and head for Masaka. A group of about 180 commandos was to be airlifted from Arusha to Entebbe, which they would capture and hold, and then move on to Kampala where they would capture the radio and announce the capture of the government.

The invasion collapsed completely, a failure which has been attributed to many factors. There were three main ones. First, the men were in poor shape, and the invasion itself was badly planned and executed; secondly, Amin knew of it in advance and had his armour and fire-power ready – specifically his Malire battalion met the invaders at Kalisizo, west of Masaka; and thirdly, Amin won because he still had the support of the civilian population of the invaded areas. The jubilation which the people were expected to

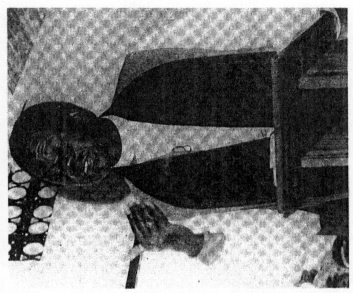

Janani Luwum, Anglican Archbishop of Uganda, murdered by Amin, February 1977.

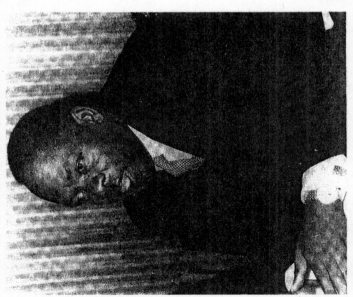

Benedicto Kiwanuka, first Prime Minister of independent Uganda (1962) and Chief Justice (1971–2), murdered by Amin, September 1972.

show when they saw the invaders did not materialise; the latter, particularly those who fought at Kyotera and Kalisizo, were harassed and many of them killed by inhabitants of the area who came across them as they wandered in swamps and forests.[25] It cannot be doubted that when the invasion took place Amin was still generally popular, particularly in Buganda, through which the invaders had to pass on the way to Kampala. For instance, on 18 September, the day following the invasion, he drove himself in an open jeep from State House, Entebbe, to Kampala and in all the many places he passed through, such as Katwe, Nakulabye and Wandegeya, he was cheered with shouts of *'Amin yekka'* ('Amin only').

The Arab world, as expected, gave Amin its full support, Libya actually sending troops to assist him. Although they never took part in any fighting, having arrived after the invaders had been routed, it was an important show of solidarity and consolidated the friendship between the two countries. Libyan assistance was welcomed by Ugandans at the time and was not seen by them as interference in the country's affairs, as Obote claimed in a letter circulated to the heads of state and government at the OAU summit held at Addis Ababa in May 1973.[26]

On the home front, the invasion had given Amin an opportunity to eliminate his enemies, both civilian and military. Benedicto Kiwanuka, the Chief Justice, was arrested in his chambers and later murdered. Kiwanuka had earlier released a detained British businessman named Stewart and commented that the soldiers had no right to detain individuals arbitrarily. It is also said that Amin killed Kiwanuka after finding out that he had agreed to work with Obote for his overthrow. This has been disputed by Grace Ibingira who says that, from what he knew of Kiwanuka, this would have been impossible.[27] However, the point is that, whether or not Kiwanuka agreed to work with Obote against him, Amin found out that the two men were in contact with each other, and this was reason enough to eliminate the Chief Justice. The murder of Kiwanuka has also been attributed to Amin's fear of him as an alternative choice for the leadership of Uganda, due to his popularity and standing within Ugandan society.[28] Another victim of Amin at this time was Frank Kalimuzo, Vice-Chancellor of Makerere University, who was picked up from his official residence and killed later at Makindye. Amin had on several occasions accused Kalimuzo, who was from Bufumbiro/Risoro, of being a spy for the government of Rwanda – and for Amin this suspicion was conclusive. Basil Bataringaya, who had chaired the meetings that were planning to stop Amin's coup in January 1971, was dismembered alive outside the town of Mbarara and his severed head displayed on the end of a pole. His wife too was killed soon after, allegedly by Juma Bashir, the Governor of Western Province.

The reign of terror unleashed on the population did not spare the youth, particularly members of NUSU (the National Union of Students of Uganda) at Makerere and other institutions of higher learning, of whom many fled into exile. Others killed at the time of the invasion or soon after included Francis Walugembe, the Mayor of Masaka, and John Kakonge, James Ochola and Shaban Nkuutu, former ministers in Obote's government. Mr Wakholi and Alex Ojera, also former ministers, took part in the invasion and were captured and later murdered. Of the twenty cabinet ministers in Obote's government, eight had been killed and four were in exile within two years of the coup. The killings were extended to the armed forces, where of the twenty-three officers of the rank of lieutenant-colonel or above at the time of the coup, only four were still in the service three years later, including Amin, the Paymaster and the Chief Medical Officer. Thirteen of these officers had been murdered.

By the beginning of 1973, Amin's true nature was emerging – what Grace Ibingira has described as 'a combination of guile, buffoonery and utter ruthlessness in killing anyone even remotely suspected by him or his subordinates of being unfriendly'. The marriage between Amin and the population had not yet collapsed; no one was talking of divorce, but certainly the honeymoon was over. The hard realities of the regime were clear. Amin himself was not unaware of this and set about consolidating his position. We now turn to the consequences for Uganda of his reign of repression. This is the period when he became unstoppable, a 'lion rampant'.

NOTES

1. G.I. Smith, *Ghosts of Kampala*, London: Weidenfeld and Nicolson, 1980, p. 29.
2. G.S. Ibingira, *African Upheavals Since Independence*, Boulder, CO.: Westview Press, 1980, p. 29.
3. J.T. Strate, 'Post-military coup strategy in Uganda: Amin's Early Attempts to consolidate Political Support', Ohio University Centre for International Studies Papers in International Studies – Africa, Series, no. 18.
4. I. Grahame, *Amin and Uganda: A Personal Memoir*, London: Granada, 1980, p. 23.
5. E.g., among others, P. Woodward, 'Ambiguous Amin', *African Affairs*, 77, 309 (1978); A.A. Mazrui, 'Amin's coup: Ethnocracy and the Military-Agrarian Complex' in A.A. Mazrui, *Soldiers and Kinsmen in Uganda: The Making of a Military Ethnocracy*, London: Sage Publications, 1975; P. Willetts, 'The Politics of Uganda as a One-Party State, 1969–79', *African Affairs*, 74, 296 (1975); Michael Twaddle, 'The Amin Coup', *Journal of Commonwealth Studies*, X, 2 (1972); M.F. Lofchie, 'The Uganda Coup – Class Action by the Military',

Journal of Modern African Studies, 10, 1 (1972); A. Southall, 'General Amin and the Coup: Great Man or Historical Inevitability', *Journal of Modern African Studies*, 1975; D. Martin, *General Amin*, London: Sphere Books, 1978.

6. For Prince Mawanda, see *Uganda Argus*, 4 Feb. 1971; for Amos Sempa, *ibid.*, 9 Feb. 1971; for Abu Mayanja, *ibid.*; 2 Feb. 1971; for Joseph Kiwanuka, *ibid.*; for J. Mayanja-Nkangi, *ibid.*, 5 Feb. 1971; and for Francis Walugembe, *ibid.*, 1 Feb. 1971. For Jayant Madhavani's praise, see *Uganda Argus*, 13 July 1971.
7. I. Grahame, *op. cit.*, p. 117.
8. ibid., p. 98.
9. A.A. Mazrui, *Soldiers and Kinsmen*, pp. 221–2.
10. J. Listowel, *Amin*, London: IUP, 1973, pp. 131–2.
11. G.I. Smith, *op. cit.*, p. 90.
12. On Asians in East Africa in general, and in Uganda in particular, see Bert. N. Adams and Mike. Bristow, 'The Politico-Economic Position of Ugandan Asians in the Colonial and Independent Eras', *J. of Asian and African Studies*, XIII, 3/4 (1978), pp. 151–66; D.P. Ghai, *Portrait of a Minority: Asians in East Africa*, Oxford University Press, 1965; J.S. Mangat, *A History of the Asians in East Africa*, Oxford: Clarendon Press, 1969; M. Twaddle (ed.), *Expulsion of a Minority: Essays on Ugandan Asians*, London: Athlone Press, 1975.
13. B.N. Adams and M. Bristow, *op. cit.*, p. 157.
14. A.A. Mazrui, 'Soldiers as Traditionalizers: Military Rule in the Re-Africanisation of Africa', *J. of Asian and African Studies*, XII, 1–4 (1977)', p. 256.
15. *Ibid.*
16. Professor Mazrui has warned us not to underrate the importance of dreams in African society. He says that although 'some of the Ugandans, particularly the intellectuals, might dispute the validity or authenticity of this or that particular dream claimed by Amin, . . . perhaps the great majority would not dispute the proposition that some dreams are intended to be guides for action, and that supernatural forces might at times be in communication with a leader.' See A.A. Mazrui, 'Soldiers as Traditionalizers', op. cit., p. 246.
17. *Uganda Argus*, 9 Aug. 1972.
18. *Ibid.*, 7 Aug. 1972.
19. I. Grahame, *op. cit.*, p. 134.
20. However, not all could be got away before the deadline. The United Nations High Commission for Refugees (UNHCR) was very worried about their safety, and therefore commandeered the Sikh and Hindi temples, declaring them to be UN territory. All the remaining Asians were kept there until they could be got out, and a number of expatriates were hastily enrolled as UN officials and fitted out with armbands declaring them to be UNHCR staff. This bluff worked. (See D. Humphrey and M. Ward, *Passports and Politics*, Harmondsworth: Penguin, 1974, pp. 45–6.)
21. The citation for the decoration was read by Colonel Toko, the then Commander of Uganda Air Force. See *Uganda Argus*, 11 Sept. 1972. Toko was among those who later lived in exile during Amin's rule.
22. *Voice of Uganda*, 18 Dec. 1972. (On 1 December 1972, the *Uganda Argus* was taken over by the government; it was then managed by the Ministry of Information and Broadcasting, and its name changed to *Voice of Uganda*).
23. *ibid.*
24. D. Martin, *op. cit.*, p. 206, to which this account and what immediately follows below is greatly indebted.
25. Personal interviews of people in Kyotera and Kalisizo.
26. A.M. Obote's letter to the Assembly of Heads of State and Government, the OAU, Addis Ababa, May 1973, appears in A.A. Mazrui, *Soldiers and Kinsmen*.

27. G. Ibingira, *op. cit.*, pp. 288–9.

28. A prominent politician, who was a minister under Amin and who is serving the NRM Administration in a high office, is suspected by many Ugandans of having been involved in the death of Chief Justice Kiwanuka. This may eventually be investigated by the Ugandan Human Rights Commission sitting in Kampala at the time of writing. See Richard Muscat, *A Short History of the Democratic Party, 1954–1984*, Kampala: Foundation for African Development, 1984, p. 88.

8

LION RAMPANT:
AMIN'S CONSOLIDATION OF POWER
AND THE ENSUING VIOLENCE

Introduction

By January 1973, the second anniversary of the coup, Ugandans had experienced many changes. The Israelis had gone and been replaced by the Arabs, and the traditional friendship between Uganda and Britain had received a severe shock with the expulsion of the Asians and the taking over of British businesses. Amin was still popular after the September invasion and the people were prepared to give him a chance. Judith Listowel observes that if he had been killed or deposed around this time, Uganda would probably have reverted to internecine warfare, and that, whatever one felt about him, there was no one in Uganda who could have done better at that time.[1] This may well be true, but by the beginning of 1973, Amin's politics had thrown the country into such confusion that no one would have wished to inherit the problems he had created by taking over the government. It looked as if he alone could handle them, particularly since they included security.

But this is not to say that the people were contented. The economic difficulties which the Economic War was designed to solve were still there and taxes were still heavy, and in November 1972 the first severe shortages were experienced. Disillusionment began to appear; there was still support for Amin, but the enthusiasm was waning. Then, early in 1973, a spate of resignations hit the regime: Wanume Kibedi, the Foreign Minister and perhaps Amin's closest civilian associate, and Edward Rugumayo, the Minister of Education, resigned. Some prominent people – ministers and high-ranking officials – went into exile and wrote damaging accounts of Amin and his regime. His murder squads had become more prominent in eliminating civilians after the September 1972 invasion, and these killings could no longer be blamed on guerrillas from Tanzania. People had lost relations and friends, and suffering and fear were spreading. Amin knew that his popularity was on the wane, but he merely set out to consolidate his power, allowing no one to stand in his path. The period between January 1973 and August 1975, when he was elected Chairman of the OAU, can be considered as one of consolidation; at the end of this time he had built such a strong security system and so cowed his people that he seemed to have become invulnerable, particularly to enemies from outside. It was from the end of 1975 onwards that the greatest acts of repression took place.

Consolidation of Amin's power

The period of consolidation was an important one because this was when the structures – particularly in the military and administrative spheres – were established which were to see him through the next few years before he was eventually removed from power.

Amin's strategy was twofold. He decided to tighten his hold on the army and administration by ensuring that they were in the hands of trusted men who would stand or fall with him. The second strategy concerned foreign affairs. Here, in order to enhance his prestige at home and abroad (particularly in Africa and the Arab world), he embarked on a militant and radical foreign policy that was to result in Uganda changing sides in international politics. Overnight he became the champion of the liberation of Africa, the arch-anti-imperialist crusader of all time and the leader, as he saw it, of a large part of the Third World. It is no wonder that in 1975 he had become such a force in the politics of our continent that he was made Chairman of the OAU. This achievement was a culmination of his attempts to achieve a new image *vis-à-vis* other African leaders, regardless of what the Ugandan people themselves were experiencing.

To take the security situation first, 1973 opened with numerous problems for Amin. Within the country he still faced opposition from the Acholi and Langis, as well as from some parts of the Eastern Province. The security forces were even fighting among themselves. The guerrilla activities, particularly those mounted by Yoweri Museveni's Fronasa organisation, were increasing, and Kampala and other urban areas were full of rumours about their impending arrival. Amin's main danger at this time – that of guerrillas – was not completely eliminated but was dealt with temporarily. A few of them were arrested in Kampala, Jinja and Mbale and put on trial. Amin was determined to make an example of his captives and eleven guerrillas and one *kondo* were, as expected, found guilty by a military tribunal and sentenced to death. They were executed by firing squad on 10 February 1973 at their respective district headquarters. It is sad to record that thousands of people voluntarily travelled to these places to witness the executions.

Most, if not all, of the local newspapers – including the Catholic monthly magazine *Musizi* – supported Amin's action. This was not a case of supporting Amin's brutality, for he had not yet come out in his true colours, but they simply voiced the views of the majority of people, particularly the Baganda, who saw any resistance against Amin as aimed at returning Obote to power and therefore bad. Whatever our views may be today, this is something which we must take into account and appreciate as a fact in looking at these events. But, as was to occur time and again in Uganda, those who supported Amin's brutal actions against others soon fell prey to his wrath themselves. For instance, Father Kiggundu, the editor of *Musizi*, was murdered soon afterwards and his body burnt in his car; while two months later Dr Sembeguya, a leading surgeon in Kampala, was also eliminated. These were leading personalities, but there were many less-known people who died at the hands of the state following the departure of the Asians and the capture and execution of the eleven guerrillas.

In an endeavour to tighten security the Military Police were given greater powers even than the regular army, police and prisons. A new decree (no. 19) empowered them to arrest people without a court order or an arrest warrant. They could arrest a wide range of 'criminals', on the basis of suspicion only. As for the armed forces, some promotions were made in May 1973 to keep them contented, but these did not stop some officers from thinking of ways of changing the leadership of the country, and the first major coup attempted by some of the most senior officers took place in March 1974. It was an event that had a lasting effect on Amin and influenced subsequent events.

However, this coup attempt was not the first against Amin since the September 1972 invasion; there had been one led by Colonel Wilson Toko, commander of the Air Force, in April 1973. It was Toko who had read the citation for the decoration of Amin after the expulsion of the Asians! Up to that time, the threats to Amin had come from outside Uganda, particularly from Tanzania; this was the first major coup attempt mounted from within. The 1974 coup was organised and led by Brigadier Charles Arube who, with Elly and a few others, had just returned from attending a course in Moscow. It was spearheaded by the Malire Reconnaissance Regiment whose commander, Major Juma, did not participate. Arube's coup almost succeeded; all the important installations – Malire, Makindye and Kampala – were captured, and all that remained was to announce the overthrow of the government on Radio Uganda. In fact, the coup started so well that in the early hours of Sunday, 25 March 1974, Arube started celebrating its success with a dancing party at his house, but he was then arrested by soldiers loyal to Amin and shot and killed there and then. It would seem that one of the major causes for Arube's coup attempt was dissatisfaction at Amin's appointment of non-Ugandans to key posts in the army and government agencies. For instance, he had elevated Malera, a Sudanese, to the high post of Army Chief of Staff, and he later relied heavily on Brigadier Taban, Lt.-Col. Gole, Lt.-Col. Sule (all Sudanese) and Brigadier Isaac Maliyamungu (a Zairean). Other influential Sudanese nationals in Amin's regime at that time were Farouk Minaawa, Chief of the State Research Bureau, and Ali Towelli of the Public Safety Unit. According to some sources, the aim of the coup organisers was to arrest Amin, Brigadier Malera and the other notorious killers from southern Sudan and place them on public trial at the Clock Tower in Kampala, where the guerrillas were executed in February 1973.

Amin was shaken by the attempted coup, which had been organised and led by Kakwa officers, his fellow-tribesmen. He felt betrayed and abandoned, but because there were very few Kakwa officers whom he could appoint, he decided not to eliminate his betrayers. Instead, officers such as Lt.-Col. Elly were sent abroad as ambassadors. Throughout 1974 Amin continued to feel threatened from all sides. On top of the abortive coup of March 1974, reports of guerrilla invasions from Tanzania in August and Sudan in November alarmed him further, and caused him to live in constant fear of being toppled by Obote. He also believed there was an international conspiracy to unseat him, engineered by international media such as the BBC and British and Kenyan newspapers. That was partly why, early in June 1974, his government banned all 'imperialist' newspapers in Uganda 'for, among other points, their perpetual stand against the Ugandan government'. It was in these circumstances that so many innocent Ugandans died or disappeared, all suspected of working against him. It is impossible to fathom the extent to which Amin really believed in these stories of invasions, but those who were in Uganda at that time cannot forget the tension that existed between Tanzania and Uganda, which put the country on a war footing.

Because of the increasingly serious security problems from the time the Economic War was declared, and particularly in view of Toko's attempted coup in June 1973 and Arube's in March 1974, Amin took measures to strengthen his position in the army. After Arube's attempt, Amin was never the same man again, a point to which those who served in his cabinet at the time have testified.[2] However, the reorganisation of the army to bring it directly under his control began well before March 1974, although it was speeded up thereafter. Thus in November 1974 Uganda was divided into five military commands. At the same time, civilians and non-West Nilers were removed from cabinet posts and key positions in provincial administration.

The way in which the cabinet was selected was only part of Amin's consolidation strategy. Alongside the cabinet itself, he created and nursed the Defence Council which, though originally meant to deal only with major military matters, increasingly encroached on the powers and duties of the cabinet. It had been created soon after Amin's take-over in January 1971, but only around February 1973, perhaps due to increasing guerrilla activity, did it assume greater importance and begin to replace the cabinet as the major decision-making organ. Indeed, major policy and security decisions, and the hiring and firing of ministers and senior officials, were being taken by the Defence Council and then communicated to the cabinet by the President, so that to all intents and purposes it was the supreme authority in the country. Its precise composition was never established, but it certainly included the Chief of Staff, the Commander of the Air Force, the Minister of Defence and the most trusted army officers commanding vital units such as Malire Mechanised Specialist Reconnaissance Regiment. It was, of course, chaired by Amin himself. An additional body was the less well-known State Security Council (SSC), which appeared to have rather similar duties to those of the Defence Council. Despite its potentially large powers, it nonetheless seems not to have played a great part in Amin's administration.

The appointment of army officers and Nubian or Muslim civilians as ministers or senior officials in the government and parastatal bodies was one aspect of Amin's consolidation of power. Another, equally effective, was the reorganisation of administration, especially at provincial level. According to the new plan announced in February 1973, Uganda was divided into nine provinces, to replace the existing five regions. The new provinces, with their capitals, were: Southern Province (Mbarara), Central Province (Kampala), Buganda Province (Bombo), Kiira Province, later renamed Busoga (Jinja), Eastern Province (Soroti), Karamoja Province (Iriri), Northern Province (Lira), West Nile Province (Arua), and Western Province (Mubende). All the governors of the new provinces were high-ranking officials of the army, the prison service and the police.

We have emphasised Amin's moulding of the army into a state instrument for the consolidation of his personal power.[3] Another aspect of this development is that by about 1975 he had transformed the army, which had been predominantly Luo-speaking (dominated by the Acholi and Langi) up till the 1971 coup, to a predominantly Sudanic-speaking body of West Nilers, from his own region. This change of fortune naturally hurt those displaced by Amin's policies

– the Acholis and Langis, who had always seen the army as their preserve. For the southern Bantu-speaking people, it was no more than a changing of the guard. For them the army remained what it always had been – dominated by northerners, and used by a leader from the north, whether Obote or Amin, to subjugate the people of Uganda, particularly those of the south and west who did not contribute large contingents to the army. The fate of the southerners remained unchanged: harassment, torture and wanton killing at the hands of military thugs from the north.

Simultaneous with these internal measures, Amin carried out a foreign policy which, because of its militancy mixed with adventurism, earned him, particularly among Africans, a reputation as a tough fighter against imperialism and colonialism, the two enemies which every African leader, if he is to survive at all, has to condemn and fight in the name of the African Revolution. This tended to impress the ordinary African, whose instincts Amin appears to have shared, and to have won the admiration, mingled with fear, of most of his countrymen.

Here we can identify two major features. The first was the alienation of Uganda from its traditional friends in the West and the embracing of new ones to replace them, namely the Soviet bloc and the Arab world, in particular Libya and Saudi Arabia. The second feature was his 'African policy', especially towards the liberation struggle of the continent which was then one of the OAU's main preoccupations, or objectives. Amin's pro-Arab policy, initiated early in 1972 when he expelled the Israelis from Uganda, was reinforced thereafter. He continually blasted off against the Israelis, on whom he urged the Arabs to avenge themselves for throwing the Palestinians out of their homeland. This policy reached its height in the Yom Kippur War of October 1973 when, through untiring efforts so far unmatched by any non-Arab head of state, he persuaded almost all independent African states to sever relations with Israel. Thus the entire OAU, including moderate Francophone states, came solidly behind the Arab world during that war.

To what extent did Amin use Islam as a means to tighten his hold on the country? Certainly the Arabs, who supported Amin financially and so propped up his regime, believed that it was part of their cause to spread Islam in a country which was so centrally placed on the African continent. Leaders such as Muammur Gaddafi of Libya and King Khalid of Saudi Arabia believed Uganda to be predominantly a Muslim country. Indeed, addressing staff and students of Makerere University on his visit in March 1974, Gaddafi, believing that 70% of the Ugandan population were Muslims, condemned Christianity as an agent of imperialism and extolled the virtues of

Islam as a faith to which all Third World people should adhere. The Arab leaders certainly expected Amin to use his influence and their dollars to enhance Islam in Uganda, especially by expanding education for Muslims. The opening of a Libyan cultural centre in Kampala in January 1975 had this intention, despite the official explanation that it was there to cement cultural links between the two countries.

In Uganda itself Amin did several things that incensed the Christians, who were in fact the majority of the population. Islam was made to seem the religion of the establishment and of all those who aspired to gain power and influence. No one was actually coerced openly into embracing Islam, but it was made clear that those who did so would be rewarded. Conversions increased and were always given wide publicity in official media. There were other causes of annoyance to Christians; for instance Amin's announced intention to build a mosque on the very site of the Christian Martyrs' Shrine at Namugongo, near Kampala. The Christian majority of Ugandans also did not take it lightly when Uganda was listed among Islamic countries, and especially when it was admitted to the Islamic Conference held at Lahore in February 1974.

The OAU summit conference held in Kampala in July 1975 was an occasion of special importance for Amin in his endeavour to increase his prestige and support inside Uganda itself, elsewhere in Africa, and even beyond. The summit was held amid many protests against the flagrant violations of human rights in Uganda. However, Africa's leaders – with a few exceptions such as Julius Nyerere of Tanzania, Kenneth Kaunda of Zambia and Seretse Khama of Botswana – decided to attend the meeting at which Idi Amin, now rejoicing in the rank of field-marshal and Life President of Uganda, was elected Chairman of the OAU. Significantly, it was the first time since the organisation was founded in 1963 that President Jomo Kenyatta of Kenya, who could not fly for health reasons, attended a summit of the OAU. It appeared as if these African leaders, by attending, ignored the cries of agony of ordinary Ugandans, and cared only for their own high politics. They came and left. Ugandans have felt betrayed by their fellow-Africans who remained silent during all the years when they were suffering at the hands of dictators such as Amin and, later, Obote and Okello-Lutwa.

Lion rampant

By the end of 1975, Amin had indeed consolidated his power over Ugandans. He had survived a few coup attempts, and he had reorganised the army and administration so that the key positions in the state at all levels were held by men on whom he could rely. He was pursuing a foreign policy as vigorous as it was nationalistic, and this won him applause in the Third World, where he was perceived as challenging the hated imperialists. To crown it all, he was now OAU Chairman. Amin's hour had come. What more could this rural peasant, born in a hut, desire in this world? The gods had delivered his boat across the turbulences of the world to the highest position attainable. He believed he had become an international statesman who would mediate between one African state and another. At home he felt no challenge whatsoever. After all, was he not a field-marshal? In the issue of *Voice of Uganda* of 8 August 1975 a letter to the editor was published, with six signatures, suggesting that Field-Marshal Amin should become Life President. And so it was proclaimed. He had become a lion; he could now roar.

During the year from July 1975 to July 1976 when Amin was OAU Chairman, Ugandans experienced a period of relative peace because of his preoccupation with international affairs. He obeyed his instinct to play down his tyranny over those he ruled in Uganda for fear of losing credibility in the international forums which he was called upon to attend and address as nominal leader of Africa. But as soon as he became 'ex-current Chairman', as he always referred to himself after relinquishing the post, the lion became rampant. Amin spared no one – at home or abroad.

In 1976, Amin announced that he would annex part of western Kenya. Kenyatta fumed, demonstrations were staged throughout Kenya, and Uganda's oil supply was cut off. For the first time it looked as if external pressures could dislodge Amin from power. Amin hesitated, but in the end he gave up his wild scheme and peace was restored between the two countries.

Amin's foreign misadventures also landed him in the hands of the Israelis, whose nationals he had kicked out of Uganda in 1972. In June 1976 an Airbus belonging to Air France was hijacked by Palestinian terrorists to Entebbe, with more than 100 passengers, mostly Jews. Amin tried his old tricks again. He took sides with the hijackers and detained the plane and the passengers of Jewish origin. The Israelis struck. In an attack that has become a carbon-copy for others in dealing with air pirates and other terrorists, the Israeli state carried out a 90-minute operation at Entebbe airport in which the hostages were rescued and carried back to Israel.

After this event, which had been an appalling humiliation for Amin, there were many stories of harassment of civilians by his soldiers. For instance, it was dangerous to be seen laughing when they went by, for fear that they would think you were laughing at them and at Amin himself because of the Israeli raid at Entebbe. In fact, Amin and his army became a laughing-stock. It was said, for example, that the Israelis actually entered the State House at Entebbe and scribbled messages on the walls of toilets, saying 'We have been here' or 'We could have got you' or 'We shall return one day'!

So things drifted on till the late 1970s. The violence and murders became institutionalised, and for the first time in the country's history, citizens lived in spite of, and not because of, the existence of the state, and individuals and communities found themselves without protection against humiliation, molestation and dispossession. Liberty, life and property were at a discount. In such a state of chaos many lives were lost, including those of leading personalities in the land. One occurrence which sent a wave of horror throughout and beyond the Christian world was the wanton murder of the Anglican Archbishop, Janani Luwum, in company with ministers Erunayo Oryema and Charles Oboth-Ofumbi. Why Amin killed the Archbishop has never been explained. However, it appears that at that time an attempt to stage a coup was being organised by some Acholis and Langis based in Nairobi. Archbishop Luwum was never involved, but he was informed of it by some Acholis in Uganda. When the Archbishop was asked to join the group, he declined, saying that as a churchman his concern was with preaching and not fighting; the plotters then left him. What led to Luwum's death was the fact that he did not tell Amin of this plot. Other people who knew of it warned Amin, and among these were a senior consultant at Mulago hospital and a senior police officer. Amin then personally accused Luwum of failing to warn him of the danger from outside the country, which meant that the Archbishop too wanted to see him overthrown. Perhaps the killing of Oryema and Oboth-Ofumbi, who like Luwum were Luo-speakers, was for the same reason.[4]

The Archbishop's murder was followed by the banning of some twenty-six Christian organisations working in Uganda – and by an unprecedented outflow of exiles of every ethnic, language and political background. Amin received worldwide condemnation, even from those who had hitherto been his friends. The United States House of Representatives passed a resolution condemning his gross violation of human rights.[5] However, the lion (or *Kamunye* [= a kite] as Amin's killer-squads were called in Buganda) remained rampant, and people began to believe that their Life President was truly irreplaceable, and that they would never see another leader. It seemed as if the people's prayers were not being heard, and that God had forgotten the ill-fated people of Uganda.

But God had not forgotten them. Amin was still vulnerable,

especially from his own army. There were disputes, as ever, among his military followers, and he could never completely weed out those who wanted to oust him from power. Other forces also came into play. Civilian groups, both within and outside Uganda, were coordinating their efforts to remove him. Anti-Amin elements were making preparations in Tanzania and Kenya: Amin's excesses had galvanised the opposition, especially the external forces living as exiles in different countries. Soon after the murder of Archbishop Luwum, meetings were held in Nairobi and Lusaka and a number of liberation groups were formed, based in various capitals, and it was these which formed the Uganda National Movement in Lusaka in August 1977.[6] The Western world too – especially Britain, which had previously supplied some of the military weaponry that had kept Amin in power – was beginning to distance itself from him. The foreign powers had kept him in power but, following their normal practice, they were prepared to drop him like a hot potato if they could still secure their economic and other interests after his overthrow.

It was in these circumstances that Amin committed a major error, for which he paid a grievous price. In a moment of over-confidence bordering on insanity, he invaded the Kagera salient in north-western Tanzania with great destruction of lives and property, claiming, as in the case of western Kenya, that it had once been part of Uganda. There has often been speculation as to why Amin took this action that proved fatal to his regime. But, be that as it may, at the beginning of 1978 he began to lose control of the army, particularly at the command level. In April he denounced some of his cabinet ministers and army leaders. These included Brigadier Moses Ali, Minister of Finance; Major-General Lumago, Army Chief of Staff; Kassim Obura, Chief of Police; Lt.-Col. Nasur, commander of the Malire Mechanised Regiment; and – to the surprise of many – General Mustafa Adrisi, Vice-President and Minister of Defence. All this indicated a major convulsion 'within the innermost circles of the regime'.[7]

According to one version, at least four senior officers confronted Amin in the middle of 1978 and asked him point-blank to step down and hand over to a civilian government.[8] Amin told the officers that he would think about it and inform them accordingly, and the officers departed. He now knew that they were against him, and they realised that he would never forgive them. To escape his wrath, but wishing to continue opposing him, the officers went and joined up with the Simba Battalion at Mbarara, which they used as their defensive base against Amin. Then in October 1978, to forestall the growing opposition at Mbarara, President Amin sent the Chui

Battalion, based at Gulu, to attack it. This he succeeded in doing, but a faction of the Simba Battalion crossed the border into the Kagera salient. Convinced that these soldiers, now turned guerrillas, would come back and attack Uganda once they had reinforcements, Amin decided to pursue them across the border. He thus sent his Chui Batallion soldiers to Kagera, where they created much destruction, technicians being brought in from the copper mines at Kilembe to blow up the Kagera bridge and so prevent the soldiers crossing into Uganda from Tanzania.

For Tanzania this was the last straw. For all Amin's enemies, who till now had failed to dislodge him from power, it was the chance for which they had prayed and waited for so long. Supported by an overwhelming force of several thousands of soldiers of Tanzania People's Defence Forces (TPDF), Ugandan guerrillas from Tanzania invaded their own country. The Baganda refused to listen to Amin's eleventh-hour pleas not to support the invaders who were passing through their territory; having supported him when he needed them most in 1971 and 1972, they were among those who had suffered most during his eight years' rule. They welcomed and embraced the invaders. The Tanzanians and the Ugandan liberators arrived in Kampala in April 1979. Amin and his army fled the city. In doing so, they took the east-northern Kampala-Jinja-Tororo-Lira-Gulu route which many other expellees were to follow later when their turn came.

Amin was gone and the era of the Uganda National Liberation Front (UNLF) had come. Professor Yusuf Kironde Lule, a man who had never been involved in the heat of Ugandan national politics, became President. Obote was not among those who entered Kampala in the wake of Amin's defeat. Everyone was jubilant at the coming of peace to the country.

NOTES

1. J. Listowel, *Amin*, London: IUP, 1973, p. 188.
2. Personal interviews (names of informants withheld).
3. This has been well described by Amii Omara-Otunnu in *Politics and the Military in Uganda, 1890–1985*, London: Macmillan Press, 1987.
4. We have not sought to give an exhaustive account of this sad affair. For more information, see M. Ford, *Janani: The Making of a Martyr*, London: Marshall, Morgan and Scott, 1978, and M.L. Pirouet, 'Religion in Uganda under Amin', *Journal of Religion in Africa*, XI, 1 (1980).
5. Omara-Otunnu, *op. cit.*, p. 138.
6. *Ibid.*, pp. 138ff. for more details.
7. *Ibid.*, p. 140.
8. Personal communication (name of informant withheld).

9

GENERAL CONSIDERATIONS ON AMIN'S REGIME

Many changes were ushered in during the eight years of Idi Amin's regime that changed the face of Uganda. Most of them, however, revolve around two issues, the Economic War and the regime's brutality.

Consequences of the expulsion of the Asians and the Economic War

As we have seen, most of the expelled Asians went to Britain but some were welcomed in other Commonwealth countries such as Canada, Australia and indeed India. It was their expulsion that sparked off what became known as the Economic War. Other foreigners were also forced out. All businesses were taken over, from small *dukas* to giant organisations such as the sugar factories belonging to Mehta at Lugazi and Madhavani at Kakira and the Kilembe Mines at Kasese belonging to Falconbridge of Canada. The big companies were managed by the government while smaller businesses and estates went to a lucky few black Ugandans – free. The result is that, right up to the present, these businessmen do not care about service to their customers, because they did not have either to work or to pay to obtain their businesses. Those hit hardest were the Ismaili community who, unlike many other Asians, were willing right from the day of independence to identify themselves with indigenous Ugandans by investing heavily in a number of welfare projects, particularly schools and hospitals, to serve the needs of the indigenous population as well as their own people.

The initial distribution of confiscated Asian property had its comical aspects. Men who had recently had nothing had become rich bosses overnight. Former cooks in Asian households moved into their former masters' bedrooms. Clerks took over their former bosses' offices. Fitters became managers of garages. Even professors and lecturers at Makerere abandoned their ivory towers and joined the great scramble for businesses, or in other words the loot left behind by the hardworking, self-made Asians. Many of the original grabbers of this property were edged out of their possessions when the exercise was formalised by the state.

The Economic War of the Amin era was primarily an exercise in wealth redistribution at the expense of the Asian community who, as a result of the colonial system that allowed foreigners to exploit the indigenous people, were the richest group in the country. The beneficiaries were the holders of power: Amin's ministers, army personnel, Nubian and Muslim communities and their supporters and potential allies. The poorest income group in the country – including peasants, pastoralists and the urban proletariat – did not benefit, except for those who looted the property of the fleeing and harassed Asians.

In expelling the Asians, Amin exploited the human weaknesses of the Africans. For many years after the arrival of the Asians and their emergence as an economic power in Uganda, an economic struggle developed between the 'oppressors' (the petty bourgeoisie, mostly Asian, although some Africans joined their ranks) and the 'oppressed' – the bulk of the African workers and landless peasants. This came into the open in the 1940s and 1950s and partly caused the 1945 and 1949 riots in Buganda and the economic boycott engineered by Augustine Kamya in 1959. After independence, an African petty bourgeoisie emerged and, with powerful political allies, began to assert itself particularly against the Asian petty bourgeoisie, the wholesalers and small retailers. This was the situation that Amin exploited in 1972, especially since expelling the Asians was bound to produce considerable political dividends. It also partly explains why, in the end, the Economic War took on the appearance of a 'racial war'. In the end, therefore, it was this African group that stood to gain from the expulsion of Asians, and it was they who stepped into their shoes as the Asians departed, particularly after the first disorganised distribution of property had been formalised.

Also, in addition to the extensive disruption of economic activity as the people watched the spectacle, the country's stock of professionals, artisans and experienced importers, exporters, wholesalers and retailers was drastically reduced. This was so in spite of the fact that in the first two or three years following the expulsion, expenditure on education, in-service training, scholarships, technical assistance and extension services of all types continued at a significant level. Efforts continued to be made, in both the public and private sectors, to develop human resources, but the overall effect, as we have said, was a drastic reduction in the essential stock of trained and experienced human resources.

It was the nature of the Economic War that wealth was regarded primarily as a stock of commodities – houses, furniture, cars, trade goods in go-downs, cash, watches, gold, personal ornaments and suchlike – and not as a flow concept. It did in part include the concept of income from, say, expropriated farms and factories, but this appears to have been overshadowed by the idea of an accumulated stock. This was particularly evident in the subsequent failure to provide for the repair and maintenance of newly-acquired homes and factories, by thoughtless allocations that separated operating units from their repair workshops, and by 'Operation *mafuta mingi*' (Operation Get Rich Quick) intended to stock shops whose initial complements of trade goods had been sold out with no thought of using the proceeds to restock.

The redistribution of wealth introduced by the Economic War was not completed with the departure of the Asian community, and it became something of a growth industry. The recipients of new wealth did not remain the same. As personalities holding power or providing support to power-holders and their allies changed, so shops, houses, farms and factories were from time to time redistributed from the initial beneficiaries to others and from them to still newer owners. This added to an already serious situation of insecurity, with rivals hunting each other for the property that had been abandoned or allocated to the 'wrong' hands. Ugandans killed each other for property, for a new culture of *okuliira mu kavuyo* (literally 'eating in the confusion') had set in the minds of the people. Given a background of considerable poverty and the element of uncertainty of the new ownership, instant wealth at the cost of no more effort than that involved in gambling (praise the chief, blacken the present owner or what-have-you) diverted many away from honest hard work to concentrate on the search for titles to new assets that could be appropriated. Output kept falling, while speculation became the order of the day. The Economic War had become the continuing redistribution of a fading stock of wealth.

It is perhaps inevitable that Ugandans should try to escape the need to strike a kind of a 'balance-sheet' on this important event, especially when we consider how significant the expulsion of the Asians was in the context of the entire period of the eight years of Amin's regime. It was perhaps even more significant in the whole history of Uganda since independence, indeed since the arrival of the colonialists.

Uganda's isolation from the mainstream of world politics has to be emphasised. Because no country would or could lend Amin money, Uganda became to some extent self-supporting although it suffered in the process.

For the first time, because credit was not available, Uganda made all its purchases with cash – obtained from the coffee boom of the mid-1970s. However, the fact that Amin paid for everything with cash did not prevent the Uganda National Liberation Front that overthrew him in 1979 from inheriting any debts from his regime. The total public debt at 31 December 1978 was estimated at US$362.3 million. If the average life of a government is five years or less, and that government has undertaken development projects financed by reasonable external borrowing – as Amin's government did, especially early on – then it is likely to leave behind some external debt. In Amin's case, there was certainly borrowing from soft sources during the honeymoon period and, moreover, he himself had inherited debts to the IBRD (International Bank for Reconstruction and Development) from his predecessors, which were still outstanding in 1979.

All in all, there is no doubt that Amin ruined Uganda's economy beyond description. But it is also true that his policies ushered in a major revolution. Ugandans are now in control of their economy. But what does this mean in real terms, and to what extent are they in control of their destiny? The *dukas* and the wholesale trade in Kampala and other towns have passed into the hands of the indigenous Ugandans. It is true that a number of Asian wholesalers have re-established themselves in Kampala, and may attempt to dominate the textile import trade once again. But the measures taken by the National Resistance Movement (NRM) government, especially in providing foreign exchange to local textile importers, will ensure that this business remains predominantly – and perhaps, in the end, exclusively – in the hands of indigenous Ugandans. Moreover, although the government has declared that the departed Asians are free to return and reclaim the property that was snatched from them in 1972, it has been made clear that the government does not expect (and therefore the returning Asians should not expect) the running of shops (particularly the small *dukas*) to be returned to the Asians. This is an established position of the government, which most Ugandans support, and it has acquired a quality of permanence.

However, it is pertinent to ask to what extent Africans are in control of the Ugandan economy in spite of this – especially as concerns the bigger businesses and estates which the Asians and other foreign interests were forced to abandon. Since 1982 Asian big shots have returned to Uganda and, in partnership with the government, repossessed their businesses and estates and begun to rehabilitate them. Thus a number of major assets have gone back to the departed Asians – for example, Mbale textile mill, Madhavani and Mehta sugar factories, Mitchell Cotts tea estates and other big properties in Kampala. These businesses and others belonging to foreign interests will certainly have a marked influence on the country's economic development, and will somewhat dampen the Ugandans' claim – and aspiration – to be in full control of the economy.

There is also the overall factor that in global terms Uganda, like any other Third World country, is not and cannot be in full control of its economy. It still depends on export markets, especially those of the rich industrialised countries, for hard currency earnings. It also largely depends for manufactured consumer goods on imports from similar sources. It depends on imports of technology and of capital equipment for its development. All this means that buyers of Uganda's exports such as cotton, coffee, tea and tobacco can deliberately reduce both purchases and prices, on the one hand, and that, equally, suppliers of machinery, chemicals and other essential consumer commodities can institute price squeezes.

So far we have emphasised, as is proper, the economic consequences of expelling the Asians, but there were many non-economic aspects as well. Not only Kampala but also Jinja, Mbale, Masaka and Mbarara became de-Asianised; no longer could Asian families be seen roaming in the towns of Uganda on Sundays and thus turning them into little Bombays and Calcuttas. The country had now truly fallen into the hands of the indigenous people – *bakasangwawo*. Whether or not we like what Amin did, it is a matter beyond our ability to change. We shall never go back to what Uganda was before the expulsion of the Asians. What is not in dispute, though, is that it is an event that merits great attention from all Ugandans.

It is a paradox that while Ugandans feel sorrow about their past, and ashamed of many things that have been done, they hold their heads high because they have experienced the hell of a revolution, and this has left them in many ways the masters of their own destiny. They say today that the declaration and implementation of these revolutionary changes should be seen as part of their history. 'When the future generations look back in history decades and hundreds of years to 1972/73,' Amin declared to the nation in a broadcast on 17 December 1972, 'if they do not remember us for any other good thing, they will at least remember us for having given Uganda her economic independence.' In the distant future, when those who experienced the agony have passed on, this may be seen as the only notable legacy of Amin's eight-year regime. Indeed many Ugandans today, including leaders and educated members of society, are embarrassed when asked to comment on Amin's expulsion of the Asians. This undoubtedly was, and remains, a popular action. What people regret is not what was done but the way it was done.

But when we have considered the effects of the Economic War on the economic life of the country, there remains that other aspect of Amin's rule, its brutality. Here the effect on the politics of Uganda has clearly been negative and destructive. It brought, first, the institutionalisation by the state of violence and disregard for life; and, secondly, a chronic degeneration in morals.

The brutality of Amin's regime

When we say that violence was institutionalised under Amin, we are not saying that violence and wanton killings had not occurred earlier, in Obote's first regime. It is only that with Amin they reached a previously unimaginable scale. We do not need to repeat the litany of statistics and facts on the subject, but should rather confine ourselves to the wider implications of institutionalised violence and brutality managed by the state and directed against unarmed and largely innocent civilians.

Once Amin had been removed from power, there was an unbelievable sense of peace, and the belief that it would spread among all Ugandans. Despite the looting that followed the fall of Kampala – the first event of its kind in Uganda's history – many Ugandans sincerely hoped that an atmosphere of contentment and even love would result as the natural outcome of the removal of Amin's bloody regime. But there was also a sense of sadness, doubt – and hatred. People could not believe what they had seen and gone through. They could not believe what their friends had done to their own brothers and sisters. What had gone wrong? And was this indeed the end of the violence?

For consider this. Amin was a killer, who ordered mass executions. The State Research Bureau was a state within a state, run by men who did not seem to possess the hearts and feelings of human beings. Amin's 'boys' had the licence to kill – but not all of his killers and supporters were 'boys'. Those who supported and served him for several years were men and women with whom we had been together at good schools such as Budo, Mwiri, Gayaza, Kisubi and Namiryango, at Makerere University, and at Britain's ancient universities and Inns of Court. These well-educated and trained people were those who served the regime that claimed so many innocent victims. True, they may not themselves have signed the death warrants, but there is no doubt that it was to them that Amin turned for advice on the legal formalities that were used to give legitimacy to his barbarities. They served Amin in key positions. Moreover, did not Makerere University confer upon Idi Amin the honorary degree of Doctor of Laws? And was it not a Professor of Law who, in his adulation of Amin, described him as the greatest political scientist and the greatest administrator Uganda had ever produced? Who ran the State Research Bureau? Who operated and served in those organs of human destruction which sent innocent men and women to their deaths on mere suspicion and over trivial rivalries centred on such petty issues as girl- or boy-friends or cars? Highly educated men, with post-graduate degrees, connived with Amin in the murder of such leading Ugandans as the Chief Justice, the Anglican Archbishop, ministers, professionals and others of all ranks and descriptions. Over and above these allies of Amin – for what else were they? – special condemnation is merited for those who headed the key ministries such as Justice, the Interior, Regional and Local Government, and Defence, and of course the state's security organs.

These were the people who served Amin. They were the instruments he used to destroy Ugandan property and lives – although they may later have abandoned him and written sensational articles and even books condemning all his works. Indeed, almost all Amin's allies, who fed from his hands and enriched themselves from his coffers, now claim that they served him out of self-preservation alone – fearing that they would otherwise have been killed. They are at pains to explain why they served a man and a regime from which they are now so anxious to dissociate themselves. These pleas should be dismissed with the contempt they deserve. History cannot be wiped out.

Such people are still with us today, and some who were Amin's ministers pose today as another batch of liberators. There are indeed some who are ministers or hold other important offices of state. As Oscar Wilde once remarked, 'No man is rich enough to buy back his past.' Otherwise many Ugandans would have bought back their past in order to hide or destroy it. There were, of course, foreigners who benefited from the chaos resulting from the mismanagement of our affairs. Personnel from both the Western and Eastern blocs played a role in the activities of such dreadful organisations as the State Research Bureau. Some countries surrounding us benefited from our country's misery, and have continued to do so. But in the last analysis, the wounds our country bears were caused by two decades of fratricidal conflict and tension *of our own making*, with the foreign forces on the sidelines enjoying the spectacle. It is we who brought about the agonies of the Amin era, and helped him to rape and destroy our motherland. We should not pile all the blame on those who happened to occupy the seats of power. Those leaders were given the support they wanted, and which they later used to suppress us, by the civil population. The civilians who gave support to those dictators – Obote in 1962 and 1966 and Amin in 1971 – share in the responsibility for the chaos of our politics and the resulting agony of Uganda since independence.

The degeneration of morality

We now need to consider another aspect of Amin's regime: the disturbing effects it had on the morals and values of the people. This is, of course, connected with the effects of the expulsion of the Asians and of the Economic War, and the institutionalisation of violence in the state. But the moral fibre of Ugandans was weakened in certain particular ways. First, there grew up a lack of respect for the old and for what is generally referred to as 'decency'. Because life came to mean so little during Amin's regime, people ceased to fear death, in the sense that a Ugandan saw violence committed by one person against another as a normal way of going about things. One person *feared* his neighbour (not in the sense of respect) – no longer because it was right to do so but because if he did not the other might 'finish him off'. It was a return to what Thomas Hobbes would have called 'man in a state of nature' where life was solitary, brutish and short. Children became used to seeing corpses lying around, so much so that it became common simply to jump over them if one came across them in one's path without bothering to cover them up or to report the matter to the police.

Another aspect of the chaotic conditions in which the young generation was brought up during the period of Amin's rule was the devaluation of education and the professions generally. Education ceased to be a passport to anything, and therefore lost much of its attraction. Previously it was the ambition of every young student to work hard at school and thereby make it to Makerere University. From there, no matter what paper qualification resulted, the graduate was assured of a respected position within the community and a commensurate salary.

During Amin's regime, all that disappeared. What came to be valued was money, and it did not matter how it was made. Dropouts from school were catapulted into positions of influence through violence, theft or simply influential allies in the government. Makerere became a laughing-stock and a symbol of the misguided, of those who would never make it in life. A typical remark might have been, 'Our friend — will never be happy, she is going to marry a Makerere graduate.'

The professions were deeply affected. Professional ethics, whether in teaching, law or medicine, utterly collapsed. What mattered was not how one did one's job as a professional, but only how much money could be got out of it. This has remained true to this day, to the neglect of the ethics which these professionals should adhere to strictly. An editorial in the Kampala-based *Star* of 6 July 1987 put it succinctly:

. . . . the professionals are not entirely to blame for this aberration. Unprofessionalism in most professions is a result of the emergence of the *'mafuta-mingi* culture' in the 1970s which stressed more the acquisition of material wealth than the means through which that wealth was acquired. The guiding principle was 'the end justifies the means'.

This culture and the economic hardships that afflicted the salary-earners systematically led to the erosion of professional ethics. Everyone's concern was to try desperately to beat the inflation. Out of all this also came frustration among the salaried people who resorted to excessive drinking and shabbiness; and of course, the ten per cent commission became a normal thing.

The total sum of all this has been the erosion of the pride of the work of professionals in the country.

In concluding this discussion of Idi Amin's regime, it is impossible not to feel a sense of guilt for the harm Ugandans have done to their own country. As we have already said, it is we ourselves who, in one way or another, have allowed dictators like Amin to be projected into positions of leadership and power, people with no qualification, educational or moral, for presiding over the affairs of a modern state. Amin's appointment of General Mustafa Adrisi as Uganda's Vice-President and Minister of Defence is instructive: General Adrisi himself confessed to the Uganda Human Rights Commission on 26 July 1988 that he could not read or write anything apart from his own name – his father had been too poor to send him to school. He further confessed that, although he was Vice-President, he never knew of the existence of the country's Constitution. Of such calibre were the men who presided over Uganda's destiny for eight years.

In 1971 when Idi Amin seized power, Uganda was by far the most economically viable state in East Africa. It is true that it had started experiencing some problems, but the economy was still on track. There was no shortage of essential commodities, and hunger and abject poverty were unknown. There were abundant programmes for exploiting the vast resources the country possessed. Tourism – one of the clearest indicators of a country's stability – was booming, and had almost replaced cotton as a prime earner of foreign exchange. Uganda was within rather than outside the mainstream of world development, and the burden of international isolation, such as was imposed upon it as Amin's outrages multiplied, was as yet unknown. Amin's regime squandered all the advantages the country possessed to lift itself by its own bootstraps into the modern era. When all the agonies suffered by the Ugandans as a result of Amin's atrocious rule are weighed, one cannot help wondering whether the Amin tragedy was not an act of God. Was it, as Lord Wharton wrote in 1642 of the English Civil War, then raging, 'a judgement upon us immediately from the hand of God, for which no natural or politique reason can be given'? The question has so far remained unanswered.

10

AFTER AMIN: THE ERA OF
THE UNLF, 1979–1980

From Moshi to Kampala

The year 1979 was seen as one that would herald a new era of peace and tranquillity in Uganda. Amin had gone, and the liberators had arrived. But the euphoria soon vanished. The paradox of it all was that the seven years following Amin's removal were no different from what had been experienced during the regime of Idi Amin. The old vicious circle of agony was renewed, and in the view of some Ugandans it was worse than the agony of the Amin years.

The crux of the matter was that once the Amin problem had been dealt with, the real problems facing Uganda became apparent. For many years – roughly from the time of the constitutional crisis of 1966 – we Ugandans had been treading a great staircase of which the top was hidden in the clouds and the lowest steps were hidden in a dark abyss. We could have ascended this staircase, but instead we chose to descend it. The ruins which we inherited from Amin's regime formed the bedrock on which the liberators were to reconstruct the new nation. But reconstruction was a daunting task, beyond the abilities of all those governments and the National Consultative Council (NCC), despite the high academic qualifications of their members. Institutions that should have survived the evil work of Amin and of those who assisted the forces of destruction were no longer there. Ugandans should have remembered that, as one philosopher put it, 'what is valuable is a certain ordering of things, and that civilisation has to do not with things but with the invisible ties that join one thing to another.' As it turned out, what was to join the regime of Idi Amin to the regimes of the 'liberators' who succeeded him was not the 'ordering of things' but the continued vicious circle of chaos and the seemingly permanent *dis*ordering of things. That, in short, is what characterised the era of the 'liberators', from April 1979 to January 1986.

The main problem facing the country after Amin's overthrow was that there were too many liberation movements or groups, with varying and often contradictory ideologies and aspirations. What had united the different groups – those of Obote and Yoweri Museveni in Tanzania; Tarsis Kabwegyere and Martin Aliker in Nairobi; Andrew Kayiira and Godfrey Binaisa in the United States;

Professor Yusuf Lule being sworn in as President, April 1979.

Sam Sabagereka, George Kanyeihamba and Paulo Muwanga in London; Kirunda Luwuliza and Edward Rugumayo in Zambia, not to mention so many others that mushroomed here and there as the end of Amin's regime drew nearer – completely disappeared once Amin was out of the way. More than twenty-five groups had convened in Moshi, Tanzania, early in 1979, and emerged with what came to be known as the 'Moshi Spirit'. It was well named because the 'spirit' was left behind in Moshi. No sooner did the liberators arrive in Kampala, faced with the real problems of a Uganda without Amin, than the Uganda National Liberation Front (UNLF) started to disintegrate.

The Moshi Conference was convened in the beautiful northern town of Moshi between 23 and 25 March 1979 and was chaired by Dr Tarsis B. Kabwegyere 'who had been elected, by various exile groups meeting in Nairobi the previous January, to be the Chairman of a Consultative Committee set up to liaise with Ugandan organisations fighting Amin with a view to remove Amin, establish democracy in Uganda and re-establish national independence.'[1] Obote himself was not present, but he was effectively represented by his many surrogates who formed several liberation groups at the eleventh hour in order to swell their numbers in the conference hall. Above all, he had his staunch supporters in the persons of Paulo Muwanga, a UPC member since the 1960s, and Brigadier David Oyite-Ojok, his fellow-tribesman and his man in the military wing of the UNLF. A Military Commission was set up with Paulo Muwanga as its Chairman and Yoweri Museveni as Vice-Chairman. Colonels Omaria and Maruru – former officers in the Uganda Army – were members in addition to General Tito Okello and Oyite-Ojok, respectively Commander and Deputy Commander of the Uganda National Liberation Army (UNLA). The NCC was set up to act as the supreme organ and legislature of the UNLF. While the NCC acted as parliament, the National Executive Council (NEC) was to act as a cabinet. It was agreed 'that the NEC would be subordinate to the NCC and that none of its decisions would be carried out without the ratification of the latter.'[2] Yusuf Lule was elected Chairman of the NEC and therefore, by implication, would become the future President and head of state of a liberated Uganda.

Lule, Binaisa and the Military Commission

The true circumstances that surrounded Professor Yusuf Lule's election as the UNLF's leader and therefore as Uganda's future leader will never perhaps be completely clarified. Yoweri Museveni, in his article 'The Nature and History of our Struggle', published in the first issue of *The 6th of February* magazine, tells us that 'it is generally not known that it was the Tanzanians who kept Obote out of Moshi Conference by force and persuaded some of us to accept the late Lule as a leader even though we knew little about him politically.' That would mean that the Tanzanians, including and above all Julius Nyerere, planned the choice of Lule rather than Obote to lead Uganda after Amin's downfall.

But as matters stood then, this was by no means an impossible position for the Tanzanians to take. The Moshi Conference was hurriedly convened in March 1979 when Amin was still in control, and, considering that the Tanzanian army, in company with the Ugandan exiles, would have to pass through the territory of the Baganda before they could capture Kampala, it made sense for the world to be told that it was Lule and not Obote who would replace Amin. It made sense for Nyerere – and even for Obote and his UPC – for Obote to stand aside and let everyone believe that the man about to take over power was Lule, a professor, a renowned international public servant and above all a member of the Baganda tribe – the now traditional enemies of Obote.

Yusuf Lule, the first President of the UNLF administration, was a sincere man. But he had no experience of running a country, especially one like Uganda 'after Amin', and in working with men of very diverse backgrounds who were also custodians of varying and mutually incompatible ideologies and political aspirations. Even sadder was the somewhat amateurish approach that Lule brought to politics. The net result was that his presidency lasted no more than sixty-eight days.

Lule was overthrown by forces whose composition has remained obscure, although fingers have been pointed ever since at those who came to be labelled as the 'gang of four'.[3] This, of course, is not to rule out the very clear involvement and machinations of the pro-Obote group which, as it turned out, was working under the leadership of Paulo Muwanga and David Oyite-Ojok and their masters within the Tanzanian establishment. It would, indeed, be naive to underestimate the power and influence which the Tanzanians, through military and political sections of the Tanzanian establishment in both Dar es Salaam and Kampala, wielded during the brief but important two-year period that followed Idi Amin's removal from power in 1979.

In seeking to explain Lule's sudden removal from power, one cannot ignore both the man's own weakness as a politician and the nature of the political and military intrigues that surrounded him. There were far too many wrangles and bickerings for power within the UNLF, especially in the NCC.

The amateurishness with which Lule approached his tasks is demonstrated by two things. The first was that, almost unbelievably, he failed to appreciate the crucial position of the army as an arbiter of Ugandan politics, as much at that time as before. He should also have remembered that the contribution of the Ugandan guerrilla groups to the liberation of Uganda had been minimal. It was effectively the Tanzania People's Defence Forces (TPDF) which actually liberated Uganda, and Lule (and those who immediately followed him) should not have lost sight of this essential point. Lule's second error was not to take steps immediately to reinforce his support or political base within the NCC, an opportunity he had under the terms of the Moshi Agreement, 'through the selection of sixty additional members of the NCC from among those Ugandans who had not fled into exile during the Amin years'. Lule never used this opportunity – or was never allowed to do so – and was therefore robbed of the support he would have needed in any showdown with his opponents in the NCC.[4]

However, the crisis that engulfed the professor-politician appears to have been triggered by the way in which he made his cabinet appointments. This brought him into sharp conflict with the NCC. It will be recalled that at the Moshi Conference in March 1979, it was decided that the decisions of the NEC (of which Lule was chairman, the position which *ex-officio* later made him President of Uganda) would be subordinate to those of the NCC and therefore subject to its ratification. From this it was implied, though not specifically stipulated, that the President's decisions – for instance cabinet appointments – required ratification by the NCC. Lule disagreed with this stand, arguing that under the 1967 Constitution he, as President, was entitled to make cabinet appointments as he saw fit. This argument was sparked off by Lule's removal of Paulo Muwanga from the Ministry of Internal Affairs to Labour and his appointment of Andrew Kayiira to replace him.

Coupled with this legalistic issue was the accusation that Lule was appointing as ministers or deputy ministers people of dubious character and who were either unfitted to hold their jobs or were blatantly conservative. To some members of the NCC Lule therefore appeared to be relying rather too heavily on the conservatives, whereas most NCC members, particularly the Chairman and his influential group which included the Secretary, were clearly not conservatives and were in fact opposed to them. Thus Lule failed to grasp the ideological position of those whose support was crucial to him for political survival. Even worse, in his enemies' eyes, was his apparent identification with the old 'Mengo clique' of conservative elements in Buganda. At least he allowed himself to be seen in that light which, as a result, robbed him of the stature of a national leader. As if to reinforce this latter point, Lule did not once move out of Kampala and Entebbe during his two months in power. Lastly, the NCC did not warm to his decision to appoint ministers on a regional basis. In the discussions between Lule and the NCC, the President remained adamant and, although the NCC allowed him ample time to reconsider his decisions, he refused to back down and insisted, as we have noted, that under the 1967 Constitution he was not subordinate to the NCC and his decisions could not therefore be subjected to its scrutiny.

It has also been suggested by some observers that Lule was removed from the presidency because of his decision to introduce a quota system for recruitment into the army, which would have been based on the population of each of the country's ethnic groups. This view probably received some support from Yoweri Museveni, who was Minister of State for Defence before Lule was removed from the presidency. If such a system had been implemented, it would have meant, for instance, more new recruits into the army from Buganda, home of Lule's own tribe, than from any other ethnic group – the Baganda being the largest ethnic group in Uganda. This would have threatened the dominance of the so-called traditional areas for army recruits such as Acholi and Lango, for instance – respectively the home territories of General Tito Okello, Chief of Defence Forces, and his deputy, Brigadier Oyite-Ojok. Although it is difficult to tell the full extent to which this policy was debated, there were certainly many people in the UNLF, and especially in the UNLA itself, who felt threatened by a move to increase the southern/western element in the army, which would mean a reduction, however small, of the northern – mainly Acholi/Langi – element in the national army.

What Lule was in fact suggesting was that the colonial and post-colonial basis for army recruitment would be destroyed and a truly national army recruited, cutting across all the Ugandan nationalities to introduce some kind of ethnic balance. Samwiri Lwanga-Lunyiigo commented as follows:

The unfortunate Lule had talked about what kind of army Uganda should have. He had mentioned basic academic and literacy requirements: he had stressed the importance of recruitment policies which took into account the nationalities profile. In daring to shape the new Uganda Army, the vital constituency, he was inadvertently trying to cut some raw nerves and it is because he dared talk about the future Uganda Army that Lule was actually overthrown. The other reasons were a mere smoke screen.[5]

Finally, it is probable that Lule's fall came so suddenly because he failed to identify himself clearly with those who had borne the brunt of the war that removed Idi Amin. Aloof by nature, he ignored things that excited others so easily, and it seems that he was never deeply interested in the war, even though the country over which he presided was still battling with Amin's rearguard in the east and north. Indeed, he was removed from power before the war in the north had ended. However, despite the political bickerings going on openly within the UNLF at this time and the machinations of the pro-Obote group, the NCC was not overly anxious to remove Lule from power, as would seem to be confirmed by the dilemma the NCC faced when it came to choose his successor.

Lule was replaced as President by Godfrey Lukongwa Binaisa, QC, who had been one of Obote's right-hand men in the early 1960s and had drafted the Republican Constitution of 1967 which has been seen as the source of many of Uganda's political difficulties. Binaisa, like Lule, is believed to have been elected President largely because of the 'Buganda factor' – the old story of the need to cultivate the support and goodwill of the Baganda, who inhabit the

Godfrey Binaisa, QC, President of Uganda 1979–80.

Paulo Muwanga, Vice-President in the second Obote regime, 1980–5, and Prime Minister under the Okello-Lutwa junta, July–August 1985.

region generally accepted as the heart of our land. However, it is suggested that the UNLF chose Binaisa to show that Lule had not been removed for personal reasons, because he was not a member of the NCC or even of the UNLF itself. It was said that he was chosen purely on grounds of merit and experience, as a prominent lawyer of international standing and a man who had once played an important role in the country's political affairs.

In fact, Binaisa just happened to be around at the time when Lule fell. He had come to Kampala from New York to lobby for the post of Permanent Representative to the United Nations, and it turned out that everyone in the NCC was happy that a man of his political calibre and stature was in the capital when the crisis of choosing Lule's successor erupted. However, contrary to widespread belief, Binaisa's election as President was not a walkover. There was a stiff election battle between him and Edward Rugumayo, who had the added advantage of being Chairman of the NCC, the electoral body. It was a close race and Binaisa won by the narrowest of margins. It would seem that one of the strong points in his favour was the fact that Lule's fall had taken almost everyone by surprise and thrown the entire NCC into confusion. Binaisa was therefore a compromise choice and Rugumayo was rejected largely because of his open radicalism, which was unpopular at that time and was even feared within certain sections of the NCC.

Lule's sudden removal from power caused consternation in the capital. The events of that Wednesday, 20 June, will always remain vivid in the minds of Kampala residents. People flocked on to the streets to protest, and the slogan 'NO LULE, NO WORK' in bold characters was scrawled over the walls of public buildings and commercial premises. Pamphlets denouncing Lule's removal were scattered about the town by speeding vehicles carrying angry demonstrators, some armed with stones. Large crowds gathered at Kampala City Square and outside the parliament buildings, which it seemed were about to be stormed. The situation was tense and anything might have happened. At Makerere University the supporters of Yusuf Lule carried banners, and anti-UNLF slogans and other manifestations were shouted and displayed. The University community was soon labelled a pro-Lule enclave and its Vice-Chancellor, Professor W. Senteza-Kajubi, fell a victim in the new reshuffle that was soon announced in a move to find a consensus within the UNLF administration. In the end, however, peace prevailed and Godfrey Binaisa was elected by the NCC under the stern chairmanship of Edward Rugumayo.

Binaisa, who had so quickly followed Yusuf Lule into the top job, also followed him into political oblivion. He too was a weak leader, which is not the least of the criticism levelled at him and at those who surrounded him. There was rampant corruption. Throughout his struggle with people like Oyite-Ojok over the control of the army, without whose backing political power 'was tenuous and hollow', Binaisa 'seemed to retain two objectives, to hold on to power and to enrich himself and his cronies. He had a much clearer idea how to go about achieving the second objective than the first.'[6] But, worst of all, pathetically and unbelievably, the vicious circle of suffering and brutality in the country continued.

The trouble really was that the UNLA could not be disciplined. As we have already remarked, it was the TPDF who actually drove out Idi Amin and his Sudanic-speaking soldiers, and thus there was no army to speak of when the UNLF took over control. The existing UNLA was manned by recruits of either Obote or Museveni guerrilla groups, and it was hoped that its rank and file would be demobilised once peace had been provided by the TPDF, who were now in control of the country's security. It was not inconceivable that more troops might, if necessary, have been procured from friendly countries. With this kind of arrangement, a new recruitment, coupled with intense training of a new national army, could have been undertaken and even achieved if goodwill had existed among those holding power in Uganda at the time. But this was not so, for the simple reason that the Obote-Muwanga group of the UPC wanted the creation and maintenance of an army that would retain power in the hands of the Luo-speaking northerners, representing the power-base and home area of Obote, Tito Okello and David Oyite-Ojok.[7] The result, therefore, was an army that perpetuated the old set-up which had existed since colonial days.

Unfortunately for the people of Uganda, the UNLA, apart from a few of its officers, consisted of a preponderance of crude thugs in soldiers' uniforms, who increasingly became as unruly as the soldiers of Amin. They were a world apart from the soldiers of the TPDF. Indeed, it soon became apparent that the UNLA soldiers who formed the country's army from 1979 up till their removal in 1986 were in many ways worse than their predecessors. For, while Amin – if he chose to – was capable of controlling his soldiers, who carried out most of their crimes only on his specific instructions, the UNLA soldiers were their own masters. What made matters worse was that the army, especially at command level, became more and more the monopoly of northerners, almost all from the Acholi and Langi tribal groups. The architect of all this machination for mass-murder and destruction was no other than David Oyite-Ojok who, though a deputy to Tito Okello, the Chief of Defence, was the true driving force behind politicians such as Paulo

Muwanga and Chris Rwakasisi, who were carefully plotting the return of Obote.

The period of Binaisa's presidency was therefore one of confusion, destruction and corruption, and history will only partly absolve him on account of his political foresight in trying to introduce the politics of the 'umbrella'. This meant that while the traditional and even new political parties would continue to exist, they would all come under a single political umbrella: the UNLF. In this way, Binaisa claimed, we would avoid the politics of religion, sectarianism, rivalry and hatred, and be able to work for and even achieve the politics of consensus. Although his view of politics at first gave rise to suspicion in some quarters in Uganda, especially Buganda, it is to his credit that many now concede that his formula might possibly have prevented the rape of our country that followed his removal.

In spite of his international standing as a lawyer and his experience as a national politician in the 1960s – factors which led to his being chosen to replace Lule as President – Binaisa proved an inept and amateurish leader. Indeed, it is remarkable that he survived for so long. When he assumed office, he paid little attention to creating alliances within the UNLF, or even to asserting some influence over it, especially its military wing, the UNLA. He thought that by merely manipulating the NCC members or by appearing once or twice before the army, as he did when he addressed the powerful Malire Battalion in Kampala on 9 May 1980, he would be able to manoeuvre himself through the minefield of Ugandan politics.

However, in the overall context of Ugandan politics at the time, there is no doubt that Binaisa was overthrown mainly because he tried to block Milton Obote's return to power as President; he fell victim to precisely those forces who were working to bring Obote back. In his attempt to assert the sovereignty of Uganda and to underline the right of its citizens to choose their President, he clashed head-on with Tanzania. Naively, he believed that he could trade blows with Obote's men and the representatives of Julius Nyerere in Kampala. In choosing to confront rather than cooperate with the Tanzanian presence in Kampala, he signed his political death-warrant. Moreover, there is now evidence to suggest that perhaps the senior representatives of Tanzania in Kampala did not properly advise Dar es Salaam on the situation in Uganda, both at the time of Binaisa's removal and during the 1980 general election.

However, in fairness to the lawyer-politician, there are other considerations to be taken into account in explaining the failure of his presidency. He worked under extremely difficult circumstances, more so than did his predecessor Yusuf Lule. It is only surprising that this unsuspecting politician, surrounded by wolves all baying to grab his neck, survived for so long. For Binaisa, unlike Lule who was elected in Moshi, did not enjoy the high prestige as a major contributor to the liberation war against Amin. He had not even participated in the Moshi Conference (it is said that, although he was in Moshi town at the time, he was not allowed to enter the conference hall); this was the man who, barely three months later, became both the leader of the UNLF and the President of the country.

In the end, it was the isolation in which Binaisa found himself which became one of the causes of his downfall. In an apparent attempt to break this isolation – since he was certainly an outsider within the NCC and the UNLF generally – he tried to strike up an alliance with Dan Nabudere, who worked in the UNLF Secretariat, and his political associates. The 'gang of four' wanted to use Binaisa to achieve their own political ends, and Binaisa, for his part, of course wanted to use them to consolidate his fledgling political support within the UNLF and the NCC.

It is generally known that the 'alliance' between Binaisa and the 'gang of four' planned to remove Oyite-Ojok, Muwanga and their group, and Binaisa even visited Nairobi allegedly to canvass the support of the new President Moi. It is said that Moi, who had just inherited his office from the veteran, popular and charismatic Jomo Kenyatta, was still finding his way in Kenya's political terrain and thus was not anxious to get involved in anything from which he could not discern a clear advantage. Moi therefore did not offer Binaisa and his group the support they needed. It was even more serious that Binaisa had fallen out with Nyerere, who had apparently become disenchanted by stories of corrupt tendencies in his administration. Indeed, Binaisa made a fatal miscalculation in going against Nyerere when he tried to remove Oyite-Ojok and Muwanga from their positions of influence, particularly while the Tanzanian forces were still in the country. All this not unnaturally led to the emergence of the Military Commission and his removal from office.

But notwithstanding all this, Binaisa was also the victim of the political opportunism of the Democratic Party, under the leadership of Paul Kawanga Ssemogerere. Sensing a political victory that would come riding high on the bandwagon of the anti-Obote sentiments in Buganda and elsewhere in the traditionally anti-Obote regions of Uganda such as West Nile, Ssemogerere's DP joined Obote's UPC in rejecting Binaisa's version of politics which would have meant the existence of the UNLF as the umbrella embracing all political opinions in the country. The DP decided to go it alone, no matter what obstacles the Obote forces were preparing to place in the way of a free and fair general election. The DP was to recognise rather too late its own absurd naivety and the undisguised political crudeness and ruthlessness of its adversaries. Now, as before, the DP was putting tactics before substance.[8]

All in all, however, Binaisa was overthrown by a combination of all the pro-Obote forces, now openly under the custodianship of Paulo Muwanga and Oyite-Ojok. The pretext for his removal from power was his decision, apparently taken without first having ensured the political or military support of anyone who mattered, to remove Oyite-Ojok from his post as Chief of Staff of the UNLA and appoint him as Uganda's ambassador to Algeria. Binaisa annoyed the so-called 'warrior group' even more seriously when he replaced Oyite-Ojok with Colonel Nanyumba, an army officer from Busoga, as Army Chief of Staff and thus as the UNLA's Deputy Commander.

This was seen as the last straw, and the Military Commission stepped in. Like Lule before him, Binaisa was accused of making important decisions without consulting the NCC, the removal of Oyite-Ojok being cited as a case in point. When Binaisa refused to co-operate with the Military Commission, and even declined to meet it to discuss their differences, the Commission moved against him on 13 May 1980 and took power from him. The reasons for his removal given to the public over Radio Uganda were the corruption of his regime and his attempt to turn Uganda into a one-party state.

We should note that when the Military Commission made its announcement of the take-over of government over the radio, Yoweri Museveni, himself a member of the Military Commission, was in Dar es Salaam. He had not been a party to the conspiracy or controversy that led to the removal of Binaisa. However, Museveni could not have come to Binaisa's rescue, even if it had been possible, because in February 1980 Binaisa had demoted him from the Minister of Defence portfolio to that of Regional Cooperation. On the other hand, because of the obduracy of Binaisa, who had refused to accept his dismissal by the Military Commission, Oyite-Ojok and Muwanga and their group badly needed Museveni's support for what they had done. They were therefore more than happy when Museveni obliged and accepted the *fait accompli* on his return. There is no doubt that while in Dar es Salaam Museveni must have discussed what was transpiring in Kampala with Julius Nyerere who, as already noted, was not an admirer of Binaisa. Therefore when Museveni joined Oyite-Ojok's group and was himself confirmed as Vice-Chairman of the Military Commission, Binaisa's fate was sealed.

After a week of open defiance, Binaisa was removed from State

House and kept in seclusion at State Lodge (formerly the Prime Minister's residence, near the former Secretariat in Entebbe), where he stayed in detention until Obote released him after the general elections of December 1980. Thus Binaisa became the first President of Uganda to be detained in the country after his overthrow from power. He was then allowed to go wherever he wanted. Paulo Muwanga, the veteran politician, had at last catapulted himself into the leadership of the country. He became the Chairman of the Military Commission which overthrew Binaisa, and Yoweri Museveni, who had been working behind the scenes on his own political programme, became the Vice-Chairman.[9]

It was clear that Muwanga and Oyite-Ojok had used Museveni to get themselves into power, but would not be slow to dump him once they felt strong enough to do so. Amid the continuing political chaos and destruction of lives and property at the hands of UNLA thugs, plans were made for the long-awaited general elections.

However, before we examine these elections, let us discuss here an event that took place during the time when Paulo Muwanga and David Oyite-Ojok were great in the land. This was the massacre in West Nile in October 1980. It will be recalled that when Obote was overthrown by Amin in 1971, there was a widespread massacre of Acholis and Langis especially in the new Ugandan army. In 1979 when Amin's army was overthrown, the *Kikosi Maluum*, which became the core of the UNLA after the 1978–9 war, proceeded to carry out acts of revenge in West Nile. Militias that had been formed in Acholi and Lango were now sent to West Nile under the leadership of Acholi and Langi army officers, and laid West Nile waste.

According to *The Citizen* of 3 November 1980, the Ugandan government was claiming that Zaire, Sudan and Saudi Arabia had facilitated the invasion of West Nile by forces loyal to the run-away President, Idi Amin. But when the Tanzanian troops reached the 'disturbed area', they found no hostile forces at all. Meanwhile, the Tanzanian Foreign Minister, Ben Mkapa, flew to Kampala for a meeting with the ruling Military Commission and, according to *The Citizen*, 'expressed Tanzanian dismay at reports of a breakdown in discipline in the West Nile by the New Ugandan soldiers trained in Tanzania'. According to reliable sources, the whole of Arua town, the West Nile capital, had been completely destroyed in the attacks, 'leaving only the Catholic Cathedral as the only building still standing'. All household portable property remaining in Arua itself and the neighbouring towns of Koboko and Moyo after their destruction had been looted by the Langi and Acholi soldiers and the militia from Kitgum.

The death toll was high. Among the victims were Martin Okwera, branch manager of Uganda Airlines in Arua, and his family of ten, together with a number of civil servants who had taken refuge in the White Rhino Tourist Hotel hall. Two cabinet ministers, Anthony Ocaya and Moses Apiliga of the Ministry of Planning and Economic Development and the Ministry of Supplies respectively, lost a number of relatives. A Tanzanian soldier coming from Arua told *The Citizen* that the town would be 'wiped out from the map of Uganda unless it was re-built afresh'. He further revealed that by the time he left Arua, 'bodies were still scattered all over the destroyed town and its suburbs', most of them rotting and others already reduced to mere skeletons. The only people that could be seen in the town were soldiers. The Tanzanian soldier also reported that by the time the TPDF soldiers intervened in the 'fighting', a lot of civilians had been shot dead, including women and children 'and even dogs'.

These events are still vivid in people's mind today, and the physical evidence is still clear and abundant. It is not easy for either side to forget, and hence for either Acholis or Langis to have a harmony of interests with the West Nilers.

The 1980 general election

When the time came to start the campaigning for these elections, the two major traditional parties – the UPC and the DP – were of course in the forefront. Obote returned from exile in Tanzania in May 1980, and immediately launched his political campaign. In the meantime, a new political party came on the scene, with a new approach to politics. This was the Uganda Patriotic Movement (UPM), led by none other than Yoweri Museveni, with political veterans such as Bidandi-Ssali, Eriya Kategaya and Kirunda-Kivejjinja among the leading founder-members.

We should explore a little the circumstances that led to the formation of this new party. The sheer weight of the events that led to the ousting of Binaisa, which was itself soon followed by the return of Obote, put Museveni in a somewhat difficult political situation. Certainly it was clear by June 1980 that after he had lent legitimacy to the Muwanga-Oyite-Ojok clique which had overthrown Binaisa, they were working hard to dump him. Indeed some of them had even started to question his position as Vice-Chairman of the Military Commission. They understood Museveni's dilemma, and it was no wonder when Muwanga announced that the long-awaited general election would be held in July, barely a month away. Despite the short time available for establishing a new party, Museveni and his supporters went ahead and formed the UPM. (In the event, the election was held in December.)

Around this time in mid-1980, when it was more or less clear that Obote and his supporters were determined to impose themselves on the people of Uganda, Museveni's supporters urged him to go to the bush and fight Obote's group. Museveni however declined, arguing that if he did so people would see him as an ambitious young man anxious to capture power for its own sake. It would be better, he seemed to be arguing, to wait until Obote and his men stumbled into some political blunder, which would give his opponents a *casus belli* to rebel against him. As it turned out, this is precisely what happened when the UPC stole the election from the victors in December 1980.

The return of Obote from Tanzania opened a new page in Uganda's political history. Almost everyone (except perhaps Paul Ssemogerere) knew what was afoot. Nyerere, because of either his ignorance of the political climate of Uganda or faulty intelligence reports being fed to him by his agents, or indeed because of his extraordinarily strong personal commitment to the man, was convinced that only Obote could save the situation in Uganda. It is said that Museveni was asked by Nyerere to support Obote but that he refused, which only added to Nyerere's estrangement from him. Meanwhile, UPM leaders made approaches to the DP with a view to forming a joint stand against Obote and the UPC until after the election, when the two parties would go their separate ways. However, as we have already noted, the affable Ssemogerere refused, believing that the DP would be able to win the election despite the glaring evidence to the contrary.

What is not in doubt is that the UPM was a party of hope. It never, of course, believed that it would win the election and form the government since it was formed only about five months before the election was actually held. But it was a party founded on principles, and it attracted men and women with the new message of hope that it had to deliver to the people of Uganda. It was to remain a party of principle, which spearheaded the struggle for the restoration of democracy and a state of law and order in the country. It was therefore no accident that most of those who founded and later supported the National Resistance Movement came from the UPM – soon after the December 1980 election.

This election was neither fair nor truly free, despite the remarkable and, no doubt, well-meant statement by the Commonwealth Observer Group (COG) that 'surmounting all obstacles, the people of Uganda, like some great tidal wave, carried the electoral process to a worthy and valid conclusion'.[10] The result was clearly rigged and by means of glaring political corruption, robbery and thuggery Paulo Muwanga enabled the UPC to be swept to power with its leader, Milton Obote, as the President of Uganda. It is noteworthy that Obote himself did not stand for election to parliament, arguing that as an experienced politician he was above what he called 'the politics of constituencies'.

Because of the importance of this election – the first to be held in Uganda since April 1962, five months before independence – we should look at it in rather more detail. As we have remarked, its main feature was the way in which the people of Uganda were cheated and humiliated. Although it was clear from the start of the election campaign that Obote – through his henchmen in the UPC – would stop at nothing to secure victory, it was not expected that people like Muwanga would stoop so low in their determination to swindle the majority of the Ugandan people out of the victory they had won.

First of all, the registration of voters was carried in a way that was designed to ensure the success of the UPC group. At the start of this exercise, fourteen District Commissioners (DCs) were dismissed so that they would be prevented from acting as Returning Officers. The reason given by Muwanga, the Chairman of the Military Commission, was that the DCs 'were incompetent and dilatory and had refused to conduct the registration of voters in accordance with the law', a clear lie because it was generally known that they had been dismissed because of their unwillingness to support the UPC candidates. Moreover, the dismissal of civil servants – which the DCs unquestionably were – was in the domain of the Public Service Commission and not of the head of state.[11]

Earlier in the electoral process, doubts had been expressed about the way in which the Electoral Commission itself was appointed. It has been credibly suggested that because Uganda had not had a general election since 1962, it was an exercise of which few Ugandans had any previous experience and for which the country should therefore have called on organisational help from abroad, as Zimbabwe did, to ensure that the election was free and fair. This suggestion was turned down, although several Commonwealth countries would have been willing to render such assistance. As a compromise, the COG was agreed upon. What is more, when the Electoral Commission was appointed, most of its members were suspected of being members of the UPC.[12]

The process of nominating candidates for the 1980 general elections was marked by some astonishing episodes as the UPC group, headed by Paulo Muwanga, strove to frustrate the candidates of other parties. Adoko Nekyon, a would-be DP candidate, was physically prevented by the UPC supporters from reaching the nomination centre in Lira Central constituency and was thus unable to have his nomination papers processed. Ridiculous and spurious reasons were used to bar opponents of the UPC from standing as candidates. Chango-Macho, a senior tutor in the Department of Continuing Education at Makerere University who stood for the UPM, was disqualified on the grounds that he was deficient in the English language! The same pretext of deficiency in English was applied to Father Okoth, a former Deputy Minister and member of the National Consultative Council, to bar his candidacy. Victor Muhindo, a DP candidate in Kasese District, was duly nominated, against heavy odds, but was soon afterwards killed by the UPC big shots in Kasese.

The happenings in West Nile during the nomination of candidates were even worse. We have already mentioned the massacre and devastation carried out there in October 1980 by a Kitgum militia led by Acholi and Langi officers, particularly in Arua District. This was a clear act of revenge for what Amin had done to the Acholi and the Langi in the early 1970s, but as such it was purposeless because by October 1980 there were no supporters of Amin left in the region, most of them having escaped into Zaire and Sudan after the dictator's expulsion in 1979. But the timing of the massacre provides the clue to its aim, which was to destabilise West Nile so that no one would dare vote for the DP (the party enjoying most support in the region) and some would be intimidated into voting for the UPC. As a result, in the districts of Arua, Nebbi and Moyo no registration worth mentioning took place.

The case of engineer Sam Drale, a DP candidate, is instructive. He was arrested at a roadblock near Moyo town on the pretext that he was involved in a plot to overthrow the government; he was held in police custody till evening and then released after the nominations were over. In fact, all the DP candidates in Arua District, contrary to the government's promises, were left without the security they needed to present their nomination papers. They were also barred from nominations by means of the non-payment of tax or tax-clearance trick, although the government had waived this proviso for all intending candidates. The Commonwealth Observer Group commented on the scandal in West Nile, especially Arua, that 'the condition of the Office of the Returning Officer in Arua was testimony to the plight of the district as a whole; doors hanging loose, the windows smashed, papers scattered and furniture looted.'[13]

As a result of this confusion, all the eight UPC candidates in West Nile were returned unopposed, and in all the twenty-one constituencies in the northern region of Acholi, Lira and West Nile, the DP managed only to nominate nine candidates, while the UPM had two candidates and the Conservative Party (CP) none. The UPC registered a 100 per cent victory in all constituencies throughout the whole northern region, besides taking twelve seats unopposed and all these in the predictable districts of Apac and Lira and, surprisingly, Arua as well.

Thus, as it turned out, by the end of the nomination exercise, the UPC had bagged seventeen seats unopposed, although this fell short of the figure of forty-three which the UPC Secretariat had hoped to secure. Yet, although the UPC went into the election with a seventeen-seat headstart over the DP and other parties, Paulo Muwanga and his UPC were so worried they might not make it that they took even further measures to block any unforeseen eventualities. For instance, just before polling took place, the only four Western correspondents based in Uganda were either expelled or barred from entry if they were outside the country because the UPC did not want any impartial reporting done on the polling day. Then, in an attempt to pre-empt any petitions from the public that might be brought against some victorious UPC candidates, the Chief Justice of Uganda, Justice W. Wambuzi, was dismissed with no explanation by the Military Commission a few days before polling day. His successor was named as George Masika. It is likely that Justice Wambuzi would have declined to swear in a government elected 'on the strength of an electoral fraud', and the UPC group did not want to take any chances.[14]

But, almost unbelievably, not all these measures were able to prevent the UPC from losing the 1980 general elections. Many of the results were declared on the evening of 10 December and on the morning of the following day. In fact, it is known that by 11 a.m. on 11 December, 'the DP was on the brink of victory with 63 seats certified by the Returning Officers'. As the results came in from up-country areas, even the DP leaders must have been astonished by the landslide. That night, the UPC chiefs reviewed the plight in which the UPC found itself and drew up a strategy. It is said that Obote and some of his lieutenants were prepared to concede defeat and allow the DP to form a government, but then to undermine it by using the army, especially as the DP leaders were believed to lack 'experience'. Some friends abroad were allegedly consulted over this strategy, and their reply was curt and simple: there was no question of letting the UPC lose an election when its men were actually in power and, even more significant, while the Tanzanian forces were still in charge of security in the country. What followed is now well-known. The UPC lawyers immediately sat down and drafted the now infamous Legal Notice no. 10 of 11 December 1980, opening the way for the UPC to steal the victory from the DP.

By means of this document, Paulo Muwanga, in his capacity as

Chairman of the Military Commission, decreed that from the previous day, 10 December 1980, no Returning Officer or any other
person would be allowed to announce an election result without the
prior clearance of the Chairman of the Military Commission, con-
travention of the decree being punishable by a fine of 500,000 shillings or up to five years' imprisonment or both. Many results had
already been declared by the Returning Officers by the time the
Legal Notice was issued, but even those had to be frozen and then
manipulated by the Chairman of the Military Commission. For
instance, Okwenje* and Butagira had already accepted defeat by
their opponents in the DP, but were now told by the UPC National
Headquarters staff at Uganda House in Kampala that they had won
the election. Dr John Luwuliza-Kirunda, a UPC candidate, was
declared the winner in Iganga District several weeks after Paul
Wangola, his opponent and the actual winner, was forced to flee the
country and his house was ransacked. Samuel Mugwisa was declared
the winner in Mubende North East constituency several weeks after
the DP winner, Dr Paulo Sebuliba, had also been forced to flee
carrying with him the signed papers confirming his victory. Thus
by the time the manipulation of the votes was over, the UPC had
bagged seventy-four, leaving the DP with fifty-one and the UPM
with one.

The 1980 general election was a landmark in Ugandan history. It
had been looked forward to as a means of redressing the wrongs of
the past, but the way it ended was a major disappointment and, as
the result, a major cause for the opposition against the administration that grew from it.

There are a number of observations to be made about this election. First, there is the way it affected the Uganda Patriotic Movement (UPM), the latest of the political parties to join the race for
parliament. For the first time the former king of one of the kingdoms of Uganda stood as a candidate. This was Prince Patrick Olimi
Kaboyo, son and heir to the late Omukama of Toro, who stood on
the UPM ticket in Kabarole Central constituency, where his palace
and the town of Fort Portal are situated. In the general election, he
polled 12,501 votes against Timothy Tigaikara Katindibwa of the
UPC (14,973) and the DP candidate P. Kaboha (17,375). There is no
evidence of any serious tampering with the votes in this constituency,
considering that the DP won the election. Thus out of 44,849 electors, more than 30,000 Batoro rejected their own prince and the heir
to their kingdom (he was not just a prince, but the *crowned* King of

*Okwenje was defeated by the DP candidate Wafula Wanyama.

Toro), thus making it plain that although princes and princesses may still be quite popular in those areas of Uganda where they once held sway, the institution they once represented is less so. This example may not, of course, be an accurate representation of what people in other parts of the country feel today about the institution of the monarchy; but it may illustrate a trend concerning an institution which some Ugandans still regard with awe and admiration. The only UPM candidate elected was Dr C. Kiyonga, who defeated the UPC candidate (Musa Kiwusu) by over 900 votes. The UPM's President-General, Yoweri Museveni, was narrowly defeated in his Mbarara North constituency. It is said that, in order to embarrass Museveni, Obote ordered his own supporters in that constituency to vote for the DP candidate – who, as it turned out, won the election. This, however, was not the first time in Uganda that the leader of a political party failed to win a parliamentary seat: Benedicto Kiwanuka, President-General of the DP, failed to enter the National Assembly after the pre-independence general elections of April 1962.

The second point to make about the general election of December 1980 concerns the DP as a party. On the positive side, this was the first time since its inception that the DP went through an election and won it – it did so because it was truly national and cut across regional, religious, ethnic and other boundaries. The DP, as one of its strongest supporters admitted, was no longer a party of Catholics.[15] However, some commentators have failed to grasp that in voting exclusively for the DP, the Baganda were not endorsing the DP as their party but rather showing that they could not vote for the UPC as the party of Obote and Muwanga. The Baganda's vote was thus an anti-UPC vote; they were voting DP not from their hearts but with their heads.

However, the negative aspect of the DP's attitude during these elections was the way in which vested interests (apparently of long standing) were used to block the return of Professor Yusuf Lule from Nairobi in June 1980 when the DP convened a delegates' conference to select its leaders. It was clear to all that Lule's return to Kampala was being blocked because it would have led to his election as the President-General of the party. Although this episode did not lead to a division within the DP, it points to a weakness of political principle and the way Ugandans have continued to view politics as a personal preserve from which others, even when they are close to us, can be seen as outsiders to be excluded.

We must finally draw attention to two other aspects of Ugandan politics that were demonstrated in the general election of December 1980. The first was the readiness with which political leaders will espouse courses or policies not because they will lead to stability or the strengthening of the country's democratic institutions but because they will pay short-term dividends. We have seen above how the DP joined the UPC in blocking Binaisa's concept of an 'umbrella', which could well have paved the way for the establishment of a political culture based on consensus rather than sectarianism. Instead Paul Ssemogerere and the DP leadership, sensing a landslide that would be achieved on the anti-Obote sentiment then running so strongly in the country, opted for and advocated a pluralist approach to the 1980 election. Indeed, even the UPM's offer to the DP to form a united front against the UPC was dismissed as a manoeuvre to rob the DP of victory!

The second aspect of Uganda's politics demonstrated by the 1980 election was the way politicians resorted to simple expediency in changing parties just because the new parties they were joining would deliver the goods to them. Prominent men who had spent more than half their political careers fighting the DP now embraced its policies. What, one might justifiably have asked them, was new in the DP – which had been hidden from them since the 1950s and early 1960s when they fought tooth and nail to kill it off, but which had been revealed to them now that its popularity was spreading to everyone in the country like an infectious disease? It is the belief of many that Abu Mayanja, Adoko Nekyon, Mikombero-Mpambara, Mathias Ngobi, George Magezi and many others did not join the DP in 1980 out of sincere belief in its principles and policies, which had not changed since its formation and had in fact become more entrenched. Time will tell whether they change their political uniforms again. Such political behaviour, we contend, had some influence in deepening the agony of Uganda rather than being in any way its result.

Some general considerations on the period

Looking over the period of the UNLF, one cannot fail to feel a sense of lost opportunity. There was so much hope when Amin was swept out of power, yet so much despair, despondency and in the end indifference after the farcical elections of 1980. After Amin, Ugandans genuinely believed that a new chapter had begun. With the coming of the election, enthusiasm gripped young and old, together with a feeling that the final victory of justice and good over injustice and evil was within our grasp. All, however, was to be spoilt, and the people's hope trampled on, by a few political gangsters.

But we must return to the opening theme of this chapter, namely the sheer uncertainty that was everywhere when Amin left and the liberators entered Kampala. There was exuberance everywhere, but no appearance of any serious appreciation of what was at stake. Leaders arrived from all corners of the world, with genuine as well as empty claims to join the governors. It was difficult, especially for those who had stayed in the country through the Amin period, to tell genuine liberators from the swindlers. Even the government leaders themselves were not sure of the credentials of those with whom they were now working and sharing power.

Three administrations held office within a space of less than two years, which meant that the UNLF leadership was highly transitory. Those who took over from their fallen predecessors always considered themselves temporary sojourners, and as such were not anxious to unpack their bags. Many of them did not even bother to bring back their wives and children. After all, many of those in the government had been away for seven or eight years and had not yet identified themselves with the population who had stayed in the country and whom they were now called to serve. They sensed that as soon as the bubble burst they would be on the run again. Indeed this is what happened throughout this period. The exodus began with Lule's fall in June 1979; increased when Obote returned from exile in Tanzania and Binaisa was overthrown in May 1980, and became a stampede when Paulo Muwanga installed his chief, Obote, in power in December 1980. The net result was to be disaster for the country. The UNLF personnel came, helped themselves to what they could, and left. Those who hung around for longer than others did not do so with the true interests of the country in mind: they merely continued to accumulate savings for the day when they would join others in exile.

These operations did not go on unobserved by the 'stayees', the silent spectators who had endured the eight years of Amin's brutal rule. Many of them did not participate in the present chaos, although they would have been the very people to play a part in the reconstruction of the country; they were not allowed to do so because they were not liberators. The stayees left the liberators to run 'their Uganda'; after all, during the violence of the 1970s under Amin, prosperous Ugandans had abandoned Kampala city and retreated to the suburbs to escape Amin's torturers and murder squads. The UNLF leaders now took charge of a country of which they knew little. This was to be the pattern of governing Uganda during the first part of the 1980s, which included Obote's second regime.

It is surprising not so much that the UNLF administrations failed so lamentably in their task, but that civil war did not erupt openly among the many factions that competed for power so intensely during the brief period following Amin's fall. Undoubtedly, the presence of the Tanzanian forces assisted in preventing the outbreak of civil war during this period, especially during the presidency of Godfrey Binaisa.

So, in December 1980, the UPC with Milton Obote again at the helm had placed themselves in charge of the country. Obote had again shown his 'genius' for winning power. The challenge of his second presidency was whether he could be equally good at using it.

NOTES

1. See R. Muscat (ed.), *A Short History of the Democratic Party, 1954–1984*, Kampala: Foundation for African Development, 1984, p. 89.
2. A. Omara-Otunnu, *Politics and the Military in Uganda, 1890–1985*, London: Macmillan, 1987, p. 142.
3. The NCC 'gang of four' consisted of Tash Tandon, Dan Wadada Nabudere, Edward Rugumayo (Chairman) and Omwony-Ojok (Secretary).
4. R. Muscat, *op. cit.*, p. 96.
5. *Ibid.*, pp. 91–2.
6. Avirgan and Honey, quoted in A. Omara-Otunnu, *op. cit.*, p. 151.
7. R. Muscat, *op. cit.*, pp 91 ff, where this subject is well discussed.
8. The DP supporters behaved in the same way as in January 1971 when Amin overthrew Obote. In 1971, as now in 1980, the DP hoped to capitalise on the anti-Obote sentiment in Buganda and elsewhere to win the forthcoming general election, which Amin had promised in his bid to win civilian support for his coup.
9. During this period of the Military Commission, a triumvirate was set up to act as the 'head of state' of Uganda, consisting of S. Musoke, Wacha and Nyamuchoncho. However, the effective head of government was the Chairman of the Military Commission, Paulo Muwanga.
10. Report of the COG, para. 147. It is not without interest that the details of the Report are somewhat at variance with its conclusions.
11. *Ibid.*, para. 42, quoted from R. Muscat, *op. cit.*, p. 110.
12. The Electoral Commission which organised the 1980 general election was appointed on 25 June 1980 and within a period of less than six months it arranged, organised and supervised what its report called 'the historic elections in the country' on 10 and 11 December. In view of what the world now knows of this election and of what happened subsequently, it is ironic that the Commission informed President Obote, when they submitted their report on 25 June 1981, 'that 10th December will be remembered in the annals of this country as a day when restoration of the People's Government took place'. The Commission members were K.M.S. Kikira (Chairman); S.E. Egweu, A. Akera, Haji Y.B. Biraali, M.B. Matovu and A. Tamale (Members). V.B. Ssekono was Secretary to the Electoral Commission (up to 11 December 1980) and J.J. Obbo was Special Assistant to the Chairman.
13. Report of the COG, para. 39.
14. R. Muscat, *op. cit.*, pp. 112 ff, to which I am indebted for this account.
15. Samwiri Lwanga-Lunyiigo. See R. Muscat, *op. cit.*, pp. 125 ff.

11

OBOTE'S SECOND REGIME, 1980–1985

The tragedy of Uganda is that each round of misfortunes that comes seems to be much more calamitous than the one before. Some believe that Obote's second presidency ushered in a period of grievous destruction and agony surpassing anything we had yet seen, including – incredibly – the regime of Idi Amin.

Obote started his new regime with a promise of no revenge and of reconciliation with all his opponents. People listened; the words were sweet, but the tone remained that of the old Obote of the 1960s. Such remarks were disarming, but they also contained chilling premonitions of the true Obote who was to emerge later as the dust of the general election started to settle. All this, as it turned out, was no more than empty rhetoric – no doubt intended for the international media and the financial institutions which chose to believe what they were told by Obote rather than what those inside Uganda were actually seeing with their own eyes and hearing with their own ears.

'One of the hardest things about wielding power is knowing how to let go of it gracefully', a commentator has said. That Obote did not recognise this in the late 1960s when he had lost popularity was unfortunate; his determination to cling to the power he obtained illegally in 1980 can only be regarded as a tragedy.

Aftermath of the election

On the evening of Saturday, 11 December 1980, Milton Obote was sworn in to his second presidency of Uganda, the only man in Uganda's history up to the present to regain power after once being deprived of it. This was a remarkable achievement, negative though it may have been in the eyes of many. Obote can be denied many of the honours he may claim as his right, but almost no one will deny his great agility in scheming, outmanoeuvring and outwitting his political opponents; friends and foes alike agree that he is a ruthless tactician. It surprised no one when he chose as his chief lieutenant in presiding over the nation's affairs Paulo Muwanga, the man who had engineered his transformation from a mere returnee from Tanzania into the head of state and government.

It was natural, after capturing power in spite of having clearly lost the general elections, that Obote and his UPC government should have relied heavily on the military. During the election campaign,

Obote had promised to form a national or broad-based administration after a UPC victory, but once in power his group forgot this commitment and instead formed an administration composed entirely of UPC members, with the military as its ultimate source of support. Had Obote fulfilled his promise, it is possible that he would have mitigated some of the harm done in stealing the election. Indeed, had Obote formed such a broad-based government, it would have brought a measure of consensus to the confrontational style of politics that has existed in Uganda since independence. But power to Obote is like oxygen to man, and there could be no compromise with those with whom he disagreed.

Thus, the UPC government did not have the support of those who mattered, particularly in central Uganda which was the heart of the nation containing the capital. It soon became clear that, much as in the late 1960s, Obote's regime operated from within an enemy's camp, surrounded by hostile Baganda with whom he had now established a relationship of intense mutual suspicion and hatred. Thus it is important to understand the thinking of the Baganda and other southerners on the one side and of Obote and his military men, headed by Tito Okello and Oyite-Ojok, on the other at the start of Obote's second presidency.

The mere return of Obote from exile in Tanzania in May 1980 had cast a chill over a large section of the Bantu nationalities of southern Uganda who were not in the UPC camp; it was regarded as an ominous event. When, on 11 December 1980, they saw on Uganda TV Obote taking the oath as President, the bad dream had come closer to reality. The people in Kampala and Buganda generally felt that they were in an occupied territory – mere local inhabitants who would be looked upon as hewers of wood and drawers of water for the ruling group. Lacking guns, they resigned themselves to what Obote and his military establishment would mete out to them.

For his part, Obote came to power with a well-worked-out plan of action. Not for nothing had he campaigned as a man of experience who was returning to take up the post he had held before Idi Amin snatched it away from him. In 1966 he had started on a mission which he was in the process of accomplishing when he was interrupted by Amin, whom he had 'brought up by the hand'. It was a mission he had to complete now, even if the circumstances had changed considerably since he had been chased from State House in January 1971.

Luckily for Obote, he still had many of his former lieutenants around, some of a younger generation than himself – men with whom he had lived in the sweltering tropical forest of Owiny Ki-Bul in southern Sudan in 1971 and then in the heated politics of

Tanzania, and who finally had planned his return to the presidency during the UNLF administrations. Obote knew that he was disliked by the DP, CP and UPM and the people they represented. It did not matter; what mattered was the power and influence he would use in the service of himself, his close lieutenants and the native regions of most of his supporters, both civilian and military. He did not ignore the political wrangles going on outside his encamped headquarters: time and guns, he mused, would take care of those problems and of those responsible for such misguided doings.

In this, perhaps, lies part of the real cause for Obote's failure in his second administration: his inability to accept that the Uganda to which he had returned in 1980 was very different from what it had been in 1971. Obote came back as a wounded buffalo, determined to crush all those whom he believed had supported Amin in the early days of his rule, and he was not prepared to offer any real reconciliation or compromise. If Obote ever knew what the English philosopher Thomas Hobbes taught three centuries earlier – that 'there is no valid reason for sovereigns to desire to oppress their subjects, for the strength of sovereigns is directly dependent upon the strength and wellbeing of their subjects' – he ignored it now. To Obote there was no common ground, no common strength and well-being, between himself as a 'sovereign' and the people, his hapless and helpless subjects. It is for this reason that Obote is felt to have lacked a clear vision of his country's future when he assumed power for the second time in 1980; he was a fighter at a time that demanded conciliation, a short-sighted politician at a time that demanded statesmanship.

Obote was able to defy his opponents because of the assurance he had received that the army – the UNLA, headed by the veteran soldier Tito Okello, with David Oyite-Ojok as Deputy Commander and the driving force behind its strategies – would support him. It was clear that Obote regarded the UNLA not as belonging to the nation but as his own and the UPC's army that would keep him in power at all costs. This was partly demonstrated during the 1980 election campaign, when Obote would challenge the DP leader to show him *his* army. Obote knew that although he did not, like the DP, have a civil constituency, his own military constituency was solidly Nilotic. He knew that the Acholi-Langi hegemony which provided the underpinning for his administration was sure and strong, and supported by other soldiers from the peripheral areas in the east (such as Teso) and some Bantu-speakers from the south and west.

As we know, confronted with the decision whether or not to join Obote and the UPC in parliament after the disastrous December

1980 election, the DP leaders grudgingly swallowed their pride (some say they also swallowed their principles) and decided to join parliament. It is said that after the UPC coup, the UPM leaders approached the DP and asked what course it intended to take. According to some sources, the DP leaders replied that they were joining the parliament because they had been rightfully elected. 'Not all votes were stolen,' they appeared to be telling Museveni's party; otherwise the DP would not have won fifty-one seats. A staunch DP member has stated that there was a long debate on the issue of whether or not the elected DP members should take up their parliamentary seats.[1] But they eventually did agree to take up those seats, perhaps in response to Obote's promise to give them the post of Deputy Speaker and the nomination of four of the ten Specially Elected Members who would be chosen. Obote, with 'magnanimity', agreed to Paul Ssemogerere becoming the 'Leader of the Opposition' and Alex Waibale 'Opposition Whip'.[2] The DP parliamentarians would continue condemning the UPC government for its rigging of the elections, but Obote and his supporters saw the DP's presence on the Opposition benches in parliament as the party's acknowledgement of the validity of the 1980 election.

However, some Ugandans (prominent among them being Yoweri Museveni) refused to give support to a government that had obtained power through fraud. Museveni has been blamed for rejecting the results of the 1980 election since he had been Vice-Chairman of the Military Commission that organised it. Indeed, one critic has even said that not only was Museveni 'a key person in ensuring that the election was not rigged . . . [but] if anything, he could have been in a position to rig the election in his own favour.'[3] Such criticism is not only unfair, but also shows how some commentators on these events had little idea of what was actually going on in Uganda at that time. Those with eyes to see knew that Museveni was no more than a figurehead within the Military Commission, as indeed was reflected by the nature and size of the room he occupied on the third floor in the parliamentary building. The real rulers in the Military Commission at the time we are talking of were Paulo Muwanga and David Oyite-Ojok.[4]

Be that as it may, the UPM refused to accept the election results and some of its members, soon joined by other peace-loving Ugandans in other parties but especially in the DP, decided to oppose Obote through the use of the gun, since that was the only language Obote understood. They started a guerrilla war against his regime. The outbreak of this guerrilla movement from the moment when he stepped into State House once again compounded Obote's problems right from the start of his administration. But before we discuss this guerrilla war and indeed other aspects of Obote's regime, we will turn to some aspects of its economic policies.

Economic policy

Between 1981 and 1984 there was heavy devaluation of the Ugandan shilling, a floating exchange rate was established, producer prices for traditional exports were periodically revised upwards, there was extensive dismantling of price controls, great efforts were made to control overall government expenditure, the tax structure was changed from specific to *ad valorem* rates, and interest rates were largely decontrolled. The result was a partial recovery between 1981 and 1983 and a further decline for 1984–5. In constant 1966 prices, the real output of the economy recovered from 6.1 billion shillings in 1980 to 7.1 billion in 1983 before falling back to 6.4 billion by 1985.

The change in the total output of the economy over the five-year-period was an average increase of 1% a year. Over the same period the population was increasing at an annual average of 2.8%; thus average annual income per head of the population fell by nearly 2% in each year. This apart, the Ugandan shilling was still falling compared with foreign currencies, inflation if anything was rising even faster, the government budgetary deficit of some 30% was still very high, and overwhelming balance of payments pressures made foreign exchange very scarce.

The highlights of economic policy were all excellent turn-around prescriptions for a declining, inflation-ridden, over-administered, export-dependent, entrepreneur-deficient economy, weak in foreign earnings and with a chronic budget deficit. Why were the results so disappointing?

Standing out in strong relief is the fact that a number of counterpart measures for the highlights of economic policy were missing in the policy package. Devaluation of the currency was not followed by sufficiently strong measures to eradicate the factors that had made devaluation imperative. Extensive efforts to control overall government expenditure were intended as the central counterpart to devaluation, but there was no detailed cutting of excessive or unnecessary government spending. Emphasis was on overall expenditure ceilings in a manner reminiscent of efforts to prevent a pot from boiling over by holding the lid down while continuing to stoke the fire underneath it. For example, officers denied funds for customary but largely meaningless tours and surveys gradually found ways of securing finance for at least some of those activities and later for most of them as often as in the past. The periodical upward revision of producer prices for export crops was not accompanied by sufficient control of inflation, and thus gains were soon wiped out. Moreover, ensuring prompt payment to farmers on delivery of their produce was not accorded priority. Efforts to control overall government expenditure were not followed by insistence on accountability.

The underlying problem was that those who managed the economy did not have the interest of the country at heart. The ministers, army commanders and other officers and all their associates and hangers-on were united in one major exercise: milking the cow. The 'liberators' who surrounded Obote were men who had returned to Uganda determined to make up for the shortfalls they had suffered during their ten years in the political wilderness in Tanzania or elsewhere. They had been away for a long time, and few, including their boss Obote, had prospered while languishing in their Tanzanian, Kenyan or Zambian exile. In the words of one observer, they 'felt that they were entitled to the fruits of independence and "liberation" which had eluded them for so long'.[5] Thus they embarked on an unprecedented plundering of the country's wealth, which has left a disastrous legacy to the Ugandans of today.

We should particularly observe that this group of the 'liberators' was headed by those who came from the north, although some of the Bantu leaders were allowed to pick up what they could from the dispensers of largesse. Thus the 'O'[6] filled the ranks of management in parastatals and government-owned financial institutions and, of course, in the civil service itself. It is true that some government financial institutions were in the hands of southerners, particularly Baganda and Banyankole; these headed the Bank of Uganda, the Uganda Development Bank, the Cooperative Bank and the Uganda Commercial Bank; but these were 'heads' used by their masters and they were there largely because they had made themselves indispensable to the corrupt system. The 'O' also took their fill of businesses left by the Nubian-Amin élites. In this sharing of the spoils, the most favoured were those from the 'royal' clan of the Langi, something which did not please the other members of the northern alliance and was therefore a factor in the later rift within the uneasy Acholi-Langi alliance. However due to history – something which Obote and his associates could not really change overnight – Bantu-speaking people, especially Baganda, continued to hold key positions in the public service. They were also in charge of seemingly important portfolios such as Defence (Paulo Muwanga), Internal Affairs (Luwuliza-Kirunda) and Industry (Adonia Tiberondwa). NASA, which harassed so many innocent people, was the preserve of the Banyankole.

Another element which Obote's regime introduced in the game of economic plunder was the Asian community, who now became important in the manipulation of the economy. They became the regime's agents, the linch-pins of the whole system of economic exploitation; most of the money exported from the country went through the hands of some Asians whose return the regime engineered. Asian firms were thus enabled to borrow money from government financial institutions without firm guarantees for its return. The largest single loan, issued at Obote's direction and guaranteed by him in writing in his capacity as Minister of Finance, amounted to 14.7 billion shillings (old currency).

Guerrilla warfare: why they took to the bush

Before we discuss Obote's reaction to the outbreak of guerrilla warfare against him, we should briefly examine why the fighters took up arms. What made certain men and women who, far from being destitute, were people of high academic and professional standing and some quite wealthy, decide to go to the bush and remain there for over five years? The NRM's detractors, especially Obote and associates of his like Paulo Muwanga, used to accuse them of having done so because they did not want democracy. By this they meant that the NRM refused to accept the verdict of the people, as expressed in the general election of December 1980 – for the UPC and their supporters, that election was free and fair and did indeed represent the verdict of the people.

We have already said that the reason – actually the pretext – for Yoweri Museveni and his NRM going to the bush and fighting Obote's regime was the rigging of that very election, but that is only half the story. The crucial issue, which many of the commentators on these events have not properly grasped, is that the NRM and National Resistance Army (NRA) went to the bush to remove a repugnant system of government based on an army dominated by northerners, especially the Acholi. It was claimed in a public lecture at Makerere University in 1988 by A.G.G. Gingyera-Pinycwa, Professor of Political Science, that the NRM/NRA went to the bush to remove the northerners from power.

This is far from the truth. The rigging of the election may have been the last straw that brought about the guerrilla war against Obote. But more fundamental was the fact that people had had high hopes of that election, which they had seen as a means of escaping from the sufferings they had been subjected to for several years. However, with the rigged election result it was clear that the old story would repeat itself. If it were not resisted, the primitive and fascist regime of the UPC would continue, and the people of Uganda would continue to suffer and die. Thus the reason for the NRM taking up arms against Obote went beyond the mere installation of Obote in power by Muwanga and Oyite-Ojok with the support of the UNLA. As we have noted, other Ugandans who shared the NRM's view about the 1980 elections and refused to accept their result were prepared to work with Obote, notably the DP Members of Parliament. They decided to work *within* the system to fight against dictatorship and political fraud. But the system within which they agreed to work was Obote's own system; not only that, it was also the system of Idi Amin and the system Obote had used to rule Uganda back in the late 1960s. It was the colonial system. Those in the NRM decided to fight Obote not only because he and his party had stolen the 1980 elections. Their taking up arms was a crime; but not so much so as the continuation of the system which had been used by all of Uganda's leaders since independence to subjugate and terrorise the people of the country:

. . . . the system of institutionalised violence unleashed upon the people of Uganda; the system of government which allowed its soldiers and armed agents to go on rampage of looting, wanton and indiscriminate killings of people and even entire villages; the system that allowed soldiers to rape women (including children and old women); the system of road-blocks which were used to rob the people of their money and property; and the system of '*Panda Gari*' ('get on the lorry') during which innocent men and women were rounded up and taken to places of torture and death from which many never emerged alive.[7]

The NRM went to the bush to remove a bad and repugnant sys-tem, and this was the stand which the NRM/NRA took throughout their protracted war up to January 1986. When Obote was removed from power in 1971, Ugandans hoped democracy would return to Uganda, but instead they were suffocated under Amin's murderous regime for eight years. Amin was overthrown in 1979 but peace did not return because the governments of the UNLF which then fol-lowed one another did not remove the system that had bred Obote and Amin. When the 1980 general election came, Ugandans saw clearly what happened. The system which had been created by the colonial power and then inherited at independence, to be perfected by Obote after the 1966 crisis and matured under Amin's dictator-ship, and which the UNLF had failed to remove, was still there. It was the system which brought Obote back to power in December 1980.

Thus it was clear to the freedom-fighters that using the *existing* system to fight Obote and his followers was not enough. But it was one thing deciding to fight Obote; choosing the method to employ in this war was quite another. The choice of strategy varied from group to group.[8] The strategy of conventional war, involving regular units facing each other in straight battles, with identifiable frontlines and large-scale modern equipment such as aircraft, artillery and rockets was beyond the capacity and the intentions of the NRM/NRA fighters at the time. The alternative strategy of insurrection would have needed a high degree of coordination and was therefore equally unrealistic in the prevailing circumstances. A coup would not have worked because of the effective deployment of Obote's army and the presence in Uganda of the Tanzanian troops, which could always be reinforced from home. This left the strategy of a protracted 'people's war' against Obote's regime. This went through the three classic phases of guerrilla warfare, mobile warfare and finally conventional warfare. The first stage began on 6 February 1981, at 8.30 a.m., with the attack on Kabamba School of Infantry. The attackers overran the camp by capturing the quarter-guard, the communications room, the military transport depot and all the administration quarters. They took all the vehicles and other equipment. The next day, 7 February 1981, the fighters went to Kiboga town, where they attacked the police station and captured a few guns. It was thus here that the war of liberation truly started. Two days later the liberators were attacked by Tanzanian soldiers and forced to leave the area. They proceeded to Lukoola. Thereafter – the phase of mobile warfare – the NRM established themselves in various areas of central Uganda, particularly in the region immediately surrounding the capital which later came to be known as 'Luwero Triangle', and started launching surprise attacks. The final conventional stage of the war lasted from the second half of 1985 until the enemy was defeated and driven from Kampala on 26 January 1986.

Some northerners, who stood to gain from the continuance of the *status quo* which guaranteed them power and influence because the army was northern-dominated, have accused Museveni and the NRM of playing on ethnic and linguistic sentiment during the guerrilla war to win support against Obote's regime. A. Omara-Otunnu, an Acholi and a nephew of Tito Okello, has said that 'although he [Museveni] made general statements of his opposition to "tribalism" for the benefit of the international media, within the country he presented the struggle for power as a confrontation between Bantu and non-Bantu speakers and more specifically as a struggle between southerners and northerners.'[9] In fact, those who conceived and started the war against Obote were, and remain, against 'tribalism'; but because of the area in which the war was fought, those who came to form the backbone of the army that fought against Obote were Baganda, because it was they particularly who were being victimised by the UNLA. It was the orphaned children of those who had been butchered who in desperation joined the freedom-fighters in order to drive out men who were totally alien to a civilised society, who represented backwardness and death. It was thus natural that those who supported the NRM/NRA were Bantu-speakers, mostly Baganda. Their enemies, unavoidably, were the Luo-speakers, mainly from the north.

In the eyes of Luwero people the killers and rapists of their people were the men from the north. The soldiers, it is true, were sometimes led to their victims by Baganda UPC supporters, but this in no way mitigates the inhuman crimes of the soldiers.

Much has been written about the 'tribalism' and 'apartness' of the southern people, about a 'north-south divide syndrome'. This is an unfortunate development, but we cannot unmake history; crimes were committed by one group of Ugandans against other groups. This is something which those who committed the crimes would like to hide and forget, but the victims cannot and should not keep quiet because it is through looking the reality of the crimes in the face that a repetition can be prevented.

Here we should make a distinction. The northerners responsible for the massacres in what became known as the 'Luwero Triangle' and other regions of the south and west were generally Langis and Acholis, especially the latter. However, the non-Luo soldiers in the UNLA had to match their Luo masters in cruelty, otherwise they would have shared the fate of their victims.[10]

Obote's reaction to the guerrilla warfare

When Yoweri Museveni, then a young intellectual involved in the turmoil of Uganda's politics, started the armed struggle against Milton Obote, 'a man of experience and backed by powerful friends in Africa and in the Western world', the conventional wisdom was that he and his few followers would die in the bush. If that was not to be, Obote would find them there and leave them there. However, that was not to be. In the end it was Obote's UNLA soldiers who were either left in the bush or driven back to Kampala, where other hostile forces – the Acholi coup-makers led by Tito and Bazilio Okello – were to annihilate them and drive them from power.

The NRM started its war against Obote in Buganda early in 1981, basing this peasant-supported guerrilla movement in the Luwero Triangle, which also happened to be an ideal area for guerilla resis-tance. We shall not dwell too much in this chapter on the manner in

The Luwero Triangle: areas of
combat between the NRA
and UNLA

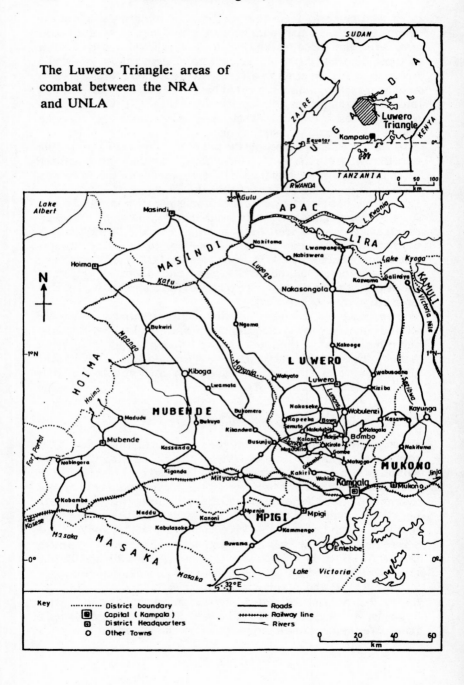

which this guerilla warfare was carried out, for this is a subject that is dealt with in other studies.[11] Here we shall confine ourselves to the manner in which Obote reacted to this event, the first of its nature in the history of Uganda since independence.

Obote's reaction to the outbreak of guerrilla resistance was a military one, as was only to be expected. No government, faced with such an emergency, will remain passive, least of all one led by a man of Obote's calibre, character and experience. Obote accordingly accepted the challenge posed by the guerrilla fighters with urgency and savagery.

The military aspects of the matter were straightforward.[11] The 'bandits', as Obote always called Museveni's NRA fighters, had to be routed and those living in their area of operations – the Luwero Triangle – were to be wiped out too. In a speech broadcast on Radio Uganda, Obote told a rally held in Seroti in 1981 that if the Baganda did not behave themselves, they (the Acholi–Langi alliance) would do to them what they did to the West Nilers in 1980. He always claimed that the trouble was confined to a tiny area which should pose no problem to the rest of the country. He evidently did not care how many deaths and how much suffering were caused in the process. As he and his close ministers agreed, most of the blood that was flowing was that of the Baganda, the stubborn tribalists who had always caused him political problems. It is possible to exaggerate the extent of the massacres in Buganda, but conservative estimates are that about 300,000 people may have been killed and another 500,000 displaced in Buganda alone. 'For the first time in Uganda's history', Samwiri Lwanga-Lunyiigo of Makerere University has remarked, 'Ugandans were put into concentration camps which really became death camps.' People were horribly tortured before being murdered. 'Obote did all this', Lwanga-Lunyiigo grimly concludes, 'to bring down the proud Baganda to their hobbling knees and he succeeded with a vengeance unprecedented in African history – possibly only equalled by Pol Pot.'[12]

Thus the Luwero Triangle, where most of the guerrilla war was fought, became the laboratory for these experiments of genocide to be carried out. Soldiers and other agents of the regime were turned by the system into instruments to wipe out a whole nationality. The callousness of the UNLA soldiers is shown by the kind of graffiti they left on the walls of the houses whose inhabitants they had hacked to death. At Kilolo, some 15 miles north of Kampala, one soldier wrote: 'Killing a Muganda or a Munyankole is as easy as riding a bicycle', followed by his Acholi name.

Obote did all this before the apparently blind eyes of world powers and their leaders including, above all, Britain, whose Prime

Results of atrocities during the second Obote regime, Luwero Triangle

Minister Margaret Thatcher was so keen on lecturing Third World governments on human rights and the rule of law. Obote's superb public relations succeeded in fooling some highly reputable academics and journalists who spared no effort to praise and exculpate him. His envoys abroad, such as the High Commissioner in London Shafiq Arain, were able to convince such people, for some reason, that nobody but Obote was capable of ruling Uganda. He was further supported by Western financial institutions, the International Monetary Fund (IMF) and the World Bank, which gave him large loans. They believed he was now a reformed capitalist, although at this very time he was using North Koreans in the war against Museveni's guerrilla fighters.[13]

However, the brutality of the regime evidently aroused the consciences even of some prominent figures in Obote's own government and armed forces. Even if the Baganda had supported the guerrilla warfare, did that mean that the carnage had to go on for ever? Frequently the people of Uganda and the world at large were being told that the troubled area of Luwero would soon be pacified, and yet the war was fast spreading with equal ferocity into other areas. Where would it all end? Differences began to surface between Obote and his lieutenants in both the civilian and military establishments. Some of Obote's associates saw a need for negotiations, however limited, with the so-called bandits; but Obote would have none of it.

There was general consensus on the goal to be attained, which was to suppress Museveni's guerrilla war and to continue in power. The disagreement was on the means of attaining this goal.

Within the civilian administration, the negotiations lobby was led, so it is now said, by Obote's Vice-President and Minister of Defence, Paulo Muwanga, and included some Bantu ministers such as Samwiri Mugwisa, the Minister of Agriculture. Whether this was because of the 'kith and kin' syndrome; or another ploy to manoeuvre themselves on to safer ground from which to gain power at an appropriate time later with Muwanga as leader; or a genuine desire to see an end to the massacres in Luwero – we shall never know the answer for certain. What is clear is that from early in 1984 Muwanga and his close associates started advocating negotiations with the NRA fighters and that Obote saw in them a source of disloyalty.

Within the military the Acholis Tito Okello, the Army Commander, and Bazilio Okello, commander of 10 Brigade Northern Zone, based in Gulu, also felt that the time had come to negotiate with the NRA fighters. For the Acholi soldiers, who formed the bulk of the army, the war which Museveni's guerrillas were fighting against Obote was quickly becoming a war against the Acholis only. The soldiers who were being sent to the war front were virtually all Acholi, and the Langi officers and men were manning safe areas of Kampala and being deliberately kept away from the war zones. In short, those who were dying in hundreds to prop up Obote's fledgling regime were not Langis but Acholis. Thus Acholis' concern over Obote's determination to continue the war against Museveni was less humanitarian than due to the realisation that if the war did not stop, their sons would continue to die at the hands of the NRA. They joined the negotiation lobby to save their skins, and thus in Obote's eyes they became a disloyal group – marked men.

Obote did not want to listen to the pleas for negotiations. His paranoid hatred of the Baganda (and now the Banyankole, the ethnic group of Museveni)[14] left no room for cool and reasoned assessment of the options still open to him. He disdainfully opposed all negotiations with the 'bandit' Museveni to end the war, in the mistaken belief that the NRM/NRA would never succeed in undermining his regime, forgetting that guerrilla warfare does not necessarily have to achieve a military victory in order to influence the political system it is fighting against. As all save Obote and those closest to him could clearly see, the fighting would continue until the guerrillas had obtained what they wanted.[15]

In view of Obote's responsibility for the sufferings of the Ugandan people, particularly those in the Luwero Triangle, it is remarkable that he has never expressed any feeling of remorse or compassion towards the survivors of the families who died in their thousands at the hands of barbarous soldiers acting under his command.

Because of the sufferings of Baganda in the Luwero Triangle, we should not forget those of the people of West Nile and Ugandans of Rwandese origin in the south-west of the country. It is estimated that by 1982, some 250,000 Ugandans had fled across the frontiers into southern Sudan and Zaire. On the other hand, in 1982 over 25,000 people of Rwandese origin, most of whom were Ugandan citizens and who had been in Uganda for many years, were evicted from their homes, had their lands confiscated and, in the case of some, lost their lives. The difference here was that the Rwandese victims suffered at the hands of the party rather than army personnel of Obote's regime. According to one source, 'the UPC official regarded as responsible for spear-heading the Rwandese evictions in 1982 was the son of the first Bairu Prime Minister of Ankole Kingdom, in 1956, at a time when Ankole politics was centred on the Bairu-Bahima cleavage within the Kingdom. For many Banyankole this symbolised the continuity with the past.'[16]

Obote's support even within the UNLA, which had always supported him since his exile in Tanzania, ran adrift in the military quicksand in which all was lost. This was partly because of his refusal to negotiate with the NRM/NRA, but the real crunch came when it became obvious to all that Obote was ignoring the Acholi factor in the Acholi-Langi alliance on which the fortunes of the 'liberators' group of the UPC had depended since Amin's overthrow. The Acholis began to see that Obote was pursuing a deliberate policy of discriminating against them in favour of his own tribe, the Langi. It was the time-honoured game of using allies to get into power and dumping them when he could use them no longer.

It was not only in the civil service and the management of the economy that the Langis were taking the lion's share. In the military too they were being pushed into positions which others thought they did not merit. The most celebrated example of this development came when the Army Chief of Staff, David Oyite-Ojok, was killed when his helicopter was shot down by the NRA at Kasuzi near Nakasongola in December 1983. All eyes were focused on Obote to see whom he would nominate for this crucial post. Did he have a Langi to put in the shoes of his long-time comrade-in-arms and confidant, Oyite-Ojok? All those best qualified to replace Oyite-Ojok, most notably Bazilio Okello, were Acholi. Obote mused to himself. He did not have a suitable Langi for the post, but after postponing the decision for almost six months, he appointed Smith Opon-Acak, a Langi but a man who lacked a solid record of leadership and did not command respect.[17] There was general amazement, but to the Acholis this was the last straw. The writing was on the wall. Perhaps it was this act alone that dissolved the seemingly impregnable Acholi-Langi hegemony which had effectively ruled Uganda since the removal of Amin, and sparked off events that led to Obote's overthrow.

For Tito Okello, Bazilio Okello and other disgruntled Acholi officers who wanted negotiations of some sort with the NRA, the appointment of Smith Opon-Acak removed the element of doubt. Hitherto their opposition to Obote had been unfocused, but with the decision to throw in his lot with his own tribesmen, the Langi, a clear decision appeared to have been made against them. To the wavering Acholi army officers it brought relief, especially in the lower ranks. Their spirits were no longer troubled, their souls and bodies no longer divided. They now knew that they had to remove the man who had humiliated them. All that remained was to work out the strategy.

We should remark, in passing, that the death of Oyite-Ojok, the Eichmann of Luwero, was received with great jubilation in parts of Uganda, particularly in the south; in some Kampala homes there were quiet celebration parties. Yet there are those who describe him as 'one of the most celebrated army commanders in Ugandan military history'.[18] There is no doubt that he was 'celebrated' – for the atrocities that he committed.

The coup

Thus by the end of 1984 Obote was in deep trouble of his own making. Then on 27 July 1985, for the second time in his political career, his own army, which had brought him to power, removed him in a coup d'état. The circumstances were similar to those of the Amin coup of January 1971. His tendency to abandon friends and allies who had helped him to attain power seemed to have become a habit. Equally remarkable was his apparent inability to weigh the consequences of his actions, especially since he himself had fallen victim to a previous coup. It is astonishing that he did not anticipate what would happen if he decided to by-pass such experienced and long-standing allies as Bazilio Okello and reach for Smith Opon-Acak merely because he was a Langi, as if to emphasise the Langi officers' belief – and the Acholi officers' fears – that the Langi were born to command and not to be commanded. It is true that there were disputes between him and the two Okellos, especially the more robust and younger Bazilio; but to allow personal animosities to intrude into affairs of state at such a crucial point in his presidency was unstatesmanlike.

With this blindness, it could not be surprising that he did not take pre-emptive measures against the counter-attack from his enemies which was sure to come. By the beginning of 1985 Obote was not in control of what was going on in Uganda generally, but especially not in the field of the military which was clearly in the hands of the aggrieved Acholis.

In June 1985, at the crucial moment when his personal presence at the scene of events was of paramount importance, Obote left the capital to officiate at a not very important ceremony at Mbale – one is reminded of his trip to Singapore in January 1971, leaving the road clear for the coup by Idi Amin. Oblivious of the true significance of his enemies' plans and actions, Obote started issuing orders and sending emissaries from Mbale. He directed his lieutenants in Kampala to take charge of the situation, and to arrest and detain the associates of Brigadier Okello. He sent an emissary – a Mr Wacha-Olal, who had acted as one of the members of the presidential triumvirate during the time of the Military Commission in 1980 – with proposals for peace-talks to Bazilio Okello, then in Gulu, but the Acholi Brigadier was no longer interested in such proposals from a man whom he could not trust. Instead, Bazilio Okello sent a message to the north across the border with Southern Sudan where the supporters of Amin and former soldiers of the FUNA (under Major-General Lumago) were living. An agreement was concluded between the Acholi and the West Nile FUNA remnants, on the basis of which an Acholi-West Nile alliance was established to collaborate in Obote's overthrow. The FUNA fighters and other West Nile elements arrived in Kampala a few days before the coup.

As everything was collapsing all around him, Obote made a last desperate appeal to his 'godfather', Julius Nyerere, to send troops to quell the Acholi coup, but Julius did not act. Perhaps he had had enough of Uganda's problems, and in any case Nyerere, with his *Ujamaa* policies in tatters, was in the process of packing his own bags to make way for his successor, Ndugu Ali H. Mwinyi. Nyerere told Obote that as he was soon leaving office he could not commit his successor to policies which would in effect be open-ended. Many Ugandans sighed with relief, to see that at last the great Tanzanian leader had realised the folly of endlessly propping up a man, however close a friend he might be, who was so unpopular in his own country. Tanzania's policies towards Obote and his government had in fact begun to shift from as early as mid-1984 – to the extent that it started quietly supporting the NRA's fight against Obote.

While his UPC parliamentarians were waiting in the National

Assembly for the start of a meeting which he himself had summoned, Obote boarded his Mercedes and drove towards the Kenyan
border. This time he overflew Tanzania on his way to Zambia. His
regime was over.

NOTES

1. R. Muscat (ed.), *A Short History of the Democratic Party, 1954–1984*, Kampala:
   Foundation for African Development, 1984, p. 121.
2. *Ibid.*, p. 122.
3. A. Omara-Otunnu, *Politics and the Military in Uganda, 1890–1985*, London:
   Macmillan Press, 1987, p. 155.
4. It is of interest to note that strictly and constitutionally the head of state was not
   Paulo Muwanga, the Chairman of the Military Commission. Rather the role of
   the head of state of Uganda was hidden in the triumvirate that was appointed
   by the Military Commission. It consisted of Mr S. Musoke, Mr Wacha and
   Mr Nyamuchoncho.
5. S. Lwanga-Lunyiigo, unpublished papers.
6. The names of most of the people who come from the north – and to a certain
   extent from the east – start with 'O'. Hence the term 'O' signifies northerners or
   easterners – the Obotes, Otais, Okellos, Ojoks, Omaras, Odongs, Obongos,
   Ottis, Odyeks, Olaras, and so on.
7. Quoted from *The People's Struggle Since Independence*, published by *Recent*
   newspaper, Jan. 1987.
8. These strategies are explained in an article which Yoweri Museveni wrote in
   August 1981 in the issue of the NRM official newsletter, the *Uganda Resistance
   News*, and reproduced in Yoweri Museveni's *Selected Articles on the Uganda
   Resistance War*, which first appeared in 1985, p. 8, ff.
9. A. Omara-Otunnu, *op. cit.*, p. 176.
10. My judgement of the soldiers from the north in regard to the atrocities they
    committed in the Luwero Triangle may be thought by some to be too harsh, and
    that bitterness has been allowed to predominate over historical objectivity. But
    similar atrocities have been and still are being committed in the north by the
    rebels fighting the NRM government against innocent civilians who have nothing
    to do with the rebellion going on there. It was reported that in Gulu, one of the
    two major towns in Acholi, on the morning of 9 July 1991, a group of fifty rebels
    of Joseph Kony's United Democratic Christian Army (UDCA) raided the Sacred
    Heart Girls School and abducted forty-four students, in addition to raping and
    maiming many others, and looting and destroying property. In addition they cut
    off their victims' ears, noses and lips. The abductions were designed to procure
    the girls as their concubines. Many civilians were hacked to death, using axes and
    machetes. Such actions have been condemned by leaders from the north itself,
    most notably the former Prime Minister of Uganda and the Chairman of the
    Uganda People's Democratic Movement (UPDM), Eric Otema Allimadi. A
    statement by the UPDM Executive Committee, released on 12 July 1991, con-
    demned the massacre in Gulu and the horrific atrocities committed by rebels in
    all parts of the north. This condemnation, we emphasise, came from the Acholi
    people themselves, including prominent leaders and elders.
11. See issues of *The 6th of February: The Magazine of the National Resistance
    Army* for more detailed information on the war.
12. S. Lwanga-Lunyiigo, unpublished papers.

13. Ironically, while capitalist countries such as Britain and Communist ones such as North Korea were supporting Obote, that very capitalist institution, Lonrho, and socialist countries like Libya were, for their own reasons, supporting Museveni.

14. Although we have said that Obote had now added hatred for the Banyankole to that for the Baganda, we should make a clarification here. In many ways, the Banyankole were, as one observer has put it, 'the UPC/Obote courtiers after the Langi'. The prominence of Rwakasisi, Rurangaranga, Tiberondwa and numerous other personalities testifies to that. Obote wooed other tribes, especially Banyankole, to be his allies against the Acholi. Bushenyi, for instance, became the Mecca for Obote's so-called 'hero's day', a most wasteful, corrupt and extravagant celebration at the taxpayer's expense. But this does not in any way mean that Obote did not harbour the kind of hatred described for the rest of the ethnic group, to which Museveni, his greatest adversary, belonged. (I am grateful to Mr Justin Okot for his clarification of this and many other points in this chapter.)

15. My attention has been drawn, by a Ugandan colleague who was well-acquainted with the situation as it then was, to the fact that General Tito Okello, the Army Commander who disagreed with Obote and later ousted him from power, wanted to facilitate free and fair general elections. According to Mr Justin Okot, to whom I am indebted for this valuable information, Tito Okello had hoped to arrange for these elections after the signing of a genuine peace agreement in Nairobi. Okot believes that if such elections had been held, 'power would certainly have gone to the Baganda in particular and Bantu ethnically in all probability'. He suggests that Tito Okello and his junta 'were fully aware of the pending change in the country's political fortunes'. All this tends to suggest that there were, therefore, fundamental differences between Tito Okello and Obote in dealing with the NRA.

16. Quoted from Cherry Gertzel, 'The Politics of Uneven Development: The case of Obote's Uganda', unpublished paper, fn. 187.

17. A. Omara-Otunnu, *op. cit.*, p. 160.

18. *Ibid.*, p. 152.

12

THE OKELLO-LUTWA FIASCO, JULY 1985–JANUARY 1986

Acholis and Langis

General Tito Okello's regime was swept into power on the crest of a military mutiny that caught the people of Kampala in a frenzy. The main characteristic of Brigadier Bazilio Okello's coup – for essentially it was he who masterminded and carried it out – was that it was an Acholi affair directed specifically against the Langi. The long-standing Acholi-Langi alliance and hegemony over the affairs of Uganda was thereby dissolved, and new alliances and hegemonies had to be looked for and formed. The six-month Okello-Lutwa regime brought together some very unlikely bedfellows.

The coup, as we have seen, was directed against the Langi, and it had been sparked off by the deteriorating military situation and the successes of the NRA, of which the Acholis had had to bear the full brunt. However, in spite of this, the two Okellos – Tito, the leader, and his fellow-tribesman Bazilio who effected the coup – needed the support of the civilian population of Kampala if they were to legitimise their seizure of power. This explains why Bazilio Okello's soldiers, when they arrived in Kampala from the north on the morning of Saturday 27 July 1985, showed clenched fists, the DP mobilisation symbol. By this they meant to proclaim to the people that the coup had been staged on behalf of the civilian constituency represented by the Baganda, who had all along defied and rejected Obote. This was the first mistake the Acholi coup-makers made; the people refused to be fooled.

The coup was bloodless because there was no outward resistance to the arrival of the Acholis; yet, on their arrival in Kampala, the Acholi soldiers embarked on a totally malicious looting of the city and its environs. The clenched fists with which the Acholis entered Kampala had been intended to attract instant applause from the alleged DP capital, but it soon became apparent that the same old soldiers of the 'liberators' had returned. They promptly wrecked shops, stole private vehicles and emptied petrol stations. The ghastly evidence of their handiwork was everywhere to be seen in the streets of Kampala. If the coup was a reconciliation, it was so only within the victorious ruling group of the Acholis themselves.

After seizing power the Okellos set about forming a new

administration, and this was the first of many challenges the two soldiers would face in the next few months. First of all, they promoted themselves, thinking about their names in particular. Tito soon discovered that he had always had a third name – Lutwa – which he now began to use; at the same time, Bazilio remembered he had been called 'Olara', which he threw in as his second name. General Tito Okello-Lutwa was the Chairman of the Military Council and the head of state, while Brigadier Bazilio Olara Okello was Lieutenant-General and Chief of the Defence Forces. The two were *ex-officio* members of the Military Council, the effective body governing the country, which also included the commanders of the various fighting groups that had joined the military junta, namely the Federal Democratic Movement; FEDEMU (2); FUNA (1); the Uganda Freedom Movement, UFM (1), UNLA (7) and Uganda National Rescue Front, UNRF (1).[1]

To establish some sort of continuity with the previous regime, the Military Council appointed Paulo Muwanga, who had been Minister of Defence in Obote's government, as Prime Minister. Some observers have remarked that Paulo Muwanga was appointed Prime Minister at the insistence of the Tanzanian leaders who were worried that their interests, particularly financial ones, might not be taken care of if there were not a civilian in the government who had been closely associated with the fallen leader – who had always had close contacts with Julius Nyerere and other Tanzanian leaders. Muwanga's appointment was short-lived because of the very adverse reaction which greeted his appointment – he did, after all, share with Obote the responsibility for the atrocities in the Luwero Triangle. He was therefore soon dropped in favour of a fellow-Muganda, Abraham Waligo – who, in a public address to his fellow-Baganda from the steps of the National Assembly, had thanked Tito Okello for having rid the country of the Baganda's enemy, Obote. To reward him for this achievement, Waligo gave the General the name 'Lutwama' (from Lutwa), a Kiganda name belonging to the Fumbe (civet cat) clan. It was not said whether or not the head of the clan had been consulted. Waligo, a highly educated man and an engineer, had served Obote loyally as Minister of Housing for more than four years, yet was now denouncing him, thus displaying a strange inconsistency.

The next people the coup-makers fraternised with were the politicians and the fighting groups. Thus as soon as Obote was overthrown the Okello junta, anxious to convince Ugandans and the world that theirs was not a purely military government, called upon all the political as well as military forces in the country to join them in forming a national administration: with the removal of

Obote, who had always refused peace negotiations of any kind, there could be no reason for continued confrontation with Kampala. It was an attractive message. But needless to say some of those who responded were self-seekers. The unsuspecting and naive Okellos could not cope with the blatant ambitions of the politicians and some so-called freedom-fighters, all of whom wanted to 'fall into things'.

Reaction of the fighters and the politicians

But what was the response or reaction of the fighting groups? They, after all, had precipitated the Acholi coup that sent Obote on his travels once again. The NRM/NRA had been the main force fighting against the Obote regime, and it had been fully supported and held together by the Okellos. However, it refused to leave the bush not because it did not welcome Obote's overthrow, for which it had created the conditions. The fighting groups were very happy with it. They refused to join Okello-Lutwa's government because it was not merely Obote they had been fighting against. He represented a system of darkness and oppression, and the NRM knew that the removal of Obote by itself would not remove the system. New men using the same bad system would be no better than their predecessors.

In a statement issued by Yoweri Museveni in Nairobi in August 1985, the position of the NRM on the question of joining the Okellos' military junta was clearly set out.[2] The NRM informed the Okellos, that it was ready to co-operate with them, despite their tainted past, provided a political settlement was worked out between the two principal opponents, the UNLA and the NRA. The issue that could not be left unresolved was the control of the instruments of force – especially the army, which had exemplified the bad system the NRM had gone into the bush to fight. It had been the army which Ugandan dictators had used as an instrument of murder and torture over the past twenty-three years.

However, the NRM's opponents would not address themselves to this fundamental issue. When, therefore, Okello-Lutwa started his reorganisation of the country by appointing the Military Council, the Prime Minister and the army commanders, the NRM realised that what had happened was a mere changing of the guard because the structure of state power and the security forces had remained intact. To the NRM this meant that the same old problems of *insecurity* would continue, with the army being used to dragoon the politics of Uganda in a particular direction. The NRM therefore rejected the administration of the Okello-Muwanga clique, which was trying to perpetuate the system that had caused the death of a million Ugandans since independence and brought about the stagnation of the whole country, and called on the people to do the same. To be rejected too were the civilian politicians who had agreed to serve in the new government. In the eyes of the NRM, they were opportunists who had always betrayed the people of Uganda but were now doing it in a more dramatic way than ever before: they were traitors and should be treated as such.

In short, when the NRM's conditions were not met by the junta of the two Okellos, it decided to continue the struggle in the bush against the regime. In his statement referred to above, Museveni exhorted the people not to throw away their victory but to await the orders of the NRA 'to complete our hard-won victory'. He called upon the people of Uganda to go ahead and defeat the remnants of the Obote-Amin regimes which had resurfaced in the form of the Okellos and Muwanga – if the latter were not willing to work out a good and secure peace. He concluded his message by saying that it was the duty of the combined patriotic forces of the NRA and others sympathetic to its cause 'to launch a final offensive to clean Uganda, once and for all, of criminals, thieves, corrupt elements and opportunists'.[3]

The reaction of the other fighting groups was perhaps not unpredictable. Some of them, such as the Uganda Freedom Movement (UFM), had long ceased to be operational although they had been among the fiercest fighters against Obote's regime at the beginning of the struggle. The Federal Democratic Movement (FEDEMU) was also in the doldrums by the time Obote was overthrown. Neither group was unhappy when Okello-Lutwa assumed power and invited the fighting groups to join his administration. Dr Andrew Lutakome Kayiira, leader of the UFM, rushed to Kampala from his home in the United States and joined the Military Council. He had no fighting force at the time, since many of his followers had either been captured and imprisoned or had simply given up the adventure and returned to civilian life. This did not deter him, particularly as Tito Okello had released all political prisoners, and hundreds of these men – some of them thugs and criminals – poured into the UFM's ranks. Others, again including the worst criminals, entered the FEDEMU and were issued with uniforms and guns. The FEDEMU fighters, especially those based in Mukono District, were the only Bantu fighting group which joined UNLA and fought against the NRA until the very end of the conflict and the fall of Kampala in January 1986.

The politicians, for their part, saw these issues differently from the NRA. The DP, which had never enjoyed power since April 1962, saw the Okello coup and the fall of their enemy Obote as a God-given opportunity for them to regain the political prominence in the country which had been denied them by Obote and the UPC in 1980. After the elections in December 1980, it should be recalled, they had decided to join Obote's system and participate in parliament even though their votes had clearly been stolen by the UPC, but they saw no inconsistency now in joining the Acholi group led by the Okellos, especially as the Okellos, like Idi Amin before them in 1971, had promised a speedy return to civilian rule and the holding of elections within twelve months. They of course knew that the future was uncertain but they believed they would/be in a position to influence the course of events from within the national government. However, the DP leaders who joined the Okello-Lutwa junta forgot one important thing: the Okellos were part and parcel of the UNLA that had butchered and were still butchering the Baganda in the Luwero Triangle. Paul Ssemogerere's DP believed that by joining them they could influence these barbarous soldiers and minimise, if not eliminate, the atrocities – like someone who tries to please a crocodile in the hope of being eaten last. The DP was far from being alone: the leaders of the other two parties – the UPM and the CP represented by Bidandi-Ssali and Joshua Mayanja-Nkangi respectively – also joined the junta, and they too were rewarded with ministerial appointments.

Perhaps the action of the DP and the other smaller parties in joining the Okello junta can be understood considering the circumstances in which the decision was taken. But what is baffling is that they continued to serve in the Okellos' government despite the continued bloody oppression by the regime after Obote's overthrow – that people who had been denouncing and fighting against the destruction of life and property should have continued to serve in a regime that was about as bad as Obote's regime, if not worse. The DP leaders argue that they joined Okello-Lutwa's administration because he had accepted the principle of a dialogue with all the political parties and the fighting movements that had been opposed to the UPC and the UNLA and because he had agreed to their participating in a national government. Persuasive as this seems, it is a naive way of looking at politics in Uganda. The system, which had already proved its unworthiness over and over, was unchanged.

The other people who were drawn into the Acholi regime were the West Nilers. Since the removal of Idi Amin in 1979, when power had slipped from their grasp, they, particularly the Nubians, had formed a number of fighting groups to oppose Obote, the major one being the Uganda National Rescue Front (UNRF) led by Brigadier Moses Ali and his deputy Major Amin Onzi; Onzi went to Kampala and was made a member of the Military Council. The former Ugandan army, as it had been under Amin (FUNA), re-emerged with the Okellos' capture of power, under leaders who included Wilson Toko and Major-General Isaac Lumago.

With the dissolution of the Acholi-Langi alliance, the Acholi embraced the West Nilers. The latter of course had suffered grievously in October/November 1980 at the hands of the Acholi-Langi militia, but when positions of influence were dangled before them, they quietly forgot those massacres. The result was a reconciliation of the Acholis and the West Nilers. In the bargaining for places that followed, Wilson Toko became Vice-Chairman of the Military Council which was headed by Okello-Lutwa. Other West Nilers soon emerged from political oblivion, some of whom were made ministers or appointed to other important offices of state; for instance, Peter Uchanda became head of the civil service. Toko proceeded to recruit several hundred soldiers from Acholi and southern Sudan to come and fight the NRA in the south; they were hurriedly brought to Kampala in Uganda Airlines Fokker Friendships, and later returned home on foot. It was also through Toko's contacts with the leaders of Egypt and Pakistan that those countries were drawn into the war against the NRA. One school of thought has it that it was the plan of the Nubians, headed by Toko, to oust the Acholis from power, since they believed themselves to be more experienced in fighting and to have better leaders. A victory for the Nubians over the Acholis would have led ultimately to the return of Amin to power in Uganda.

Politics, war and peace

The Acholis, faced by guerrillas who would not accept their unreconstructed government, offered to hold negotiations with the NRM in Nairobi. This proposal was finally agreed to. However, by the time the so-called 'peace talks' began, the NRA was no longer fighting an exclusively guerrilla action. The war was now partly a conventional one since the NRA was occupying fixed positions in many parts of the country. For instance, in August 1985 it overran Fort Portal in the west and set up an interim government there in October. This administration was led by a Kampala businessman, Haji Moses Kigongo, who since 1981 had been the second Vice-Chairman of the NRM and leader of the National Resistance Council (NRC), its political organ. The formation of the interim administration in Toro meant that, for the first time in Uganda's history, there were two governments in the country; indeed the seizure of the Katonga bridge on the Kampala-Masaka road by the NRA in September meant that the country was also divided physically into two separately governed territories.

With the benefit of handsight, it is difficult to see what was to be gained from the Nairobi talks. This is not to belittle the efforts of those who tried to make peace between the two warring factions, notably Nyerere of Tanzania and Daniel arap Moi of Kenya. Nyerere's efforts did not go far because he was offended by Okello's flirtation with Amin's former soldiers, notably Toko. Moi had the additional interest of enhancing his international stature by presiding over the talks, as well as of continuing to exercise political and economic influence in Uganda. No doubt too the Nilotic politicians in Kenya were not sorry to see the continued hegemony of Luo-speakers in Kampala. This would partly explain Kenya's ambivalent attitude to Museveni's government, which it accused of abrogating the peace agreement over which Moi presided.

It is difficult to tell to what extent the NRM was committed to these talks. It undoubtedly wanted peace to be achieved, but it was naturally suspicious of the actions of the two Okellos, and especially so of Wilson Toko. The External Mission of the NRM was probably keener to hold these talks than those who were fighting in the bush, and it is not inconceivable that it was the latter who forced the abrogation of the peace agreement when it was signed in December 1985. The NRM feared being led into a deal which would mean a sell-out, and the Okello regime's way of negotiating was such as to raise and then frustrate expectations through vacillation and bureaucratic delays. Thus what was intended to create trust succeeded in doing the opposite.

In the mean time, while the talks were going on in Nairobi, the junta had to run the country. It was not easy for the Acholi and other northern soldiers who had come to power with Obote's fall, and who had lived for so long by looting property and murdering unarmed civilians, to become civilised overnight. Considering the enormity of the problems facing the Okellos and their limited intellectual equipment, one can even feel some sympathy for them. They made genuine efforts. Part of the tragedy was that they surrounded themselves with men whose main interest was in acquiring power and wealth. As to the roles which the civilian ministers and administrators such as Paul Ssemogerere, Bidandi-Ssali and Mayanja-Nkangi (who headed the DP, UPM and CP respectively) played in affairs of state at that time, more research needs to be done. But it is certain that dubious characters were promoted to positions for which they were not qualified; young Acholi intellectuals saw themselves as the future rulers of the country and started empire-building.

Foreign influence on events in the country was also felt. During the second Obote period, the United States government had down-graded its representation in Kampala to the level of *chargé d'affaires*, but in November 1985 a new US ambassador presented his credentials to Tito Okello-Lutwa – on the same day as a new Zairean ambassador. At this time it was clear that the entry of the NRA into Kampala was imminent. As already mentioned, it had closed the route to the west at Katonga bridge on Kampala-Masaka road, and the barracks of Mubende, Mbarara and Masaka had been captured. This was going to be the first time in post-independence Africa that a guerrilla movement, without external support and supported only by unarmed peasants and workers, would take over power after defeating a heavily-armed government army. The NRA was about to prove that with the support of the people it was pos-sible to overthrow a constituted government. It was an unwelcome precedent, and the Americans and other Western powers were not slow to realise what this could mean for the whole of East and Central Africa, or to seek ways of preventing it. 'Friendly' African countries were enlisted in this attempt and it is believed that certain non-African countries – notably the Netherlands, Belgium and Israel – were used to act as conduits for the supply of arms to the Okello regime in a last-minute attempt to foil the success of the NRA's offensive.

Tito Okello-Lutwa's regime lasted only six months, but they were eventful months that will be remembered by Ugandans. One major achievement stressed by Okello's supporters (mostly those who enjoyed power and wielded influence during that brief period) was the conclusion of the peace agreement of December 1985 between the regime and the NRM, signed by Okello and Museveni them-selves. They speak highly of Okello's statesmanship in concluding such a pact and point to the fairness of the agreement, and were depressed by its failure – understandably, since its conclusion was the only positive achievement that could be claimed for the regime.

In different circumstances the agreement could perhaps have paved the way to some sort of a lasting peace, but the pact had many weaknesses, the major one being that its main concern was to per-petuate the regime in power. True, the people of Kampala cheered Tito Okello on his return from Nairobi, but this was more by way of welcoming the supposed end of fighting than the perpetuation of the Military Council under the Okellos and Wilson Toko. In truth, there was little confidence that the fighting would suddenly end just because the pact called for an immediate ceasefire. This could only have happened if the peace pact had marked the beginning of a true and meaningful reconciliation of Uganda's peoples.

The truth of the matter was that the peace pact was a trap for the

NRM/NRA, who were called in to join the round table in a room where the doors would be locked once they had entered. It was the old game again: bring in your opponents, use them for as long as you need them, and then eliminate them. The NRM/NRA, after waging a people's war for five years, was not to be fooled by men whose only interest was to subjugate the people of Uganda, especially those in the south, to a permanent position of subservience to those who still enjoyed the monopoly of terror. And, what was more, the violence which the peace agreement had been supposed to end actually increased.

However, the NRM/NRA's attitude towards the Nairobi peace agreement signed on 17 December 1985 needs to be understood. Right from the start of the peace talks, they were not considered a priority in the programme of the NRM/NRA whose main task, which they never shirked, was to fight the UNLA and remove it and the regime it supported. The NRM/NRA knew that the Okello regime needed the peace accord more than the freedom-fighters did. If no peace agreement were signed, the guerrilla war would continue and the only outcome could be the removal from power of the Okello junta. On the other hand, with the signature of the accord, the military junta would have a gentleman's exit that might still leave them with some sort of power. The freedom-fighters knew that the accord was not a major factor in the politics of Uganda, but there could be no harm to them in signing it. They knew that the Okello regime was in no position to implement the specific measures provided for in the accord.

First, the regime could not induce its own soldiers to return to barracks as was required by the accord; they had now taken to the streets and were bent on looting before they were demobilised. They also refused to lay down their arms. Indeed, the soldiers of FUNA and UNRF (Moses Ali's army) categorically refused to be demobilised. The government could also not stop the killing of innocent and unarmed civilians in the city and elsewhere – an imperative condition of the accord – because such abuses had become a habit. In short, the regime could not implement the peace agreement in the area of security, which happened to be its most important part. Therefore, the NRM/NRA – which could have effectively fulfilled all these provisions – could not simply take its fighters, who had been in the bush fighting the UNLA for five years, to Kampala and hand them over to the very soldiers of Bazilio Okello who had been massacring the people of Uganda; to do so would have been a betrayal of the principles on which the NRM/NRA was founded. The NRM/NRA knew that it had already won the war against the UNLA, and that it was no longer a matter of 'if' but of 'when' it would enter Kampala. Hence the differing perception of the Nairobi peace agreement by the two sides.

The end of the regime

It is said that at the height of the guerrilla war, a former Ugandan leader arrived in the country with an urgent message for Bazilio Okello. The two men met in Kampala. The essence of the message was that the former leader could recruit for the Okello junta some 500 British SAS soldiers to come as mercenaries and fight (he called it 'flush out') the NRA guerrillas from Katonga bridge. For his services he demanded US$2 million. Desperate though they were, the Okellos could not entertain the offer and it was turned down.

After the failure of the Nairobi peace agreement, the two Okellos were at the mercy of events; from then on, it was a day-to-day policy which left the initiative with the NRM/NRA. Above all, violence increased to an unprecedented level, which undermined whatever respect the regime still commanded. It is understandable that the supporters of the Military Council – largely the Acholis and especially the young Acholi élite – should feel downhearted by the collapse of the regime from which they benefited and which would have ensured their continuing dominance. When the peace agreement was signed in December 1985, some of the Acholi and Nubian soldiers saw this as a signal for their dismissal since, according to the agreement, the NRA was to be given 3,580 out of 8,480 soldiers of the army recruitment.[5] They therefore started to loot, rob and murder the people of Buganda, particularly in and around Kampala; it was, in fact, this which prompted the NRA to march on the capital earlier than it might otherwise have done.

Internal divisions in the Military Council were also becoming more pronounced, with Onzi of the UNRF and Lumago of the FUNA reluctant to see their soldiers disarmed after the peace talks. The army continued to disintegrate, and the population of course remained hostile. Indeed, as time passed, there developed a situation of acute uncertainty when it appeared as if no one was in control of the country. The peasants in the liberated areas and the mass of people in Kampala fully supported the NRM and wanted the NRA to force a military take-over rather than make compromises in Nairobi with Amin's and Obote's soldiers now masquarading under a new banner – that of the Okellos.

It is clear that there was a virtual absence of any planning by the Acholis under the two Okellos when they launched their coup against Obote and his Langi tribesmen; the implications of their programme had not been thought out and their view of long-term

Ugandan goals was vague at best. Indeed, by the time the Nairobi peace agreement was signed, they had become trapped in a dangerous, costly operation on a major military scale against the NRA, with no end in sight.

Naively Bazilio and Tito Okello, advised by Toko, believed that by adding more soldiers from Karamoja and Acholi they would increase their security against the NRA. The youngsters from Acholi and Karamoja who were lured south to fight were promised all sorts of things, including beautiful brown-skinned girls to take back as part of their booty after the war. The Karamoja were told that all the cattle they had lost had been taken by the Banyankole (Museveni's ethnic group) and were now ready for collection in Kampala. And so hundreds at a time were brought south in trucks and even in Fokker Friendship aircraft. These unfortunate new recruits from Sir Samuel Baker College, Gulu, and from the Karamoja villages only increased the vulnerability of the Okellos and provided more targets for the NRA guns. Unfamiliar with the terrain where the fighting was taking place, many died at Katonga bridge and, in the case of those who arrived as the NRA was wrapping up its victory, at Natete and in other parts of Kampala. The few survivors, like their cousins from southern Sudan whom Toko brought south to fight, were to return to their homelands on foot. To underline their victory, the NRA allowed the veteran UNLA soldiers to escape, following the railway line, along the east-north route, which they knew so well. In effect, the UNLA and its allies (FUNA and some UNRF) was now running to the north of the country and even beyond into southern Sudan and north-eastern Zaire to take refuge among their relatives.

So it was that on 26 January 1986, about forty days after the signing of the Nairobi peace agreement, the Acholi bubble burst and the NRM/NRA entered Kampala. The Okellos military might, which all along had appeared like paper tigers to the NRA *kadogos*, collapsed. It had been a long struggle, but finally the NRM/NRA's mission had been successfully accomplished. Its administration now began.

NOTES

1. This is competently discussed in A. Omara-Otunnu, *Politics and the Military in Uganda, 1890–1985*, London: Macmillan Press, 1987, chapter 13.
2. See Yoweri Museveni, *Selected Articles on the Uganda Resistance War*, Kampala: NRM, 1985, pp. 76–83.
3. *Ibid.*, p. 83.
4. A. Omara-Otunnu, *op. cit.*, p. 168.

5. Under the terms of the peace agreement signed in Nairobi on 17 December 1985, the army was to consist of the following numbers of soldiers:

UNLA	3,700
NRA	3,580
FEDEMU	
UFM	
UNRF	} 1,200
FUNA	
Total	*8,480*

The Military Council was to consist of:

Head of State/Chairman, Military Council	1
UNLA	7
NRA	7
UFM	1
FEDEMU	2
FUNA	1
UNRF	1
Total	*20*

For the terms of the Nairobi peace agreement, see *Mission to Freedom*, *Uganda Resistance News, 1981–1985*, Kampala: NRM publication, 1991, pp. 319 ff.

13

THE ERA OF THE NATIONAL
RESISTANCE MOVEMENT

I finished writing the preceding chapters in late 1988. Three years
have gone by since its completion, and it is now five years since the
NRM seized state power in Kampala. Much has occurred during this
time. Some aspects of the history of this period will be the focus of
attention in this final chapter.

We need, in particular, to look closely at the National Resistance
Movement's record since it came to power in January 1986. There is
the continuing insurgency in the north and north-east of Uganda, on
which international bodies such as Amnesty International and the
Minority Rights Group have commented; there is the problem, connected with this rebellion, of the army's discipline in combat zones
as well as in its interaction with the civilian population elsewhere in
the country; and there is also the need to review what the NRM has
achieved. It will be recalled that the NRM came to power with a Ten-
Point Programme which has formed the basis of its administration.
The programme is of course no more than a guide to the philosophy
of the NRM leadership – it says nothing about how the movement's
aims are carried out in practice.

The Ten-Point Programme was worked out – over a period of
3 and a half years – by the National Resistance Council (NRC) of
the NRM, together with the High Command and senior officers of
the NRA, under the chairmanship of Yoweri Kaguta Museveni. It
contains, in its own words, 'proposals for a political programme
that could form a basis for a nationwide coalition of political and
social forces that could usher in a new and better future for the long-
suffering people of Uganda'. As we have shown in the preceding
chapters, Uganda continues to experience, near the end of its third
decade of independence, a chronic state of backwardness. It has not
been able to redress the many economic distortions inherited at
independence, distortions that are characteristic of many other
former colonies in Africa. Sadly it is much worse off than at independence, and therefore continues to be in trouble and to need help
in rising from the ruins it has been reduced to. Consequently, a
political programme was needed as the basis for a national coalition of democratic, political and social forces that could at last get
things moving after years of stagnation, destruction and utter chaos.
The ten points which the NRM leadership identified for national

Yoweri Museveni being sworn in as President, January 1986.

reconstruction are: (1) democracy, (2) security of all persons in Uganda and their property, (3) consolidation of national unity and elimination of all forms of sectarianism, (4) defence and consolidation of national independence, (5) laying the foundation for an independent, integrated, self-sustaining national economy, (6) restoration and improvement of social services and the rehabilitation of the war-ravaged areas, (7) elimination of corruption and abuse of power in public life, (8) redressing of errors that have resulted in the dislocation of sections of the population, (9) cooperation with other African countries to defend human and democratic rights throughout Africa, and (10) pursuing the strategy of a mixed economy. The application of these points will be reviewed in turn.

Democracy

The much-used term 'democracy' – together with its companions justice, the rule of law and human rights – is a remarkably difficult one to define or grasp. Many of the world's most notorious dictators and tyrants have claimed not only to be democrats themselves but to have untiringly worked for – and achieved – democracy. It is not necessary here to revert to the undemocratic nature of the regimes which it was the role of the NRM to remove from power. The idea of democracy was at the core of why the freedom-fighters went to the bush in February 1981. The aim of the war was not to capture power *per se*, but to remove dictatorial regimes so that fundamental changes – and not a mere change of guard – could be instituted for the better management of Ugandan society. As Yoweri Museveni himself put it, 'The National Resistance Movement waged a protracted people's war against tyranny on a platform of restoring personal freedoms and amelioration of the socio-economic conditions of our people: that is the cornerstone of our programme.' The cornerstone of the NRM's policy is therefore the requirement that the people themselves should be the instruments of changes affecting them and in charge of their own destinies; that they should elect their leaders and participate both in the decision-making and the implementation processes. This, of course, does not mean that in practice people have lived up to the NRM's expectations; but there is no denying that there is a genuine sense of political participation in the political process, promising yet better things to come. Perhaps, for the first time in many years, the people feel committed to what their government is doing.

We should examine some of the elements of Uganda's restored democracy – starting with the Resistance Council (RC) system. This is a system of committees established from the grassroots up to the national level. Some detractors branded them as 'Communist imports', but the system has not only taken root but has won the admiration of a large section of the population, especially in the rural areas where the poorest and most exploited live. Right from the beginning of the liberation war in Luwero Triangle – and as early as 1981 – the NRM established Resistance Councils and Resistance Committees in the areas they liberated. These became, and have continued to be, the bedrock of the NRM's concept of democracy. People meet as Resistance Councils at village levels to discuss matters that affect them, and elect from among themselves their own Resistance Committees of nine officials: Chairman, Vice-Chairman, General Secretary and Secretaries for Youth, Women, Information, Education and Mass Mobilisation, Security and Finance. Every Ugandan is a member of at least one 'legislative body', because every person, even including non-citizens, is expected to attend the Resistance Council of the village or ward in which he or she lives. And Resistance Councils and Resistance Committees are formed from village levels up to parish, sub-county, county and district levels. At the national level, there is the National Resistance Council (NRC) acting as parliament, which consists of historical members of the NRC (constituted in the bush during the

Resistance War), women representatives, some nominated members and ordinary members representing counties and/or municipalities. Any elected RC official who does not perform satisfactorily can be removed from office even before his/her term of office has expired. Many people would like to see this element extended to the National Resistance Council (the parliament) itself. The RC system has been an interesting experiment in the political organisation and mobilisation of the people for the country's development; and it will not be surprising if the system is retained in some form in the new constitution that is being prepared at the time of writing. Perhaps people would like to see the term 'Resistance' changed since the political forces or regimes that were being resisted are no longer there.

The most important question at issue in appraising the merits and demerits of the RC system in establishing democratic channels through which a democratic government can emerge, is what constitutes a 'democratic state'. *The Economist* (London) has referred to a democracy as 'a state whose central government was chosen by a free and honest electoral process, open to candidates from rival political organisations, with reasonable opportunities to publicise their programmes. A better test, which by no means all our democracies would pass, is whether the people can vote out a government they are fed up with.' By this criterion the RC system, as practised in Uganda today, does not fully qualify as democratic. There is a ban on the open functioning of the political parties, and the government's justification for this is that we are establishing firm political instruments – including the writing of a new national constitution – and that until this process is completed we do not need division along political lines but unity. The elections held in February 1989 for the expansion of the NRC were carried out on a non-party basis; all candidates, in effect, were elected on the NRM ticket. But the brighter side to this political picture is that, within the NRM's concept of broad-based government and the RC system, anyone of whatever religious, social or political views is free to stand as a candidate and to be voted on by the people. Since the NRM is not a political party, no one is barred from (or admitted to) the NRM; every Ugandan is deemed to belong to it. Because the system is a non-party one, Uganda is not a state where only one *de jure* political party is allowed to operate. No Ugandan can be expelled from the NRM and thus from political activities, because the NRM does not have that power. This means, therefore, that the present political system existing in Uganda is an open one where *anyone* acceptable to the local voters can operate freely. We emphasise that this is not going to be the permanent political system of the country. It is an experiment first enunciated in mid-1981 when the NRM leaders were still in the bush, and put into practice within a free state since 1986, and it remains to be seen whether the people of Uganda will choose it as the cornerstone of their new political system. That is why, in fact, the new constitution that is being framed will be decisive for future political development. It is not without interest that other African states, including Nigeria, have sent delegations to observe how the system is working.

An important element in the restoration of democracy has been the NRM administration's appointment of a Commission of Inquiry into violations of human rights in Uganda from independence in 1962 till 1986 when the NRM came to power. Its main purpose is to redress the injustices that were commonplace when no rule of law existed in Uganda. The Commission, presided over by a judge of the Uganda Supreme Court, is investigating the activities of agents of past regimes who brought about horrific sufferings in the country. As the result of testimony already presented to the Commission, there have been arrests and even convictions of some of those responsible for gross violations of human rights, including murder, rape and kidnap. Those who perpetrated crimes under past regimes – or who collaborated with them – have naturally been unhappy with the setting up of this commission, and questioned its usefulness. It is naturally unpleasant to parade witnesses whose friends or relatives were butchered or subjected to unbelievable sufferings, and to recall acts of violence which the present generation finds too much to stomach. However, the essential fact is that nothing should be spared – no expense and no discomfort – to secure justice and redress injustice. Criminals of this kind, once identified, must be brought to book, not only to answer for their own misdeeds but as a warning to any who might go down the same path in the future. Indeed, it is disappointing to many that the inquiry is restricted to the period up to January 1986, when the NRM came to power, for many crimes and human rights violations have been committed since then. But a healthy precedent has been set with the appointment of the Commission.

Another important aspect of democracy is freedom of expression and of the press – an area where the NRM has clearly demonstrated its commitment and how different the present regime is from its predecessors. For long Uganda was a closed society, where people had to look over their shoulders whenever they moved or uttered a word; for many of us, particularly when we frequent public places such as bars and theatres, it has taken time to absorb the fact that Uganda is once again a free country. Academics and intellectuals, particularly at Makerere University, may not yet think that the freedom of speech and association that they enjoy now is sufficient;

but many would concede that not only is there formal freedom of inquiry but also the opportunity to obtain major concessions from the government by reasoned argument. Even students have had their share of the dialogue between the scholars at Uganda's 'ivory tower' and their sponsors in the government. Much remains to be won and secured, but considerable headway has already been made. Writers and scholars no longer lie low, afraid of reprisals from the adminis-tration. The paradox, as President Museveni has complained more than once, is that the people of Uganda do not know how to use the freedom they now have. There is freedom to travel, and today Ugandans are more likely to be prevented from travelling by the countries to which they wish to go than by their own country, as in the past.

But freedom of expression is most clearly manifested in the press, which, compared with many other countries in Africa, has been a clear testimony to the NRM's commitment to the tenets of democ-racy. Freedom of the press is thriving in Uganda, although this does not say much for the actual quality of the papers that are being published. Editors and reporters have at times run into trouble with the authorities, but these occasions have been rare and where injus-tice was done matters were rectified. For instance, a BBC Swahili reporter was arrested and charged in court because he asked embar-rassing questions of a visiting president. This, as it turned out, became an embarrassment for the government, and in the end the journalist was released. By arresting and charging the journalist in an attempt to appease a 'friendly' ruler the NRM was not being true to itself.

Another clear indication of the kind of freedom Ugandans now enjoy was the manner in which Paulo Muwanga, Vice-President of Uganda in Obote's second regime, was buried in April 1991. It was Muwanga who, as Minister of Defence, had presided over mass killing in the Luwero Triangle in Buganda, yet a memorial service was held at a cathedral in the capital, and the body, dressed in a grey striped suit, was carried to Uganda House (UPC headquarters) by present cabinet ministers who had served with him when he was Vice-President of the UPC, all dressed in UPC colours. He was given what almost amounted to a state funeral, although only UPC supporters took part – such was the extent to which freedom had been restored by the NRM administration. In the late 1960s the UPC government under Obote not only prevented the remains of the late Kabaka, Sir Edward Mutesa, from being returned after he had died in Britain in November 1969, but did not even allow his subjects gathered at Kasubi to mourn him. Such distinctions are the measure of a just and civilised society. This said, the NRM government's record as regards human rights, freedom of expression and the rule of law is not perfect, and the people must remain vigilant so that the country does not slip back to the dark days of the past.

Preparation of the new national constitution

One of the major tasks which the NRM set itself was the making of a new national constitution. While still in the bush, as early as 1982 if not earlier, the NRM leaders considered this question. There were some who wanted to capture power with the constitution already written, but the majority view was that it should be the Ugandan people themselves who should create the new documents and that this could only be done after the dictatorial government of Obote and the whole repugnant political system that went with it had been overthrown. Thus, early in 1986, after capturing power in Kampala, the NRM government reiterated its decision to let the people of Uganda draw up their new national constitution, and a Ministry of Constitutional Affairs was set up to supervise it.

The Bill setting up the Uganda Constitutional Commission was presented to the NRC late in 1988, freely debated and passed into law; in February 1989 the Commission itself was set up, chaired by Justice Benjamin O. Odoki, a judge of Uganda's Supreme Court, and with twenty-one members assisted by a few legal officers and research assistants. Its initial life-span was two years, but the Minister for Constitutional Affairs was empowered by the statute to extend its life if it had not completed its work within that period; this was done in April 1991, when the Commission's mandate was extended by a further year. The Constitutional Commission's role is merely advisory; it will submit the completed draft constitution, together with a report, to the government, which will have the task of convening the Constituent Assembly to debate and promulgate the new national constitution. How the new constitution will be promulgated into law – whether by public acclamations at district council level or through a national referendum – is among the issues that will be resolved by the Assembly itself. Even the way in which the Assembly will be elected and convened has not been agreed upon at the time of writing; this is among the issues for the Constitutional Commission to settle and advise on.

The Constitutional Commission began its work in April 1989. After holding a number of internal seminars, it organised district seminars throughout the country; also seminars for specialised bodies – trade unions, lawyers, churches, youth groups, teacher training colleges and subsequently women's groups, political parties and political leaders. The district seminars were attended by almost all district council executives as well as those at sub-county levels, who were expected to return to their people and instruct them on the constitutional points the Commission had identified as needing consideration in the new constitution. The Commission produced a well-researched document entitled *Guidelines on Constitutional Issues*, containing twenty-nine constitutional issues and some 253 guiding questions which it asked people to study and make the basis of their proposals on the new constitution. However, the executives who attended the district seminars fell down on their task, and the Commissioners had to carry out another tour of all the sub-counties to put the constitutional issues across to the people. This was completed in April 1991 and the Commission then started to collect the people's views by means of memoranda drawn up at village and parish levels and through oral presentations at open meetings held at sub-county headquarters.

The constitution-making process has awakened great public interest in the political development of the country. On the other hand, the constitution has become a catch-all. The government sees it as the solution for all the problems the people have voiced. And it has been the reason both for the banning of political activity by the parties and the extension of the NRM administration's life to an anticipated nine years instead of the four announced when it came to power in 1986. Both issues have been resented, particularly among politicians, who claim that the ban is unfair while the NRM remains free to mobilise the people; it is the reason given by the UPC leaders for not participating in the constitution-making exercise; they say they will only do so when the ban has been lifted. This position is shared, if not in full, by the radical wing of the Democratic Party, the so-called 'Mobilisers' Group'. The NRM administration's answer is that the activities of the political parties need to be curbed in order to cool down emotions so that the nation can reflect more soberly. It also says it must stay in power until the new national constitution is in place; otherwise, how will the new government be voted in? Both points of view are supported by strong arguments.

It seems possible that exaggerated expectations have been aroused: the writing of a new national constitution is seen by many as a panacea, a patent medicine for all that has ailed our nation. Linked to this are fears – not entirely rational, but perhaps inevitable – that we may fail to grasp the great opportunities presented with the writing of a new constitution, and that things are being rushed. People are getting heated up over the form of government that may emerge – whether it will be federal or unitary; the place of traditional rulers (some people in Buganda even question the Commission's authority to discuss the Kabakaship and claim to be unhappy that its Chairman does not come from a Bantu-speaking area); national language; the role of political parties (whether Uganda should be a one-party or multi-party state); and the political role of the army and security forces. There are even diehards who say that the whole constitution-making exercise is a fake because the NRM already has a written constitution.

The basic issue appears to be the importance of blending – or rather seeking to reconcile – two conflicting pressures that appear to have bedevilled our nation since independence: the undoubted need for strong unitary government at the centre, and the strong desire of some nationalities in Uganda to cling to national and regional identity. The success of the new constitution will depend on its ability to resolve this issue.

In 1991 there was a reshuffle of the cabinet, in which the number of ministries was reduced from twenty-eight to twenty, and the Ministry of Constitutional Affairs ceased to be a ministry on its own; it was placed instead under the Minister of Justice and the Attorney-General. This move has been seen as downgrading the Ministry of Constitutional Affairs, with a possible adverse effect on the speedy working of the Constitutional Commission. Many others wonder whether the minister in charge of making the new constitution, Sam K. Njuba, is equal to such an important exercise.

Consolidation of national unity

Here we shall consider four main issues: the security of persons and property; the establishment of a government of national unity; the insurgency that broke out in the north and north-east of Uganda; and the attempt to fight against religious and 'tribal' sectarianism.

Security of persons and property is one of the ten points of the NRM's programme and it is an important area where it is not disputed that the NRM administration has achieved success. It is true that security is mostly enjoyed in the south, east and west of the country, but for those who experienced the rule of the gun that used to prevail in Kampala and the south of the country, the peace that prevails there now represents a remarkable achievement. For the first time in many years, people can go about their business by day without being harassed by the soldiers and can go to bed at night without the fear that their premises will be raided while they sleep; and there are no longer roadblocks which have been turned into 'tax-collecting posts' where innocent civilians can be robbed by armed soldiers at will, and with state sanction. Of course armed robbery still occurs – it would be too much to expect total peace in a country that has seen so much crime and murder inflicted daily on the innocent – but there has been an attempt to make the country a safe place to live in. Here the NRM's greatest contribution has been the building up of a disciplined army, the National Resistance Army (NRA), to work and serve in a corrupt society. The standard of integrity and discipline with which the NRA started off when it entered Kampala in January 1986 has deteriorated; but generally it has maintained cooperation with the civil population. An important element in the discipline shown by the NRA soldiers, compared with those of past regimes, has been their written Code of Conduct. This lays down how NRA soldiers will interact with the public, and establishes a High Command Tribunal and disciplinary committees to try officers and other ranks who commit serious crimes, especially against civilians. This form of justice has aroused some criticism in Uganda and among international human rights organisations for the summary trials and executions of sentences that have been carried out; the NRM has argued that these measures are necessary in order to curb violations of human rights by the soldiers and to protect civilians.

The major test that has faced, and to some extent still faces, the NRM administration and the NRA, is the insurgency that broke out first in the north and later in the north-east of the country. It has not been easy to maintain the high level of discipline expected of the soldiers when they have had to fight rebels who can barely be distinguished from armed robbers. It has often been difficult to understand the reasons for this war, which has become increasingly senseless. Yet those who have taken up arms against the government certainly see themselves as engaged in a war of liberation. Thus the NRM finds itself having to condemn a rebellion against 'a legally constituted government' when it did exactly the same over a period of five years before it captured power in 1986. To many people what distinguishes the rebellion in the north and north-east from the NRM's liberation war is the way in which the rebels have turned on the civilian population instead of the government which it purports to fight. This has made it impossible for the rebels to claim that theirs is a just cause. Atrocities have also been committed by the NRA; international organisations such as Amnesty International have protested against some of the actions of the government soldiers, and at home too, bodies such as the Uganda Law Society, the Uganda Human Rights Activists and the Churches have pointed out the government's failure to observe human rights and the rule of law while trying to suppress the rebellion in the north and northeast. An interesting episode was that of eighteen men and women, including a Minister of State for Foreign Affairs and at least two Members of Parliament, who were arrested in the north and charged with the treasonable act of abetting the rebellion. The country's Attorney-General and Minister of Justice set a precedent by apologising for any mistreatment that might have been inflicted on the eighteen. *Munno*, an independent daily paper in Kampala, pointed out that Dr George Kanyeihamba's open way of answering the complaints of the Uganda Law Society on this issue would show that Uganda has changed from what it was only a few years ago. A recommendation was adopted by the Africa Leadership Forum held in Kampala in May 1991 that 'A fundamental link exists between national security, stability and sustainable development, and these conditions can only be brought about by political pluralism encompassing full respect for human rights, official accountability and popular participation.'

The consolidation of national unity and elimination of sectarianism are stated objectives of the NRM government, although Uganda's ethnic and religious differences, compounded by the political divisions which are their consequence, makes them hard to achieve. As an example of the quest for reconciliation, some former leaders of the Uganda Patriotic Movement (UPM), which Museveni led in 1980, who might have been expected to stay in high office, are now in the political wilderness, while former members of the Uganda People Congress, Obote's henchmen and members of the Okello government now hold important government positions including seats in the cabinet. Museveni also decided, in 1986, to come to an understanding with the Uganda National Rescue Front (UNRF), almost all of whom were from West Nile. As a result, the UNRF fighters joined the NRA and Moses Ali, their leader, was made Minister of Tourism and Wildlife. At first this appointment caused dismay, especially in Buganda, because of his former close association with Idi Amin whom he had served as a minister.

The essence of a broad-based national government is that ministers and other public servants are drawn from all the political parties and even non-political organisations. In Uganda at the time of writing the cabinet consists of UPC, DP, UPM and CP politicians, men and women who previously did not see eye to eye politically, but can now sit together and arrive at a national consensus on the major issues affecting the country's future. Apart from a few professional politicians who feel let down by some of their own party members whom they see as being in league with their former political enemies, and who also feel left out, there has been general acceptance of a broad-based administration as perhaps the only formula in the present circumstances that can rescue the country from the quagmire into which it was thrown by the past regimes. It is consonant with the spirit of the RC system that discourages – indeed bans – sectarian politics based on party, religion or nationality.

The war being waged against the NRM government in the north and north-east is the major obstacle to national unity. However, an amnesty law has been passed by the NRC, extending to all combatants or those assisting them, so that they can have an opportunity to lay down their arms and become resettled. The amnesty also extends to those who have served in former armies and fighting groups, the police, the prisons service and state security agencies whose past activities might make them liable to criminal prosecution. Many times negotiations have taken place between rebel leaders and the government, and at the time when a peace agreement was signed between President Museveni and the Uganda People's Democratic Army rebels at Gulu in 1988, it seemed that these efforts were bearing fruit; however the optimism was premature and the war continued. But, as we write, reports indicate that many rebels are surrendering to the NRA, since civilians have joined in the effort to fight and uproot the rebels.

The economy

There is little doubt that in the end the NRM's success or failure will be judged by its management of the economy, for while the people have embraced democracy and political freedom, what they yearn for most is an improved standard of living, which alone can enable them to enjoy the social benefits that accrue from a just society. That the NRM administration was bequeathed a corrupt society, empty coffers and an external debt running into billions of dollars is all too well known, and the story does not need repeating here; our concern should rather be to consider the NRM's economic strategy for rehabilitating the shattered economy and its results so far.

The strategy has concentrated on laying down structures that will improve on those inherited at independence. Whereas its predecessors did not seriously try to change the colonial economic structures, the NRM administration has chosen, as an enterprise inspired by patriotism, to untie the economic fetters that have always benefited our former masters rather than ourselves. It wishes Uganda nonetheless to remain in contact with the rest of the world.

To achieve an independent, integrated and self-sustaining national economy, each 'component' has to be supportive of the others. First, the economy has to be liberalised, and the NRM administration has not only accepted this but pursued it with vigour under the doctrine of 'a mixed economy'. This, together with 'the advance of science and technology' which Museveni has often emphasised, will avert the decline which can threaten political freedom. But the philosophy of liberalisation is not enough in itself for the economic development of a country such as Uganda without a clear understanding of how developing countries have remained underdeveloped. Dr Will Kaberuka, a presidential economic adviser, has argued 'that neither the complete breakaway from the capitalist world economy nor industrialisation is enough to provide sufficient means for breaking through the bondage of underdevelopment if there are no changes within the underdeveloped nations.' What is needed is the determination to break away from the colonial structures and institutions on which both the colonial and post-colonial economy of Uganda was based, characterised as it was by emphasis on the production of such crops as cotton and coffee that were required in the metropolitan states. There must be diversification too into non-traditional crops such as beans, groundnuts, sim-sim and soya beans, that can be sold abroad as easily as cotton or coffee. There must also be a move towards a breaking-away from the mere export of raw materials to production of finished products for export 'with added value'. For instance, instead of exporting 1 kilo of lint cotton, which will fetch US$1.50 on the world market, it makes more sense to turn that lint cotton into yarn which will sell at US$7 a kilo. It would be better still if that kilo of lint cotton were to be woven into a shirt that might fetch, say, US$13 on the world market. This is in line with the recommendations made at the ACP-EEC meetings at Kampala in February 1991, when East African governments were called on to help their industries 'give value-added to their commodities so as to earn foreign exchange through exports', something which has been effective in promoting exports elsewhere in the world. President Museveni was quoted in *Newsweek* of 29 April 1991 as saying: 'We are working very hard to promote alternative exports, not only raw materials but finished goods, textiles, leather goods, food products, fish products, cooking oil and other items'. Government companies, he said, would remain divided into four categories: those maintained 100% as government owned; those where the government maintains the majority shareholding and private business has a minority; those where this second situation is reversed; and finally, those sold outright to private industry. On the link between democracy and economic development, Museveni said at the OAU summit at Abuja, Nigeria, in June 1991: 'I strongly subscribe to the view that the establishment of democracy is a necessary condition for stable economic development.'

The liberalisation policy pursued by the NRM administration has led it to reconsider its former policy towards the world's financial institutions such as the IMF and the World Bank. To the chagrin of some of its greatest supporters, it has almost fully embraced the programmes as dictated by the two world financial bodies. Indeed it has had little room for manoeuvre due to an external debt that costs the country over half of its foreign earnings to service. Some important Western countries have also insisted that their economic assistance depends on Uganda's acceptance of IMF and World Bank conditions. As those who opposed this policy foresaw, this has brought problems to the government. For example, the Bank has required the government to carry out massive devaluations; lift subsidies from some commodities, leading to price rises; and reduce personnel in the civil service and parastatal bodies, causing great resentment among those affected.

The effect of the economic policies pursued by the NRM is still to be felt. In a country that has seen runaway inflation, the performance of the government has not been bad considering that inflation is falling, prices are stabilising, and money has regained some of the value it had lost. With an improving road network, transportation hazards are being overcome while the exchange of goods and services within the country is increasing. On top of this, the country has greatly benefited from its natural ability to produce its own food, for strictly Uganda has never imported food despite our many political and economic crises. With the return of peace to regions such as the former Luwero Triangle (Luwero, Mpigi, Kiboga and Mubende districts), people have returned to their old homes and farms and have even produced food surpluses. The government's liberalisation policy has enabled some foreign investment to trickle back into the country, often in partnership with local entrepreneurs, with the result that local manufacturing industries have sprung up and former ones have been rehabilitated. In the latter category are the two sugar works at Lugazi near Kampala and Kakira near Jinja, whose output will soon make the country self-sufficient in sugar with some surplus for export. Production of cotton, coffee, tobacco, tea – the so-called traditional cash crops – and of sim-sim, beans and garden produce – the non-traditional ones – is on the increase, although it is still much less than before the regime of Idi Amin. On the whole there is a great improvement and an air of optimism and determination to put to good use the peace that Uganda has today after so many years of turmoil.

But there are still many factors inhibiting a rapid economic revival, and these are due to the way our society developed through the 1970s and 1980s. Many Ugandans have forgotten the value of work as a means of earning their living, and instead have resorted to corruption and even armed robbery. Manna is expected to drop from heaven in the form of grants from the World Bank or from one of the rich Western powers. There is also little investment, a legacy from the bad old days when it was unsafe to invest money in any-thing. It is worrying to see young and able-bodied people loitering around in urban areas with small merchandise hanging from their arms; some join professional criminals in terrorising those who want to earn their living legally and decently. These are the people whose energies are needed to tap the rich natural resources in which the country abounds.

The other constraint is the emptiness of the government's coffers due to the lack of a sound taxation policy. Uganda's tax-base is narrow, and it has turned out that the government is now over-taxing the more easily taxable section of society – civil servants, public employees and peasants. While in other countries tax revenue amounts to 20%–30% of their GDP, in Uganda it is as low as 6%. Taxing public servants as much as 40% or more of their earnings has caused resentment while bringing in little revenue. As for the peasants, a recent increase in the graduated tax led to riots, with elected revenue collection officials and district administrators being harassed and assaulted. The government has announced the setting up of a Revenue Authority to be run by experts, but it remains to be seen whether it will produce the required results.

As for foreign assistance, the NRM government's liberal policies and its record on human rights have earned it such a good name abroad that aid has flowed in faster than it ever anticipated. Not only the IMF and the World Bank but Britain, France, Germany, the United States, Italy, the Scandinavian countries and others have come to Uganda's rescue with generous offers, partly in outright grants. This has been especially useful with the country's foreign earnings from its traditional cash crop, coffee, recently falling by about two-thirds. However, it is reasonable to ask what use all this money has been put to. Will it go down the drain, as so much did during the two Obote regimes? Will it return to where it came from – abroad, in the bank accounts of a few big shots?* However, the government has some tangible results to show. These include roads, particularly those linking the capital, Kampala, and the major regional towns; the construction of new industries and rehabilita-tion of old ones; and the rehabilitation of a number of important institutions: Makerere University, Mulago Hospital and tourist

---

*To those Ugandans do not know how the increasing flow of foreign aid is being used by their leaders – particularly the senior Planning and Economic Development and Finance Ministries who always accompany their respective ministers when these aid agreements are being signed at home and abroad – we would recommend John Madeley's book *When Aid is No Help*, published by Intermediate Technology Publi-cations in London.

hotels. In a move intended to attract foreign exchange and preserve what little is in the country, the government instituted the Forex Bureaux, which are free to buy and sell foreign currency at market rates. While this new policy has enabled Ugandans working abroad to repatriate their money (they can earn more from the Forex Bureaux than from the Central Bank), the system has fallen short of the intentions behind it since those who appear to benefit most from it are foreigners. The people who attract most criticism are the Asians, most of whom have been allowed to return and reclaim the property confiscated from them by Amin; they are alleged to be more interested in buying US dollars and British pounds than in selling such currency to the local people, and to be once again 'milking the Ugandan cow rather than feeding it'.

Moreover, the return of the Asians to Uganda is placing the NRM administration in a dilemma. Western countries – particularly Britain, which could block all Uganda's financial dealings with foreign states and international financial organisations, and at one time threatened to do so – have insisted that the NRM government demonstrate its adherence to human rights and the rule of law by, as a matter of course, not only allowing the Asians to return but giving them back the property snatched from them during the Amin regime. Many of the NRM leaders genuinely believe that the Amin regime did wrong in treating the Asians, especially those with Ugandan citizenship, as it did and that the wrong done to them should be redressed. This view is shared by some Ugandans but not by all, especially those who were and still are the beneficiaries of the confiscations, having obtained Asian property without paying a single shilling for it. The government's stand that genuine Asian returnees should be allowed to reoccupy their properties has been greeted with anger and resentment bordering on rebellion. The outcome of this delicate matter will affect the economic and social welfare of many Ugandans and is thus awaited anxiously.

The future of the NRM could well depend on its handling of the economy. Some people have undoubtedly benefited from its policies, but the wealth and benefits created have not been distributed fairly throughout society. Many people face economic hardship, and its causes cannot be satisfactorily explained to them. It is often seriously argued that Ugandans, like most other Africans, have very limited expectations, but the NRM ushered in an era of hope and vision in which all, rich and poor, were to share. The poor paid dearly in the armed struggle against Obote, and expect to see some improvement in their lives. People especially cannot understand why their pockets remain empty when stories are frequently heard of open and unabated corruption.

Rehabilitation and corruption

Rehabilitation is closely connected with the revival of the economy which we have been discussing; it is also connected with the disease of corruption. Rehabilitation can only succeed if the economy improves, and the economy cannot perform well if there is rampant corruption, such as exists in present-day Uganda. The efforts made by the NRM to improve the well-being of the people, particularly by rehabilitating the economic and social infrastructure, will suffer reverses if the government does not seriously address itself to this disease.

Roads, schools, hospitals and industries have been restored in many parts of the country. One can now travel on a tarmac road all the way from Malaba, on the border with Kenya in the east, to Kabale and even Katuna, on the border with Rwanda in the west – a distance of more than 500 miles. Feeder roads have proved a problem, because although graded and repaired they are not maintained for lack of the necessary machinery – an example, perhaps, of where money has disappeared into thin air instead of being used for its intended purpose. However, most of the rehabilitation has been in the regions that were ravaged in the war of liberation, most notably the Luwero Triangle, containing the districts of Luwero, Mpigi, Kiboga and Mubende. As soon as the NRM came to power, large sums of money were collected – some in donations from foreign governments and organisations – specifically to rehabilitate the war-ravaged Triangle. But much of that money is alleged to have disappeared or failed to reach the people for whom it was meant. Up to this day, the people of these districts have continued to blame the NRM government for abandoning them, when it was their support which enabled the NRM to win the war – a fact which even President Museveni has at times admitted. The peasants have even claimed that 'other Ugandans' – meaning non-Baganda – used the Baganda of the Luwero Triangle as a ladder on the ascent to power, forgetting them once that objective had been achieved. Of course, it is not true that the NRM has ignored the peasants and workers who made its victory possible; it is simply the paucity of financial resources at its disposal that has prevented the government from keeping its promises. The major complaint of these people is the failure of the NRM government to rehabilitate family houses that were wrecked by the UNLA soldiers. Some have been re-roofed, but many people who were well housed before the war of liberation now live in grass-thatched or mud-walled huts. The government has committed itself to build 2,000 houses annually in the Luwero Triangle alone.

Another constraint in the process of rehabilitation, and indeed in reviving the whole economy, has been the war in the north and north-east. Huge sums of money, which would otherwise have gone into rehabilitation, are daily being spent on fighting the insurgents in the war zones. But the major drawback, as is now generally admitted, has been the corruption that has afflicted our society. This presents the NRM administration with a serious test because not only the economy but the very moral fibre of society is affected. It makes a mockery of the government's persistent calls for the people to tighten their belts and sweat for the reconstruction of the country. Calling on the people to pay taxes for the construction of roads makes little impact when not only is there little or nothing to show for it, but when they see their society quickly being divided into 'haves' and 'have-nots', those whose children are being well educated, in the country and abroad, and those who have to keep their children at home, even if they are academically bright, because they cannot afford school fees. It hurts, in a society that was ravaged by war, to see a group of people whose rich life-style is completely out of proportion to what is surrounding them, especially when it is well known that the wealth of some well-to-do Ugandans was acquired through dubious means, especially corruption.

In Uganda today, corruption is a way of life. Those in the forefront are ministers, Permanent Secretaries and heads of big parastatal bodies – leaders who should set an example of incorruptibility. In the late 1980s, a minister said in parliament that all ministers were corrupt, and although some of his colleagues rose on points of order to refute the allegation, many within the House and outside felt that the minister had said no more than the truth. The Kampala-based monthly *Uganda Confidential* published an article castigating the ministers and high government officials for openly indulging in corruption. It pointed out that some ordinary Ugandans wonder if it is worthwhile to work – let the ministers and their cronies concentrate on governing, they seem to be saying. President Museveni – one of the few leaders generally believed to be still clean – said, while launching the Martyrs' University of Uganda at the Sheraton Hotel on 24 March 1991, that in backward countries like Uganda people enter politics not to serve but to be served. It has been said of another Third World country, not very different from Uganda, 'that ministers pick over the economy, stripping any tasty morsels they come across on to their plates on the dining-table'.

Appetite grows with eating. The ministers who are involved in massive corruption are already the most privileged section of public servants. They are entitled to huge allowances: 500,000 shillings p.m. as housing allowance if they live in their own houses (even those without houses claim the money); they are allowed to co-own expensive cars such as Pajeros and in addition are paid 318,000 shillings p.m. to maintain them (a privilege which many have abused because instead of using those co-owned vehicles they still make all their journeys in government vehicles); their electricity, water and telephone bills are met by the state; and they are entitled to body-guards, *ayahs* and house-servants. People will naturally wonder at their receiving such allowances, while they also use their official positions to acquire added wealth. In mitigation it has to be added that their constituents look to them for, among other things, material maintenance; and that allowances are not always paid in practice. Nevertheless it is their conduct which has lowered the public esteem in which Uganda's leaders are held.

Ministers are not, of course, the only culprits. Senior and junior civil servants and high-ranking officials employed in parastatal bodies, including banks, have joined the race, and on their behalf it is pleaded that their pay is very low. This is true, and one wonders how they survive on it. For instance the basic salary of a professor at Makerere is some 9,000 shillings a month,* equivalent to US$100, and junior civil servants are paid much less. The basic fee for a child in an ordinary secondary school is around 70,000 shillings a term – and there are three terms in a year. Many succumb to the temptation of stealing money from their employers, and this is why in Uganda, as in many other Third World countries, corruption is embraced, despite public denunciations. And a practice has arisen, which one would have thought was a Third World phenomenon, but which can be seen in slightly different forms in industrialised countries. This is when the former head of a government financial institution establishes his own bank a few months after leaving office. In our case the capital used to start up the new concern has actually been stolen from the government.

One disturbing aspect of corruption in Uganda is the way the courts deal with those arrested and charged with embezzlement of their employers' money. In general, the more the offender steals from the government or parastatal body, the greater will be his chance of being set free. Those who steal many millions of shillings are hardly bothered by the long arm of the law, for even if they are arrested and taken to court they are immediately released on bail and that is the end of the story. But if a peasant or worker is caught stealing some hundreds of shillings, he would be lucky to be released

---

*A professional allowance of 60,000 shillings was recently added on, although it is not always paid on time.

after six or twelve months. For him, there is no question of being released on bail. It is this blatant disparity in the treatment of offenders – effectively the lack of a proper sentencing policy – which has irked the ordinary people, who do not enjoy the luxury of legal knowledge. In the eyes of these people there must be a collusion of interests between the magistrate or judge presiding over the case and the thief who stole millions of shillings from the government. If such a person is released, even if on sound legal grounds, the people will conclude that the 'rich thief' bribed the 'poor magistrate', and think that they too might help themselves to state property. Why, they will ask, should they refrain from taking their employers' wealth when their seniors do it and are not punished?

The Department of Inspector-General of Government was set up by the NRM, where a wide range of cases including corruption are reported and dealt with, but the Inspectorate has no powers of arrest or even of prosecution of those it finds guilty, and has thus proved ineffective in dealing with corruption in the country. The President promised that the Attorney-General would be asked to amend the powers of the Inspector-General of Government 'so that he concentrates on fighting corruption only without tackling human rights issues'; but no such amendment has gone through parliament, and corruption is not only still there but is thriving at such a rate that the consequences could well be disastrous – for the country, of course, but also for the NRM leadership itself.

Uganda needs moral rehabilitation perhaps more than anything else, for without it everything else that is being attempted will end in vain. The Code of Conduct statute passed by the NRC is law, but it is no more than that; it can threaten the would-be offender but cannot prevent the determined wrong-doer from harming society. It is the NRM's responsibility to provide the right environment for moral rehabilitation.

Foreign policy

It is perhaps in foreign affairs most of all that the NRM has achieved success. Uganda is no longer the laughing-stock it used to be, but a country that is taken seriously and is fully accepted back into the comity of nations. This has been no mean feat considering how low the country's prestige had sunk. Ugandans can now attend international conferences with confidence, and their contributions are given the consideration they deserve. Much of this has been the personal achievement of Yoweri Museveni, whose leadership was rewarded when he was invited in April 1991 to address the European Parliament in Strasbourg, the first African head of state to do so. And because of the positive image that Uganda enjoys today, Kampala has been host to some important international conferences, e.g. the ACP-EEC Conference held in February 1991 (for the first time in Africa). Important conferences have been held in Kampala to discuss South Africa, and in May 1990 the Africa Leadership Forum was organised there. The Kampala Forum, as it was dubbed, was Africa's first attempt to replicate Europe's Helsinki Conference of 1977. Organised by the founder of the Lagos-based Africa Leadership Forum, the former Nigerian head of state Olusegun Obasanjo, the Kampala conference produced the 'Kampala Document' containing many far-reaching recommendations for the achievement of peace, stability, development and cooperation in Africa. In June 1990 Yoweri Museveni was elected Chairman of the Organisation of African Unity (OAU). Unlike Idi Amin, who became OAU Chairman when Uganda hosted the summit in July 1975 and it was thought too embarrassing to deny him that position, Museveni's election was in appreciation of his achievements for his country and in the belief that he represented a new brand of leadership of which the continent was in short supply.

On the other side, there have been failures in Uganda's foreign policy during the NRM's period in government. Most notably, relations with Kenya have been far from friendly right from the time when the NRM came to power.

There have been several causes of this long-lasting antagonism. First, the NRM's liberation war set a bad example in the region. Here was a group who, without outside assistance and fighting not across borders but within their own country, succeeded in overthrowing a legally constituted government which still enjoyed the support and assistance of foreign governments. The NRM's victory over its opponents, especially Obote who enjoyed considerable international backing, was a significant event and shook the confidence of many of the region's leaders. The NRM's victory aroused the admiration of the young in surrounding states, to the concern of their leaders especially in those countries where democratic institutions were under pressure. An editorial in *Africa* magazine remarked in 1987: 'Soon after Yoweri Museveni seized power in Uganda at the beginning of last year there were reports that young men [in neighbouring countries] were parading with guns on their shoulders singing "we are Museveni's children".' Museveni has repeatedly stated that the NRM revolution is not for export and that the NRM has no intention of urging other Africans to rise against their governments; but there is a widespread feeling that if Uganda's experience were to be emulated by African countries with oppressive regimes, then the NRM revolution would not have been in vain. In the particular case of Kenya, its leaders are still piqued by the failure of the 1985 peace talks over which President Moi himself presided; they still blame the NRM for the failure of these talks, whereas if they had succeeded Moi would have earned the accolade of successful international mediator and, perhaps, 'godfather' of the new post-Obote Uganda.

Ugandans are perplexed by the Kenyan antagonism towards their government. They feel genuine affection for Kenya, where some of them have fled in times of political turmoil at home. They feel a natural kinship, and a nostalgia for the days of the defunct East African Community when barriers between the two countries were abolished. Moreover, Uganda is Kenya's principal trading partner in Africa and obtains most of its essential goods from Kenya. Ugandans wonder whether Kenya is envious of the rapid rate of Uganda's reconstruction after years of chaos and turmoil, or whether Kenya fears that its revival means that it has a new economic competitor in the region. All this baffles the Ugandans, much in the same way as it baffles the friends of the two countries. A statement by Lynda Chalker, the British Minister for Overseas Development, on a visit to Uganda in June 1991, that the British government attaches great importance to the existence of friendly relations between Kenya and Uganda reflects the concern of the international community at large, since it is clear that what unites Kenya and Uganda is more important than what divides them. In November 1991 the heads of state of Kenya and Uganda exchanged state visits. On 9 November President Daniel arap Moi paid a one-day visit to Uganda and held discussions with President Yoweri Kaguta Museveni in the industrial town of Jinja. Mr Museveni then paid a one-day visit to Nairobi on 21 November; these talks were joined by Tanzania's leader, Ali Hassan Mwinyi. A three-man committee of Foreign Ministers from Kenya, Tanzania and Uganda was appointed to explore and define closer cooperation in the region. This seems to augur well for the revival of the former East African Community, which enjoyed a thriving common market in the 1960s and 1970s.

Relations between Uganda and its other neighbours have generally been correct. The only difficult incident was the invasion of Rwanda from Uganda by Rwandese refugees belonging to the Rwandese Patriotic Front. Rwanda claims that it cannot admit them because there is no land reserved for them – implying that they should stay where they have lived for three decades or (in Uganda's case) longer. The exiled Rwandese want to return home even if there is no land reserved for them, and the Ugandan authorities cannot accept that Rwanda's disowning of its citizens should be at the expense of those countries which have generously offered them refuge for so long. However, the main dispute between Rwanda and Uganda turns on Rwanda's accusation that its neighbour is supporting the invasion by the refugees, an accusation which Uganda denies.

Conclusion

Finally, having examined the agonies Uganda has suffered, we must attempt to look into the future. Essentially this must lie with the country's leaders. The NRM has tried to provide leadership based on full popular participation in both decision-making and implementation. This is the essence of the Resistance Council system it has introduced. How will it fare in the political climate that lies ahead? The other element of leadership is inspiration. The NRM under Museveni may not have succeeded particularly well in the management of the economy or in the fight against corruption, but it has provided the people, especially the young, with 'more equal opportunities of proving themselves unequal'.

During these years, when active politics has been banned, the NRM has been able to usher in a spirit of belonging together, even if there has not been consistency or clarity over what is so characteristic of other parties in Uganda and elsewhere in Africa, namely ideology. The NRM people – old and new – know each other and can identify themselves, even if they are still hidden in other traditional parties. It is this fraternity and solidarity among the NRM supporters which so frightens other parties who want clear ideologies and clear political issues – which, in Africa, can so easily lead to strife.

Yoweri Museveni is a difficult man to assess, for in many ways he has not conformed to type. He has not intentionally built a 'machine' that would keep him in power. It is true that the NRM has been there behind him, but he has not used it to elevate himself into the position of being the only unassailable man in the land. If he has towered above others, it has not been through dictatorial or legislative manoeuvres. Much to the chagrin of his supporters in the NRM, who have often felt left out in the cold, he has refused to appoint as ministers or rely only on members of his former party, the Uganda Patriotic Movement, or the NRM. Most significant of all, he has made few removals from office, and the ministers who have left government were either accused of a criminal offence or lost elections in February 1989.

Regarding Museveni as a person, it is generally agreed that he has had a great impact on Ugandan society and its reconstruction, but is he, as was said of a Church leader, 'more a prophet than a ruler, more a preacher than an administrator, more a charismatic mystic than a confirmed pragmatist'? Can he deliver the goods, or is he simply an inspirer of others?

Museveni is scheduled to govern Uganda till 1995, when he will have been President for nine years, and whether or not he will continue to rule Uganda after that date will be decided by the people, as is their right. It is to be hoped that the constitution now in the making will have laid down the necessary rules for what should happen after 1995. But till then Museveni has a golden opportunity, with the people's goodwill behind him, to lift Uganda finally out of its abyss of agony.

30 June 1991

INDEX

Acholi district and people: 1, 14, 22, 24; recruiting centre for army, 71, 72, 78; as threat to Amin, 87–8, 105, 108, 112, 130, 133, 137, 138, 141, 150, 153, 154, 157, 159; opposed to Obote, 161–3, 164, 165n; and Langis, 167–77

Adoko, Akena, 67, 72

Adrisi, Gen. and Vice-President Mustafa, 113, 123

Africa magazine, 199

Ali, Brig. Moses, 113, 171, 175, 189

Aliker, Martin, 125

Amin Dada, Idi: 4, 24, 35, 37; massacres Baganda, 39–40, 43, 60; promoted major-general, 64, 65, 68, 71, 72; falls out with Obote, 72–6; and Muslims, 73; career and character, 78–81, 83, 84, 85; orders state funeral for Mutesa II, 86; visits West Germany, 90; and Arab world, 91; expels Asians, 92–6; orders takeover of British enterprises, 96; defeats guerilla invasion 1972, 98, 101; chairman OAU, 104, 101; attempted coups against, 106–7; bans BBC and European newspapers, 107; alienates Christians, 110; field-marshal and Life President, 111; opposed by senior officers, 113–4; flees Uganda, 114, 119; brutality, 120–4, 125, 126, 130, 137, 145, 148, 149, 155, 164, 171, 172, 192

Amnesty International, 179, 188

Ankole (Nkore), kingdom of: 2, 3, 5, 10, 24, 26; erased by Obote, 59, 61, 162

Anyanya (Sudan), 73, 75, 90

Apiliga, Moses, 138

Arain, Shafiq, 160

Army (Ugandan): emerges as political factor, 36; supports Obote, 64, 71; killings in under Amin, 87–8; and Asians, 95; attempts coup against Amin 1974, 106; dominated by West Nilers, 108–9; effect of Entebbe Raid on, 111–12; senior officers of oppose Amin, 113, 128; relied on by UPC, 148–9; campaigns against Obote, 163

Arube, Brig. Charles, 106, 107

Asians in Uganda: 8; riots against in 1945 and 1949, 8, 68, 76, 78, 88, 89; expulsion of by Amin, 92–6, 97, 102n, 104, 106, 115–20, 118; during Obote's second presidency, 154; NRM view of, 194

Aswa, W.O. Samuel, 78

Baganda: agents of British, 2–3; form state within a state, 3, 5; disagreement with Britain, 5; unsuitable for colonial army, 6; sub-imperialism of, 7–8; educational superiority of, 9; anti-colonialist movements, 11; petition to Kabaka 1949, 13; dominate UNC, 13; refuse to participate in 1958 elections, 16; cultural separateness, 28; self-destructive political culture of, 30; and 1966 crisis, 38–41, 47–9; massacred by Amin, 39–40, 44; angered by Obote's measures, 60; and national unity, 61–2; refuse to come to terms with Obote, 63; support Amin 1971, 73–81; and Amin, 86–7, 106; fail to support Amin, 114, 130; and 1980 election, 144; hostility to Obote's second presidency, 149; in public life under Obote, 153; backbone of NRA, 157; massacred by Obote, 159, 161

Baganda Bataka Party, 12

Bahima immigrant cattle herders, 7

Bantu-speaking people, 1, 28, 33, 55, 56, 109, 149, 153, 156, 170, 187

Banyankole ethnic group, 153, 161, 166n, 177

Bashir, Juma, 101

Bataka (clan heads), 5

Bataringaya, Basil, Secretary-General of DP: 33, 53, 75; murdered by Amin, 100

Bidandi-Ssali, 138, 171, 173

Binaisa, President Godfrey, QC: 32, 125; presidency and downfall, 130–7, 145, 146, 147

Brown, Archbishop Leslie, 67

Buganda, kingdom of: seeks British support, 1; civil war 1892, 2; British protectorate, 2; state within a state under British, 3; Agreement of 1900, 4–5,